The Feuerstein Method

This book is designed to help parents and professionals respond to the behavioral potential of children and adults diagnosed with autistic spectrum disorder (ASD) through the application of the Feuerstein method, an approach that brings an alternative and innovative treatment modality that uncovers and enhances the learning potential that traditional diagnoses and treatment methods often overlook or discourage.

The method is based on Reuven Feuerstein's formulations of cognitive modifiability and has been implemented successfully and confirmed by both research results and the experiences of teachers and parents. This book is a valued resource for treatment, including descriptions of the basic concepts of the method and their application to the assessment and treatment of those functioning within the spectrum. Each chapter is specifically written by members of the Feuerstein Institute clinical and research team. The chapters are interspersed with case studies that illustrate the principles and practices described therein and is written in an accessible and clear language for practitioners and parents.

Presenting a new and optimistic paradigm in defining and responding to ASD, this is an invaluable resource for parents and practitioners concerned about meeting the needs of the ASD individual and acquiring insights and techniques for seeking or implementing treatment.

Refael S. Feuerstein, PhD heads the international organization of the Feuerstein Institute, a researcher, creator and teacher. Among his developments are dynamic cognitive diagnosis methods and preschool intervention methods and the development of learning profiles and identification algorithms.

The Feuerstein Method

A Cognitive Approach to Autism

Edited by
Refael S. Feuerstein

Routledge
Taylor & Francis Group
NEW YORK AND LONDON

THE
FEUERSTEIN
INSTITUTE

Designed cover image: Image generated by Jo using Dall E

First published 2024
by Routledge
605 Third Avenue, New York, NY 10158

and by Routledge
4 Park Square, Milton Park, Abingdon, Oxon OX14 4RN

Routledge is an imprint of the Taylor & Francis Group, an informa business

Library of Congress Cataloging-in-Publication Data
Names: Feuerstein, Raphael S., editor.
Title: The Feuerstein method : a cognitive approach to autism / edited by
Raphael S. Feuerstein ; translator, Rosi Goldenberg ; copyeditor, Sara
Tropper.
Description: New York : Routledge, 2024. | Includes bibliographical
references and index. | Identifiers: LCCN 2023041900 (print) |
LCCN 2023041901 (ebook) |
Subjects: LCSH: Thought and thinking--Study and teaching. | Mediated
learning experience. | Autistic people--Education. | Feuerstein, Reuven.
Classification: LCC LB1590.3 .F474 2024 (print) | LCC LB1590.3 (ebook) |
DDC 370.15/2--dc23/eng/20231128
LC record available at https://lccn.loc.gov/2023041900
LC ebook record available at https://lccn.loc.gov/2023041901

ISBN: 978-1-032-58705-9 (hbk)
ISBN: 978-1-032-58704-2 (pbk)
ISBN: 978-1-003-45113-6 (ebk)

DOI: 10.4324/9781003451136

Typeset in Times New Roman
by Taylor & Francis Books

The names of all subjects in the case studies are fictitious and other details may have been changed to protect personal privacy.

Esther Mandelbaum: in memory of her father Roman Mandelbaum z"l.

The most endearing memories of my beloved father, our grand-father, and great-grandfather, Roman Mandelbaum z"l, revolve around the pure joy he expressed in the presence of children. Entertaining children with stories and funny sounds and games brought out his playful and slightly mischievous side—and a never-ending supply of chocolates and candies to boot. My father valued the ideas and interests of children; he supported their education and activities, and he took great joy and pride in their accomplishments. Born into a large and loving family of seven siblings, he experienced the deepest of heartbreak and sorrow during the war, when his beloved parents and his three youngest siblings were murdered by the Nazis. A survivor of the Shoah, he found the strength to go on and build a family as well as a very successful and meaningful life. We are honored and grateful to in some small way live up to his example and carry out his legacy of championing the wellbeing and education of children.

Esther Mandelbaum and Family

Contents

Illustrations

Contributors

Ayelet-Hashahar Aithan is an assessor and cognitive therapist in the Clinic for Child Integration at the Feuerstein Institute, Israel. She is also a yoga teacher with a specialization in children, and a group facilitator.

Gili Amorai is an occupational therapist who earned an MA in Early Childhood Studies from the Paul Baerwald School of Social Work and Social Welfare at the Hebrew University of Jerusalem.

Bruria Avichay is an occupational therapist in the Clinic for Child Integration at the Feuerstein Institute, Israel. She specializes in the MLE method.

Orit Atara Berkovich worked a special education teacher and cognitive mediator in the Clinic for Child Integration at the Feuerstein Institute, Israel.

Betty Brodsky Cohen worked as a senior social worker at the Feuerstein childrens' clinic with local and international populations for nearly three decades.

Louis H. Falik, PhD, serves as senior scholar at the Feuerstein Institute, Israel, and Emeritus Professor, San Francisco State University. He has published many articles and books on the Feuerstein Method.

Refael S. Feuerstein, PhD, is a Rabbi and president of the Feuerstein Institute. In addition to having written and edited many articles and books on the Feuerstein Method, he has developed many programs for cognitive mediation which have been translated into a number of languages: these include the Instrumental Enrichment program for early childhood, the cognitive dynamic assessment for the early childhood (LPAD-B) and the Digital Cognitive Dynamic Assessment (LPAD-D).

Rina Frei Schreiber is a speech and language therapist who specializes in work with children with special needs. Rina directs the department of speech therapy in the Clinic for Child Integration at the Feuerstein Institute, Israel.

Haya Ginton is an occupational therapist with a specialty in pediatrics. She directs the Early Childhood Assessment and Consultation Unit in the Clinic for Child Integration at the Feuerstein Institute, Israel.

Julie Jamet is a special education teacher in the Clinic for Child Integration at the Feuerstein Institute, Israel. She is part of the multidisciplinary staff that has treated children based on Mediated Learning Experience (MLE) and Instrumental Enrichment Program (IEP).

Shoshana Levin Fox, EdD, is a child psychologist, play therapist, and author of *An Autism Casebook for Parents and Practitioners: The Child Behind the Symptoms*. At the Feuerstein Institute between 1992 and 2017, she specialized in the play-based dynamic assessment and treatment of autism-diagnosed children.

Debbie Nadler is a special education teacher and cognitive mediator in the Clinic for Child Integration at the Feuerstein Institute, Israel. She is also a sports therapist.

Chana Nakav is an occupational therapist and director of the Clinic for Child Integration at the Feuerstein Institute, Israel.

Monica Paz is an educational psychologist and coordinator of Dynamic Cognitive Assessment (LPAD) at the Clinic for Child Integration at the Feuerstein Institute, Israel.

Acknowledgments

First and foremost, I wish to express endless gratitude to my father and teacher, Prof. Reuven Feuerstein, and my mother Berta Feuerstein. Their ideals, innovation and unceasing struggle to realize human potential left an enduring legacy for me—as for so many others. The many rich chapters of this book are the fruit of my father's method and vision.

I further wish to thank Ms. Esther Mandelbaum, who generously made possible the publication of *Feuerstein on Autism*. The book is devoted to the memory of her dear father, Mr. Roman Mandelbaum, who knew and admired Prof. Feuerstein and whom Prof. Feuerstein knew and admired in return. And to Chaim Guggenheim who managed the Institute's resource development, for his contribution to creating this connection.

Heartfelt appreciation goes to the members of the Feuerstein Institute's board of governors, whose support enables the Institute to thrive: Claude Bassou, Mordechai Heisler, Mordechai Chazon, Zvi Sand, Noam Shifman, Giora Roy, Prof. Yehuda Shapira, Jerry Lafair, Elad Rosenblatt, and Shaul Attia.

My colleagues at the Feuerstein Institute unstintingly contributed to this work by formulating their knowledge and expertise in such a way that children and families across the globe can benefit from it.

I wish to thank Hannah Nakav, the highly skilled director of the Children's Clinic at the Feuerstein Institute, who encouraged her team's massive contribution to this effort, despite their exceptionally heavy treatment load. I would like to thank from the bottom of my heart Rina Frei-Schreiber, Director of Language Clinics at the Feuerstein Institute, whose dedication, professionalism and determination brought this book to its successful conclusion.

I gratefully acknowledge Prof. Louis H. Falik, Dr. Shoshana Levin Fox, Dr. Betty Brodsky Cohen, Prof. David Tzuriel, and Dr. Sari Alony, who worked hand in hand with Prof. Feuerstein for decades and whose published works meticulously express his and their ideas. Appreciation is also due to Prof. Steven Gross, who has worked for many years with this population and whose insights inform this book. I thank the incredibly dedicated members of the clinical and research staff, Rina Frei Schreiber, Bruria Avichay, Julie Jamet, Ayelet-Hashahar Aithan, Debbie Nadler, Prof. Alex Kozulin, Haya Ginton, Orit Atara Berkovich, Monica Paz, Prof. David Tzuriel, Shlomit Cohen, Dr. Haim Davisheim, Merav Fleischmann, Ilana Zugman, Gili Amorai, Simha Drey, Yael Elharar, and many others who contributed their knowledge and know-how to this enormous research effort.

Thanks go as well to the talented translator of this book, Rosi Goldenberg, to our patient and professional editor, Sara Tropper, who took complicated ideas and made them accessible to the reader, and to Prof. Alex Kozulin, who contributed valuable editing advice. Special thanks to our indefatigable project coordinator, Hananel Frankel.

Special thanks to all the children and adults, the mothers and fathers, who placed their confidence in the Feuerstein Method and who taught us more than we taught them; they exemplify the Talmudic remark, "Many were my teachers, but I learned more from my students than from everyone."

Last, but far from least, I would like to express gratitude to my beloved wife, Tal, and our beloved children, Bitya and Avraham, Elhanan, Hillel, Chava and Elyasaf, Michael and Margalit, Achinoam, Noga and Avraham Kave, whose endless support and encouragement gave me the strength to engage in this labor of love.

My heartfelt thanks to all.

Refael S. Feuerstein

Preface

Refael S. Feuerstein

A little boy of five was taken by his parents to be treated by a Feuerstein therapist. Try as she might, the therapist could not get the child into the treatment room. When he finally did agree to enter, the boy wandered around aimlessly, picking up objects wherever and whenever they took his fancy. The Feuerstein therapist took a circumspect approach with the parents, taking care not to make promises but committing herself to drawing the child out of his complex condition. Notably, the therapist aimed not to adapt the environment to make it fit the child but just the opposite: to bring the child to adjust to a normative environment.

The Feuerstein therapist sets herself a highly ambitious goal—to integrate the child into a mainstream kindergarten and school, and, in the future, for the child to succeed in holding down as standard a job as possible. Obviously, this depends to a great extent on the child's intellectual functioning, as well as on a great many other factors. What sets the Feuerstein therapist apart from others, however, is her persistent quest for latent potential, her effort to pinpoint that potential and bring it to fruition. The therapist working with the Feuerstein Method is fully aware that this aim carries with it the chance of failure. Importantly, however, she also knows that the burden of proof rests on her shoulders. The team of therapists operates on the basis of an assessment that pinpoints the potential within the child. Consequently, if the child's potential is not realized, it is the therapists who have failed—never the child.

Feuerstein on Autism, written for professionals and parents alike, presents the purposeful and multifaceted method used to achieve this goal. In a reader-friendly way, it demonstrates interdisciplinary work carried out by psychologists, speech therapists, occupational therapists, teachers, social workers, researchers, clinic administrators, and parents, in their efforts to enable children and adults on the autistic spectrum to lead as normative a life as possible. The book furthers work carried out in the field over some forty years, and consolidates the tremendous experience accumulated at the Feuerstein Institute into a clear and comprehensive method available to all.

This book constitutes the product of the vision of, as well as the methodology and clinical and scientific work conducted by, my late father, Professor Reuven Feuerstein. Even as far back as when he was studying under the renowned Professor Jean Piaget at Geneva University between the years 1950 and 1956, Professor Feuerstein came to the conclusion that his scientific approach was different and perhaps even in opposition to that of his mentor. For his entire career, he would operate with an unshakable belief in human modifiability—regardless of the cause or severity of the condition, regardless of the age of the individual.

Feuerstein on Autism reveals Professor Feuerstein's methodology, and the wide-ranging knowledge that he instilled in his many students. In it, the reader will learn the principles of his theory and how they are implemented in work with people on the autistic spectrum.

Beyond the vision, the theory, and the knowledge, Professor Feuerstein endowed his students and the entire world with the belief in the modifiability of human beings—all human beings, including those on the autistic spectrum. In this volume, which contains theory, clinical-educational processes, the reader will hear a sort of accompanying internal melody that resounds with the therapists' belief in their autistic clients' ability to make significant changes in their functioning. These are not, as one might think, just congenial words, but rather a real clinical standpoint. This standpoint affects the therapists who act with the understanding that they bear ultimate responsibility for the treatment and cannot hide behind their clients' condition. A no-less-important ramification pertains to the intensity of the treatment needed in order to bring about change in the presence of long-standing difficulties, and the significant investment which must be made in each and every individual receiving mediation. Essentially, the Feuerstein Method is a generic method based on the comprehensive theory discussed in the opening chapters of the book, which describes the cognitive development of all human beings.

In contrast to Piaget, and like the Russian psychologist L. S. Vygotsky, Feuerstein maintained that the development of intelligence stems from human mediation processes that mediate culture to the child. Culture is made up of a great many things—knowledge, values, religion, social principles, customs, traditions, and so on. An important part of culture is the way in which it comprehends reality; thinking and learning strategies, then, play an important role in culture. It is these strategies that are responsible for processes of deduction and drawing conclusions, and for the way in which such processes are realized in everyday life. Every culture develops learning and thinking skills that allow its people and its different components to survive in the face of challenges presented by the environment. A culture based on the farming traditions of yesteryear is unlike an environment founded on advanced technology. A culture in which religion serves as the cornerstone will differ from one in which religion plays a minor part. Thus, every culture develops its own learning and thinking skills to suit it, and it passes those skills on to the next generation. That being the case, according to Feuerstein's approach, intelligence is acquired rather than innate.

Through the process of mediation, the child learns something else—possibly the most important thing of all: he learns how to learn. Thus, he learns to derive essential usefulness from his cultural environment, to internalize it, elaborate on it, and use it. All these factors are passed on to children in the culture by mediators, including the adults of their community. Feuerstein showed how this process unfolds, the impediments that can cause the process to fail, and the factors that can expedite and also further the process. Without going into detail, I will say here that the impediments intersect in one crucial way—they all prevent the child from learning and benefiting from his environment. According to Feuerstein, sound development hinges on one's ability to learn.

Basing human cognitive and functional development of the learning process of the surrounding culture has implications for another core principle of Feuerstein's theory: the belief in human modifiability. According to Feuerstein, the option to change is our most fundamental quality, regardless of cause or severity of condition, or age. A broad description of the theory and its major applications written by this author can be found in the introduction to the book.

Feuerstein's theory has a large number of applications. The main ones are the LPAD (Learning Propensity Assessment Device (Feuerstein, R., Falik, L., Rand, Y., & Feuerstein, R.S. (2002).)), a dynamic assessment process that makes it possible to evaluate a person's modifiability, along with a wide range of intervention methods that aim at realizing the person's intellectual potential, principal among them systematic syllabi (the Feuerstein Instrumental Enrichment Program) designed to develop students' intelligence. Owing to the generic nature of the theory and its major operating systems, it has a great many derivations that address the problems of a wide range of populations, the main one being the educational application. The Feuerstein Method is implemented in many schools all over the world, offering innovative teaching methods based on and incorporating the Feuerstein Instrumental Enrichment (FIE). In addition, there are dynamic evaluation programs for class-mapping based on both the students' learning potential and their learning profiles. The mapping system enables teachers to adapt their teaching to the different students in the class and, specifically, to systematically mediate learning and thinking skills to each student.

The other applications pertain to the clinical sphere, and these address a wide array of problems and a broad age range. One of the applications focuses on people with chromosomal impairments such as Down Syndrome; another application treats people who have suffered head injuries.

Still others address such issues as cognitive developmental disabilities and learning deficiencies.

All of the applications share three basic principles:

The Goal—a purposeful goal is set to bring about a significant change in the definition of the individual rather than just in his functioning, while maintaining throughout the constant belief in human modifiability.

The Process—the cognitive component as a basis for the individual's different and varied functions is highlighted.

The Method—Feuerstein formulated the method to be used to convey skills and even knowledge in such a way so as to instill essential thinking and learning skills. He called this method the Mediated Learning Experience (MLE).

What is special about the theory, and particularly about the third principle (the Method), is that it is void of content. Feuerstein defined it as "the quality of the interaction"; in more practical terms, speech clinicians, occupational therapists, teachers, and psychologists all conduct interventions using mediation. While all of these professionals transmit different skills, they use the same method: Mediation.

This, then, is the essence of this innovative work, which presents the Feuerstein Method for the treatment of individuals on the autistic spectrum. Our book is based on the theory and on the main systems derived from it, and deals with the following two major issues:

How to shape the basic principles of the theory to benefit individuals on the autistic spectrum; special aspects that have to be accentuated in mediation to people with communication impairments as compared to other population groups.

How the theory and its derived systems shape the work of the different specialized professionals such as speech pathologists, occupational therapists, psychologists, social workers, teachers, and even clinic administrators. And, of course, the place of the parents has not been overlooked in this book. Although it is not specifically a guide for parents, the book deals extensively with the link between parents and the professionals who treat their children.

Thus, the reader will learn how to mediate in a wide range of intervention situations.

It is important to point out that the term "autism" or "Autistic Spectrum Disorder" (ASD) is not taken for granted in the Feuerstein Method. Essentially, the Feuerstein Method takes a cautious approach towards clinical definitions of any sort.

The constitutive principle of "modifiability" in the Feuerstein ecosystem leads us to oppose fixed designations seen as unchangeable qualities. The Feuerstein ecosystem takes a wary approach to the different dimensions of intelligence such as IQ, which describe people as having fixed traits and which in fact maintain that human beings are unable to significantly change their IQ score during their lives.

Feuerstein preferred to describe human beings as being made up of *states.* Contrary to *traits,* states are not dependent on surroundings and relationships. We are all able to say that in a particular environment we can feel at ease, in another, agitated, and in yet another, tense. Are we tense, agitated or at ease? The answer is that it depends on where we find ourselves. There are environments in which we are sure of our knowledge and are able to express it with ease. However, there are circumstances in which we are tense and inarticulate *even having the same knowledge*—for example, in an exam or a job interview.

Even clinical situations that appear to be steady and fixed were considered by Feuerstein to be conditions that could change. The group of Feuerstein specialists who contributed to this book had intense discussions regarding whether it is possible and proper to use the accepted definitions for severe communication disorders such as PDD, autism and even "autistic spectrum." Some of these experts argued that in order to remain true to the dynamic spirit of the Feuerstein Method, and considering that, in our decades-long collective experience, many diagnoses given to children proved to be incorrect and we were able to disassociate so many clients from the diagnoses they originally received, it would not be justified to use the accepted definitions. We note that accepted terms such as "autism" and "PDD" were changed by DSM-5 to "autistic spectrum," and this more flexible term is consistent with the basic viewpoint of the Feuerstein Method.

Other specialists in the group maintained that in order for this book to be understood and, we hope, to serve as a source of inspiration to therapists and parents globally, the book must keep to the definitions accepted within the professional world, thereby allowing a constructive dialogue with recognized viewpoints. Ultimately, the editor decided to retain the accepted terms for the reasons given above, but, at the same time, to convey our reservations regarding the terminology, and particularly regarding the absolute manner in which they are accepted. It is not just a matter of a philosophical discussion on how parents, therapists, and particularly bureaucrats, relate to these definitions—rather, they have implications for the fate of an immense number of individuals. We would therefore ask our readers to consider the use of the accepted definitions with care, at least from the Feuerstein point of view.

The book includes this author's presentation of the theory of Mediated Learning Experience. The chapters by the late Prof. Feuerstein, Falik, and

Feuerstein discuss the different progressions of the term "autism" and its relation to the Feuerstein Method, as well as the principles of the method in relation to autism in a more specific way Levin Fox examines the term "islets of normalcy," coined by Feuerstein, and its implications for the treatment of individuals defined as being on the autistic spectrum. Nakav and Feuerstein present the unique nature of the work done in accordance with the Feuerstein Method by the professional team at the Feuerstein multi-disciplinary clinic. Ginton and Berkovich discuss the LPAD dynamic assessment used with low-functioning clients. Paz covers the LPAD dynamic assessment of high-functioning clients. Frei Schreiber reports on her work as a speech clinician in the area of communication, while Jamet and Feuerstein write on the use of the Feuerstein Instrumental Enrichment Program to promote cognition among children on the autistic spectrum, and on how the program affects their social and emotional functioning. Avichay and Feuerstein set forth advanced interventions to teach writing; Eitan and Nadler discuss Cognitive Therapy through the motor modality and Brodsky Cohen on family treatment.

We hope that our readers will appreciate the scope of the book. Its style makes it suitable both for professionals and for parents seeking to understand how the Feuerstein Method operates in the major treatment areas. On the whole, descriptions of treatment have been organized into sections each constituting a sort of treatment stage, with each stage not strictly dependent on each other but possessing a logical internal connection that makes for a clearer explanation of the treatment procedure.

Feuerstein On Autism is intended to be the beginning of a global training process for parents and therapists in the Feuerstein Method. It is our aspiration to realize the vision of Professor Reuven Feuerstein and convey the message of his method throughout the world.

Introduction to the Theory of Mediated Learning Experience

Refael S. Feuerstein

The Four Basic Principles of the Feuerstein Method

Feuerstein on Autism departs from earlier books in the Feuerstein library in that it is oriented toward the applications—rather than the overall theory—of the Feuerstein Method (FM) (Feuerstein, R., Rand, Y. and Feuerstein, R.S. 2006. Feuerstein, R., Falik, L., & Feuerstein R. S. 2010). A central application derived from the FM is mediating to individuals on the autistic spectrum. Significantly, the FM focuses on learning. Rather than engaging with specific therapies and theories, it shows how various topics are understood and assimilated by an individual who receives mediation, and how this mediation brings about structural and systemic changes. For this reason, we draw particular attention to the ways in which different topics are effectively conveyed using the FM to those on the autistic spectrum. The reader, then, will hear two distinct "messages." One of these addresses the 'what': this is the voice of the different disciplines put forward in the book—the terminology of psychology and social work, of speech and occupational therapy, and of teaching and movement therapy. All these are aimed at therapy content, that is, the 'what.' In this sense, each of the chapters in the book stands on its own. Yet, the chapters also share a profound and practical common ground: the 'how'—the way in which the different topics and skills are imparted to an individual during treatment such that they bring about real change. The change we are talking about is one that will be internalized and thus unlikely to disappear, a systematic change that will be projected into an endless number of different situations. This 'how' aspect runs like a connective thread through the otherwise diverse chapters.

This section will introduce the reader to the four basic principles of the generic FM as it is reflected in the different specialized chapters.

The first principle of the theory of Structural Cognitive Modifiability (SCM) is that all people are capable of change regardless of the cause(s) or the severity of their condition or of their age.

The second principle states that cognition is the key factor in bringing about significant emotional, behavioral, and personality change, and that

DOI: 10.4324/9781003451136-1

the way to bring about lasting cognitive change with systemic impact is what we call in the theory "Structural Cognitive Modifiability" (SCM) (this term will be explained later).

The third principle asserts that structural changes are created by means of a singular learning process which Feuerstein called the Mediated Learning Experience (MLE) (Feuerstein, R., Rand, Y. and Feuerstein, R.S. 2006). In other words, what Feuerstein called "cognitive structures" are not innate but are rather acquired by means of processes of learning/mediation. For this reason, intelligence, which is a collection of cognitive structures essential to our existence and survival, is the product of intensive mediation processes that take place during the childhood years and beyond. Put differently, human intelligence is acquired through mediation processes conveyed to children by their parents as well as their educational and family environments.

The fourth principle holds that low functioning in any area (thinking skills, academic knowledge, behavior, etc.) is the product of a lack of learning/mediation processes—a lack which can be traced to many sources. Either these processes were not given to the child, or they were blocked and prevented from being "absorbed" by him.

We now turn to discussing these different principles in greater depth.

The First Principle—Human Beings as Changing Entities

The Search for "Islets of Normalcy"

The journalist Claudie Bert, who interviewed Feuerstein for an article in the *Le Monde* newspaper, titled her piece: "For Feuerstein, Chromosomes Do Not Have the Last Word" (Feuerstein & Spire, 2006, p. 22). While it is clear that chromosomes have a powerful effect on who we are, it is becoming increasingly clear that this effect is only one among many such major effects. In fact, as early on as the 1960s, Feuerstein foretold what is today called the plasticity of the brain in neurology and epigenetics in the field of genetics—both fields espouse the notion of the brain's modifiability. Feuerstein explained the phenomenon of modifiability in terms of his view of intelligence being a product of culture, similarly to the renowned Russian psychologist Lev Vygotsky (1896–1934). Thus, intelligence is shaped by two aspects of culture: its content and its cognitive components. The first includes general knowledge, art, values and opinions that are accepted in a certain culture; the second refers to the system of learning and thinking strategies that characterize the processes of decision-making, conclusion-drawing and knowledge-formation in a particular culture. The eminent American psychologist Raymond Cattell (1905–98) called the content component, "crystallized intelligence," and the processes, "fluid intelligence." For Feuerstein, however, one's culture supplies both components—even learning skills.

This being the case, the most important process in human intellectual development is the learning process—it is the "pipeline" through which the two parts of culture and knowledge flow to the individual.

From this point of view, we are all modifiable. Nonetheless, our modifications cannot be predicted because our abilities are based—and even depend—on learning. Culture, which is in a constant state of flux, continually changes a person. From this perspective, the brain can be seen as the hardware of a computer—something which indeed is innate—while the operating system of that "computer" and different "programs" originate outside the computer. In other words, as intelligence is learned and not acquired, in principle, it is possible to find ways to teach those individuals who for physiological or environmental reasons were not exposed to learning/mediation.

Individuals on the autistic spectrum—particularly those functioning on a low level—often do not receive appropriate mediation. Owing to their severe communication problems, they are liable to be locked out of the world/culture in which they live because of their learning/mediation impediments, which, as we have said, are caused by their communication difficulties. Parents will try to talk to their ASD child, to draw his attention to things they consider important, try to tell him stories... but the child does not establish eye contact. Often, the child will look "through" the parents but not at them. Such a child will not acquire the behavioral rules, words, and concepts. Returning for a moment to the computer metaphor, it is as though this child is equipped with "hardware" but no "software." This brief explanation of the functional impairment of people on the lower end of the autistic spectrum has important practical implications.

In her chapter, the psychologist Shoshana Levin Fox discusses "islets of normalcy," which is an expression that was introduced by Feuerstein to eloquently depict how the mediator seeks out in the ASD individual tiny islets of ability, islets that are surrounded by oceans of inability in a variety of areas. Why do these miniscule islets even merit mention? After all, it would seem that they are often so few in number and so lacking in everyday importance that they can hardly be relied upon. The Feuerstein answer is as radical in its simplicity as it is profound in its implications: even if there are barely any islets at all, those that do exist were *acquired*. The individual learned them—he was not born with them. He clearly possesses a normal learning process, although it is currently limited. If we manage to pinpoint that learning process, however limited it may be, we can use it to instill in him an infinity of elements. Our job is to determine the exact "process" on which the individual is "transmitting and receiving" from the outside world—after which we will be able to bring about significant changes in him.

The systematic way to find those windows into the ASD individual's world, or, more precisely, the way to identify the learning processes that could constitute a basis to begin treatment, is by means of the *Learning Propensity Assessment Device* (LPAD) Feuerstein, R.S., Feuerstein, R., & Falik, L. (2005) developed by Feuerstein. This dynamic assessment procedure that aims at identifying learning potential is made up of three basic phases. In the *pre-test phase* the assessor evaluates the current state of the person in a wide range of cognitive contexts. In the second phase, the *intervention phase,* the assessor intervenes and tries to mediate to the individual certain skills that were noted to be absent or deficient. In the third phase, using *the post-test,* the assessor examines the extent to which the individual has put to use the strategies he has learned. Importantly, this is not a binary question—"Did he learn or not?". Instead, it is a qualitative question—"How does learning occur in this individual?" "Where is he blocked?" "What accelerates his learning processes and what slows them down?" and a great many other evaluative questions. The process of dynamic assessment (LPAD) with low-functioning individuals is presented in the chapter written by occupational therapist Haya Ginton with speech therapist Orit Atara Berkovich. The chapter in this book that outlines dynamic assessment with high-functioning individuals was written by educational psychologist Monica Paz. The purpose of dynamic assessments as it applies to ASD individuals is to identify islets of normalcy and their significance. An illuminating presentation of three case studies conducted by the late Professor Feuerstein himself is given at the end of the book in the chapter by R. Feuerstein, Falik and R. S. Feuerstein. In the chapter she wrote with R. S. Feuerstein, occupational therapist and head of the Clinic for Child Integration at the Feuerstein Institute, Chana Nakav, discusses how dynamic assessment becomes the treatment blueprint for the team of therapists mediating to the ASD individual.

This dynamic approach is the central theme of the book. The reader will learn how the different therapists work tirelessly to discover their clients' islets of normalcy upon which the learning process can be based. The chapter by Amichay and R. S. Feuerstein demonstrates the strategic efforts made by therapists to find points of interest and meaningfulness in the client. At times, the therapist has to create this sort of linchpin of meaning externally. For example, in the chapter written by Jamet and R. S. Feuerstein, the reader will see how the therapist used an instance of wedding-related confusion that formed in the child's mind to develop a structural conceptual system of family relations in the child.

Setting Treatment Goals

In the FM, the assumption of human modifiability is fundamental to the development of treatment goals. The LPAD presents an individual's latent potential—that is, potential that has not yet been realized. The results of the assessment and the premise of the possibility of change present in everyone—even the most challenging among us—require therapists using the FM to set ambitious goals. A glance at the book chapters will reveal that the ultimate goal of the different therapists in the varied areas of treatment that make up the FM goes well beyond anticipated linear development: it is nothing short of audacious. However, the reader will also see that these goals are not set naively; instead, they are laid out as units that allow for gradual development on the path to the grand objective. Alongside the "actively changing" approach, one can see the great many hours that this method of treatment requires. This extensive investment often yields excellent results. It ought to be made clear, however: in the absence of enormous effort, the desired changes will not be obtained. And, while the work is ambitious, it is also gradual, carried out with much patience. The FM approach and treatment planning are discussed at length in the chapter by Nakav and R. S. Feuerstein, which outlines considerations for determining treatment content and intensity in accordance with this governing principle of the human capacity to change.

Failure

Anyone who sets himself high goals experiences periodic failure, and treatment with the FM is no exception to this rule. Crucially, however, in the FM, the cause of failure is not attributed to the ASD individual himself. He retains the capacity to change, even if the treatment proves unsuccessful. The burden of proof is on the therapist, who cannot hide behind the individual's deficiency, or even behind the severity of the problem. Moreover, failure itself is harnessed toward the mediation goals, as therapists use the information gained to change course and try different tactics. From the FM perspective, failure is a valuable piece of the puzzle in understanding how to effectively mediate for significant change.

In this volume, readers will witness therapists' heroic struggles with individuals' difficulties. They will encounter therapists who refused to give up—even when, session after session, their clients did not relate to them. One of these therapists sat through four sessions talking to the child she was treating—receiving as her only response, resistance—until the breakthrough moment, after which the two worked together, mediating as a team. Readers will learn about therapists who worked together for months to ultimately succeed in mediating to a child with dyspraxia to sit down on a chair! Of course, therapists do not always meet with success—but, in the FM, the effort to mediate change is fierce and steadfast.

The Second Principle—Bringing about Cognitive Change

Why Emphasize the Cognitive Area?

FM goals are comprehensive—they encompass communication, behavior, everyday functioning, academic and emotional skills, and more. All of these goals are filtered through the mode of thinking. Feuerstein offered several reasons for this, the first of which he learned from his teacher, the pioneering Swiss psychologist Jean Piaget (1896–1980). Piaget held that thinking is part of everything, even the emotional sphere. Thus, there is no emotion that does not connect to a cognitive understanding of the situation. We feel happy because we assess a particular reality as being good for us. Alternatively, we might feel angry at someone because we interpret her behavior towards us as negative. Consequently, there is no emotion that does not have a cognitive basis. Relatedly, there is no behavior that is not goal- oriented. Correct functioning requires planning, and planning is a thinking process— goals are defined through thinking. Accordingly, improved thinking skills have the potential to project onto a broad range of functioning and activity.

A second reason for channeling mediation goals through the cognitive area concerns the ability to create effective communication precisely in that region. The area of emotion is rather hazy, as are factors related to the motivation to carry out certain activities, whereas cognition is by its nature structured and precise. Therefore, targeting the cognitive area allows for the creation of effective communication channels with everyone, including the ASD individual.

Thirdly, as explored in the chapter written by Jamet and R. S. Feuerstein, it is particularly the cognitive area that becomes distanced from the stormy and emotional world of the ASD individual. Hence, if we lower the level of anxiety by moving away from the emotional area, we increase the likelihood of being able to work effectively with him.

Change in the cognitive dimension is perceived as being more stable than change in the emotional realm. It is less subject to the turmoil and mood swings that in ASD individuals can be extreme. For all these reasons, the different treatment areas discussed in this book center on the cognitive sphere— the cornerstone upon which improvement in diverse functioning is built.

In the chapter by Aithan and Nadler on movement therapy, the therapists stress the shaping of movement by means of planning and control skills. Avichay and R. S. Feuerstein, for their part, emphasize the verbal identification and implementation of geometric shapes in lieu of outright imitation and copying. In her chapter on the acquisition of language skills, Frei Schreiber highlights the role of language and communication as a basis for developing thinking skills and for learning to form interpersonal relationships. These are but a handful of the many examples the reader will find concerning the cognitive factor, which governs all the varied areas of intervention and constitutes a critical feature of the FM.

"Thinking Structures" as Intervention Goals

In speaking about the notion of "thinking" or "intelligence," Feuerstein followed in the footsteps of Piaget. Thus, Feuerstein considered intelligence to be made up of what he called "thinking structures" (or, in Piaget's terminology, "schemas"). From this point of view, the knowledge that we carry around in our minds is not stored in a scattered way. Rather, it is organized in group-like formations based on specific categories. For example, the category "heat" includes the idea of an oven, sun, burn, cooking pot, frying pan, soup, bonfire, flame, candle, summer, sea, and so on; for its part, the category "receptacle" includes the idea of a bottle, glass, tanker, bathtub, swimming pool, sea, hosepipe, and so on. The cognitive changes that Feuerstein believed in are of a structural nature; consequently, he developed the theory of Structural Cognitive Modifiability (SCM).

In this book's chapter by Frei Schreiber on her role as a speech therapist, she presents the case of seven-year-old Nathan. Nathan had communication difficulties of which he was aware, and thus refused to carry out communication-related tasks. The FM (Feuerstein, R., Falik, L., Feuerstein, R.S., & Bohacs, K. 2012) defines this difficulty of Nathan's as a "closed thinking structure" on the basis of which he had formed for himself a self-image in the area of communication. Any attempt to compliment or encourage him was met with an impenetrable barrier. This is an example of a structure that must be opened in order for there to be any chance of providing treatment and advancing Nathan's communication skills.

In Aithan and Nadler's article on movement therapy, the authors discuss the case of Bryan, a ten-year-old boy diagnosed as being on the spectrum. As they put it, Bryan showed a passive behavioral pattern lacking initiative. He came to the Feuerstein Institute daily for a long period of time accompanied by his mother. The multi- disciplinary staff at the Institute worked intensively with Bryan and his mother in an attempt to increase his need to become more independent and active. Bryan showed no interest whatsoever in the cognitive treatments aimed at developing ways of thinking and learning strategies. He would sit gazing at the therapist, emit various sounds, move his hands in a stereotypical way, and take a long time to answer questions or carry out instructions.

Bryan's behavior can help us understand what we mean by "thinking structure." His behavioral pattern was made up of an infinite number of attempts that failed to take him out of the state he was in. All those factors made up a unified, coherent, structure that became impenetrable, blocking direct efforts to change him. When such attempts were made, he would "gaze at the therapist, emit sounds and move his hands in a stereotypical way." In other words, the "structure" essentially "thrust out" the many efforts made to get through to him and change him.

Moving to this book's chapter on cognitive intervention, written by Jamet and R. S. Feuerstein, we meet Joseph, who immigrated to Israel from France at the age of 14. All the attempts to teach him Hebrew were met with failure. In this case, it would appear that the thinking structure of the language did not include universal language principles. What he had learned in his mother tongue, then, precluded expansion to new languages.

In all these cases as well as in many others the reader will encounter in *Feuerstein on Autism*, the goal of intervention was to change the person's thinking structures.

The Third Principle: Mediated Learning Experience as a Primary Way to Bring about Change in Human "Cognitive Structures"

Mediation for Intentionality

Joseph, Bryan, and Nathan exhibited intransigence, each one in his own way. In his research, Feuerstein asked how the sought-after structural change could be brought about. Would it be sufficient to provide routine teaching? He, soon realized that normative teaching and even treatment would not bring about the major change in which he believed. Such radical change demanded an alternative educational technology. Feuerstein devised this technology, the powerful learning process needed to bring about structural changes and called it Mediated Learning Experience (MLE), which is also the name of the second major theory that he introduced.

In developing the MLE technology, Feuerstein first asked himself how one might penetrate the hard cognitive structure of a person—without being "thrown out of the system". Let us, for a moment, consider the image of an ancient walled city. In order to enter, one had to search long and hard for the entry gate. Analogously, as mediators, we ask: what is the opening through which we can get in to make a change in the "hard" cognitive structure of the recipient of mediation?

The first condition for a change to take place, that is *Mediation for Intentionality*, requires us to find the way "in" to reach the recipient of mediation. We, as mediators, must ask ourselves how we can most effectively present ourselves. Should we speak gently or forcefully, briefly or at length? Should we use concrete or abstract terms? Then, we have to ask ourselves how we can most effectively shape the message—through a story, a conversation, or perhaps a short film? Following this, the recipient's setting has to be "shaped"—where would be the best place to have the discussion? Would it be best for the parents to be present in the room, or should the child be alone? These are but a few of the many factors that the mediator must take into consideration in order to effectively convey her message and establish that it is assimilated by the recipient of mediation.

Feuerstein defined *Mediation for Intentionality* as the mediator's responsibility to ensure that the message (any message) is perceived by the recipient of mediation. When teachers, caregivers, parents and others talk to children, students and clients, they tend to focus more on the content of the message and less on their method of communication. For example, Joseph, discussed by Jamet and R. S. Feuersteun, became cooperative only after being given short, sharp instructions that required precise answers. Joseph's linguistic system seemed to block all intervention in the linguistic area in a foreign language, perhaps because the technical structure of French which he had acquired prevented a new language from being assimilated. The therapist's determined search for "a way in" led her to the conclusion that Joseph responded most positively to brief, focused instructions. Conversely, when he was given complex, instructions with ambiguous meaning, he became blocked. The therapist shared her discovery with the other professional staff members, who implemented the information in their work with the child. From that point on, significant change was noted in Joseph's level of cooperation. Here, the need for *Mediation for Intentionality* led the therapist to pinpoint the child's open paths. This effort was required because his existing paths were extremely narrow.

In the case of Bryan, who was described in Aithan and Nadler's chapter, *Mediation for Intentionality* led the movement therapist to investigate whether the motor channel could be open to learning and change. It turned out that when Bryan was stimulated in a motor modality, he was able to learn sequences and planning, imitated movements upon request, persevered in doing activities, and even initiated some of his own. The movement modality was found to be a way into his cognitive development. The case of Nathan described by Frei Schreiber reveals another interesting discovery that made it possible to get through to Nathan's cognitive structure. As she wrote:

> *Taking this sensitivity into account, the speech therapist first explained to Nathan how the assessment was structured, increasing incrementally in difficulty, and so mediating for challenge so that Nathan would be prepared to search for novelty and complexity within a task. Then, he was shown how to signal as soon as he felt a task was difficult. When he did so, the clinician reminded him of the tools that they had learned that would equip him to carry out the task. Nathan was also given the choice of how many pages of the assessment he wished to complete during a given therapy session; he and the therapist would place a marker on the page where he chose to stop. The therapist thus gave Nathan autonomy over his learning process. He appreciated that his opinions were valued and that he knew what to expect during the assessment.*

We can see, then, that Nathan's linguistic structure was characterized by a sense of lack of control and uncertainty, which led him to become anxious. The effort of *Mediation for Intentionality* allowed the therapist to understand that by letting Nathan take control, she would increase his confidence and create in him the desire to cooperate. FM therapists do not just offer treatment; they work intensively to solve the riddle that envelops the individual in treatment.

It is important to note that Feuerstein did not believe in laying down a precise treatment protocol. Instead, he offered guiding principles for mediation. In the examples above, the therapists used a wide range of approaches—which makes sense, as the recipients were different children. The underlying principle remained the same, however: *Mediation for Intentionality*.

Mediation for Transcendence

Even after they have been assimilated, the message, skills and knowledge conveyed to the recipient of mediation can remain local and concrete. As such, they may fail to have a broad, systemic impact on the functioning of the recipient.

In the chapter written by Avichay and R. S. Feuersteun, they describe the process of mediation for writing. One of the accounts introduces us to Steve. Not only did Steve not know how to write, he found it difficult to draw a square even by copying and imitating or by breaking the square up into its components (four lines, angles, etc.) The cognitive structure on which we focused was that of "part- whole" (analysis and synthesis). This cognitive structure is key to controlling the perceptual field, which, in Steve's case, turned out to be very fragile. With the help of this skill, the perceptual field can be broken down into components which are easy to grasp and, using assembling procedures (synthesis), put them together again into one "whole." *Mediation for Part-Whole Structures/Skills* is made up of three expanding circuits. The initial circuit is about taking apart and assembling simple geometric shapes. Once this first, concrete circuit has been assimilated, the mediator expands the skill acquired to the sphere of letters and words. Next, the mediator further expands the mediation message to the sphere of sentences, paragraphs and themes. Mediation to Steve was concluded with an attempt to see the connection between the "part"—the basic theme about which he wanted to write—and the "whole," that is, the internal and social context of the theme. To illustrate the notion of transcendence: the email that one writes to one's parents is likely to be very different than the email one writes to one's siblings—even if the same message is communicated in both correspondences. In Feuerstein's view, the ability to create a "conceptual structure" with a systemic influence on the child's function depends on the mediator's active effort, which moves from the concrete message to other areas of functioning and thinking, and that the mediator actively connects the concrete message, which is the point of departure of the mediation, to the expanding fields of functioning. Piaget claimed that this transcendence takes place in an automatic way. Feuerstein, however, maintained that the mediator must connect the pieces of the puzzle—that transcendence will not automatically take place for many of the children with whom we work.

Of course, the mediator cannot link the message to every past and future event. Yet, the knowledge that permeates fits together like Lego blocks, constructed in such a way as to be ready to fit into more and more "blocks of information"—those that already exist and other, future ones. This is dependent on the mediation of transcendence of different pieces of knowledge and skills, making them open knowledge that can fit together with ever-increasing information and skills that permeate the system.

Mediation for Meaning

At one point, a certain change was brought about in Steve. He developed the ability to look at the world as being made up of parts that come together and form whole pictures made up of those parts. He learned to look at social relations and communication in a broad context, a context that takes into consideration behavior norms, and, of course, his own internal world. Yet, the structural change that came about within him could have remained untapped. For Steve to make use of the acquired skill, the mediation process required an additional parameter which Feuerstein called *Mediation for Meaning*. The parameter of *Mediation for Meaning* is responsible for the energetic side of the cognitive structure, for the motivation to make use of skills and knowledge that have been acquired. In our discussion of *Mediation for Transcendence* in the previous section, we mentioned the "what," that is, the message that we convey to the mediation recipient. Now we are talking about the "why." Why should the mediation recipient make use of the change that came about? What is the motivation that makes him do so? In this instance, the mediator should impart an emotional significance to the conveyed content. It is important to note that emotional significance changes in accordance with the content of the mediation. Being cautious around dangerous things or the ability to communicate effectively within social surroundings are examples of content that is critical to our ability to survive in our society. There are less important content matters, too. The ability to correctly distinguish between different animals, for example, is important— but less so than some social communication skills. When the content matter is something that the mediator deems crucial to the wellbeing of the recipient, she must adopt a serious tone in speaking with him. Additionally, she must repeat the message several times, and she chose where to best convey the message and the most suitable time to do so. The mediator uses all these means and more to give the message the appropriate emotional significance and thus ensure the correct use of the content acquired.

In Steve's case, Avichay and R. S. Feuerstein recounted their considerations in choosing which letters to begin their intervention. FM therapists prefer starting with letters that are meaningful to the child (e.g., those that make up his name) rather than letters which are easier to learn but lack meaning for him.

Aithan and Nadler describe *Mediation for Meaning* in their effort to develop in six-year-old Jon the ability to make eye contact. To quote the authors:

> *The activity was accompanied by Mediation for Meaning of communication and emotional reflection: "When you express your needs, I can respond to them and then you will feel good." "What fun it is playing together like this." "I am so glad you are looking into my eyes and holding my hand." "I'm pleased to see that you are happy and calm." The appearance, duration and quality of eye contact, connection and communication increased and slowly and gradually Jon responded to the mediator's eye contact. Eventually he even established contact himself. An increase in reciprocity, cooperation and enjoyment was observed. Close and warm contact was established.*

Frei Schreiber discusses four-year-old Nicky in her chapter. Nicky communicates with her own private speech, which is unintelligible to those surrounding her. In order to arouse in Nicky the motivation to use language that others could understand, the speech clinician presented her with an imitation of her way of speaking—not as a criticism, but to demonstrate to her the problems involved in the way in which she was communicating. As she was doing this, the clinician offered a brief sentence reflecting Nicky's intentions instead of the jumble of sounds she had produced. The purpose of this intervention was to demonstrate to Nicky the meaning of the alternative that the clinician was proposing.

Mediation for Reciprocity

The ultimate goal of the mediator is to bring the recipient of mediation to a state of self-mediation. Parents, teachers and therapists will not mediate forever. Thus, the recipient of mediation must become an independent learner. The way to turn the recipient of mediation into an independent learner is through his consciousness; in professional terminology, this is called *meta-cognition.* In *meta-cognition,* the recipient of mediation partners with the mediator. The mediator does not "teach" him in a top-down manner, as someone who possesses particular knowledge that she passes on to her student. Unlike a non-mediating teacher or therapist, the mediator includes the mediation recipient in the process of learning. Thus, mediation appears like a dialogue in which the recipient has an active role to play. He is asked questions, and he receives instructions and responds. Crucially, the mediator tries to introduce the process into the consciousness of the recipient of mediation. In the course of the mediation, the mediator begins to build up the recipient's independence.

Returning to Steve: the child arrived at the clinic one day in a state of high excitement. Contrary to regular practice, his father had brought him in rather than his mother. The therapist used the insight she had created through ongoing mediation and assisted him to use the principle he had learned, namely, to express his feelings. In fact, he went on to write down on a sheet of paper "I am excited that my father is here." He was able to make this transfer because he understood the process he had undergone (i.e., expressing his feelings). *His understanding allowed him to make use of the process.*

In the same context, another interesting case has been described in the chapter written by Ginton and Berkovich. They present Ian, who was diagnosed as being on the autistic spectrum when he was four years old.

> *Over the years, Ian learned writing and reading skills, but he did not attain a level at which those skills could constitute a basis for the expansion of knowledge and the development of high-level thinking skills. Ian's communication modalities were limited. He made an effort to communicate but the way he expressed his needs and feelings verbally was restricted.*

Ian was presented with tasks of a high level of abstraction (analogical thinking). Note the mediation he was given:

> *… Ian was asked to solve the problems in the Raven (Colored A, AB, B) test. Throughout the test he was asked to provide logical proof for his choices as he used verbal concepts and superordinate concepts….*

This request is a good example of *mediation for reciprocity.* It was not enough for Ian to solve the task successfully. He needed to create meta-cognition, to understand and express the strategies that he had used.

> *This task was not easy for him. In the beginning, his answers indicated concrete thinking based on visual perception. He had trouble transferring strategies to solve problems from one problem to another. A break-through was observed when he was asked to solve shape analogies in the Variations test. At that point Ian began offering logical explanations spontaneously. Giving logical explanations requires a fair level of abstract thinking. In this way, Ian learned to be careful not to give answers for which he did not have logical proof.*

The assessor thus mediated to Ian at a meta-cognitive level, incorporating an awareness of the strategies he had used to help him become a more independent learner who applied his acquired strategies to new and complex tasks.

The Four Essential Dimensions of Mediation in Brief

The four dimensions of mediation that were mentioned above—*Mediation for Intentionality; Mediation for Transcendence; Mediation for Meaning;* and *Mediation for Reciprocity*—are defined as the four conditions for interaction between the child and the mediator (parent, therapist, teacher, or anyone else) to be mediated and for the desired structural change to come about. If even a single one of those parameters is missing, the interaction cannot be considered mediated learning.

Beyond these four mandatory parameters, there are nine optional ones that are available for use. Let us turn to these optional parameters now.

The Nine Additional Parameters of Mediated Learning

The nine optional parameters of Mediated Learning are responsible for the way cognitive styles vary between cultures and individuals, as well as for the shaping of responses to stimuli, whether internal or external. To detail all the nine parameters would be beyond the scope of this Introduction, but we will delineate the principles mentioned in the different chapters.

- *Mediation for a Feeling of Competence:* Many ASD individuals have a fear of failure, owing to the fact that they have experienced so much of it, and this fear can block learning. Therapists put a great deal of emphasis on mediating for feelings of competence. The task being worked on is broken up into small steps, thereby ensuring that the child successfully accomplishes each stage. Tasks are selected so that, on the one hand, they help the child make progress and, on the other hand, enable him to be successful, after which his success is mediated to him. Mediation for a feeling of competence is accompanied by explanation, with the aim of creating a computational structure that will enable the child to change his self-image.
- *Mediation for Control of Behavior:* Many people on the spectrum characteristically show a high level of impulsivity. They are easily distracted by environmental/external stimuli as well as internal stimuli. For this reason, the therapist must assist them in setting specified goals for their processes of input, elaboration and output so as to aid the suppression or at least reduce the effect of internal and/or external distracters.
- *Mediation for Specifying Challenges:* The therapist prepares the client for the task presented. A large number of ASD individuals feel uncertainty when faced with a new task. They do not know how to assess their chances of success; they do not know how to evaluate failure, and so, in many cases, anxiety paralyzes them, and they are unable to cooperate with the therapist. The reader will note not just

how the different therapists mediate specific skills or tasks, but also how they prepare the client for the task. Thus, they demonstrate the task at hand, and, from the very beginning, indicate expected success and failure, which is presented in the context of tackling a challenge.

- *Mediation of the Awareness of a Human Being as a Changing Entity*: This mediation parameter is important on at least two dimensions. The first relates to the child and his emotional state before attempting a task, whether or not the therapist believes in his ability to change. In some of the case-studies in this book, we will see that the children tested the patience and determination of the therapist, and perhaps even the affection she felt towards him. The children would not cooperate with therapists who did not demonstrate these qualities in the face of the children's own testing. The second dimension is mediation for parents. The parents bring the child for treatment, and they are often quite desperate. Deep down, they fear that their child will remain autistic for the rest of his life. With the correct mediation from the therapists, the changes that the parents see as a result of treatment with the Feuerstein Method will lead them to perceive their child as someone who can change and develop. This factor is vital when bringing the parents into the treatment room (see detailed discussion in the chapter by Nakav and R. S. Feuerstein) and in making them active partners in the therapy process of their child.
- *Mediation for Sharing Behavior*: Thirteen-year-old John, who was discussed in the chapter by Jamet and Feuerstein, would shout rudely at passersby and be surprised that they were offended; immediately upon entering the treatment room, eighteen-year-old Anna would destroy a game that had been carefully prepared for her. These behavior patterns are familiar to all those involved in this field: life in a social bubble is one of the prominent characteristics of people on the spectrum. This requires *Mediation for Sharing Behavior*, in which what is mediated is the individual seeing himself as part of society and him seeing society as a system that organizes its parts. The chapter by Jamet and Feuerstein considers the use of Feuerstein's cognitive tools to change the clients' perception through mediating to them the ability to identify facial expressions—and even through direct cognitive intervention—aiming to create feelings of empathy.
- *Mediation for Individuation and Psychological Individualization*: "Barry, a five-year-old boy, was frustrated when his clinician did not understand his attempts to communicate," reports Frei Schreiber in her chapter. Barry did not see himself as an entity distinct from his surroundings. He expected that whatever he felt and desired would be understood by his surroundings in one way or another; in other words, the environment was responsible for responding to his needs. Thus, he perceived himself as being symbiotically attached to his environment. Mediation focused on the effort to mediate to Barry that he was a distinct entity—not

transparent to his surroundings—and that he must therefore make an effort to communicate coherently to those around him.

- *Mediation for the Search of an Optimistic Alternative*: In the chapter by Nakav and Feuerstein, Nakav writes of a low-functioning client who came to the Feuerstein Institute for treatment: "As a young therapist, I consulted Prof. Feuerstein, and he recommended that I write down everything the child knew how to do. It should be noted that my notebook remained empty. On one occasion, I noticed that the child showed considerable interest in cars, really inspecting them closely. From that point on I concentrated on cars in my treatment, examining the cars' size, color and shape..." Prof. Feuerstein's advice made the therapist look for an optimal alternative in the client. She had made it clear that the "islets of normality" in the child's functioning were few and far between—to say the least. Feuerstein mediated to his therapist to actively search for an optimal alternative.
- *Mediation of Challenge: The Search for Novelty and Complexity*: The behavior of individuals on the autistic spectrum is very often stereotypical. In their chapter, Feuerstein, Falik and R. S. Feuerstein describe the classic case of a child who, upon entering the treatment room for the first time, failed to notice special objects within the overall context of the treatment room. The therapist set himself the goal of building awareness in the child to the wide range of items in the room, both people and objects. Mediation of Challenge: The Search for Novelty and Complexity is essential in assisting the child to begin to be able to learn from the world around him.
- *Mediation for a Feeling of Belonging*: Returning to Steve in Jamet and R. S. Feuerstein chapter: Steve became confused when his beloved sister got married. He did not know whether his relationship with her would continue after her marriage. As far as he was concerned, he was losing her. Steve had a rigid of "belonging"; any disturbance of the family structure made him confused and anxious. The therapist used a tool called "Family Relations" from Feuerstein's Instrumental Enrichment series, which aims to give individuals the tools to organize the cognitive structure of family belonging in particular and social belonging in general.

To conclude, four fundamental parameters for Mediated Learning Experience were described above: *intentionality, reciprocity, meaning,* and *transcendence.* When the encounter between parent, therapist or teacher, and the child is not characterized by these four parameters, the desired cognitive-structural change will not come about. We have briefly reviewed the nine additional parameters of mediation. While not essential, these parameters can determine our learning style. We have taken a brief look at their relevance to individuals with communication disorders, many of which are defined as being on the autistic spectrum. We have offered case histories with explanations taken from the book's different chapters in order to illustrate the connection between the general theory and the implementation as discussed in this book, involving treatment of individuals defined as being on the autistic spectrum. The purpose of this section is not to repeat the theory that has been set forth in so many other Feuerstein books. Readers wishing to expand their knowledge are encouraged to turn to those books, which are available in many languages. Instead, this chapter aims to provide a brief description of the theory and, particularly, its basic connection to the theme of this book.

The Fourth Principle: Disability is Caused by a Lack of Mediated Learning

The Importance of Mediation to Human Development

In the previous chapter, we described mediated learning as a highly effective therapeutic technique because it addresses our basic thought structures and enacts a kind of "cognitive re-engineering." In fact, however, mediated learning experience theory makes an even more radical claim, namely, that *the development of a child's intelligence* stems from exposure to mediation processes by his parents, his educators, and his environment. Our theory argues that the four mediation parameters mentioned above (*intentionality, transcendence, meaning,* and *reciprocity*) naturally characterize the connection between parents and children in all cultures of the world. Many studies have indeed confirmed this claim. Parents and caregivers focus their children on the most relevant stimuli at that present moment. A mother says to her baby "look at me" and directs her gaze to his. If necessary, she gently moves his little head so that their eyes meet. Parents will slow down their speech, almost instinctively, so that their child can understand what they are saying. They will teach him about color and size, and about temporal and spatial concepts. They will mediate to him when they read him a story or simply speak to him. Alongside all the general knowledge they provide him with, the child's parents, teachers, siblings and other family members all mediate the thinking and learning skills that he needs. In this vein, Penina Klein, in *A Smarter Child* (1985), presented a host of longitudinal studies demonstrating that children exposed to intensive mediation by their mothers had a higher IQ than those who were not sufficiently exposed to mediation.

Children on the autistic spectrum frequently experience only minimal mediation. Their communication difficulties make it difficult for them to perceive the mediation directed at them. Their parents speak to them, but their receptive communication difficulties make it difficult for the child to understand what is being said and so affects the child's ability to learn.

Feuerstein distinguishes between *distal* factors (an underlying vulnerability for a particular condition or event) and *proximal* factors (a direct vulnerability for a particular condition or event). The distal factors for a lack of development are the child's communication difficulties, but the proximal and direct cause of damage to intelligence is the lack of mediation (due to his communication difficulties).

Thus, Feuerstein looks for "islets of normalcy" (as Shoshana Levin Fox discusses in her chapter) which indicate the existence of a learning process. Even if minor, these islets indicate that the child has certain abilities that are the product of learning. The cognitive-dynamic assessment—the LPAD (described in the chapters written by Paz, and by Ginton and Berkovich)—aims to identify the learning mechanisms that are present. These can be described as tiny slits in a fortified wall which act as a buffer between the child and the human environment that tries to mediate to him, with limited success. If we can identify the open slits—the learning mechanisms that exist in the child—we can use them in order to mediate (artificially at first) to the child and provide him with the skills he needs to learn and think. The LPAD creates a variety of learning situations around different types of tasks, in order to identify learning processes in the client that can later be built upon in order to mediate necessary skills, social understanding, rules of conduct, and so on.

The Search for "Islets of Normalcy" Using the "Cognitive Map"

According to Feuerstein's theory, one of the most important methods of seeking out the islets of normalcy—to locate the person's ability to learn and change—is the *cognitive map* (Feuerstein, Feuerstein, Falik, & Rand, 2006). The cognitive map is a tool that enables task analysis in terms of its cognitive characteristics. For example, mathematics requires a high level of abstraction, in contrast to manual labor in a factory. Factory labor, however, requires a much higher level of efficiency than that required by the mathematician. The mathematician can think about a problem for days or even months, whereas the production worker must keep up with a high rate of productivity. The complexity level, that is, the total amount of information that the architect must consider when planning a high-rise building, is much greater than that of the gardener who maintains a large garden. The modality of the tasks in which the mathematician deals is symbolic, while the modality of the gardener's tasks is motoric and the architect's is figural.

The Feuerstein therapist asks himself in which tasks the child's learning channels are more open and effective. Ayelet-Hashachar Aithan and Debbie Nadler's chapter on movement therapy shows that, with some individuals, working on certain skills can be more successful in the motor modality than in other modalities. They recount parents who were concerned that their ASD child was not able to play with his brother, who was close to him in age. All efforts to advance in this area proved fruitless,

except for an activity using movement, which led the children to cooperate. The motor modality often creates modes of change where other
modalities, such as the verbal and pictorial ones, do not.

Avichay and R. S. Feuerstein note that the grapho-motoric modality
(writing) may lead to breakthroughs in the communication ability of a child
with ASD because it provides fast and efficient tools in which a person can
express himself. Often, the child has a history of failure in using the verbal
modality and so cannot express himself using this channel. In their chapter
on cognitive mediation, Jamet and R. S. Feuerstein demonstrate that the
cognitive modality is often more effective in dealing with the complexity of
family and social relationships than behavioral and emotional modalities. In
these examples, we illustrate the efforts of various therapists to locate the
"open slits" in order to use them to produce learning and change.

In their chapter on the treatment of a person on the autistic spectrum
with a multi-disciplinary team, Nakav and R. S. Feuerstein present the
tremendous advantages of teamwork. In an efficient team, therapists who
come from different disciplines report to the others on learning processes
that they have found effective. This mutuality significantly expands the
efficacy of the treatment.

The Cognitive Map

The cognitive map examines how the characteristics of a task relate to the
performance of the subject. These characteristics are:

- Content of the task—the sort of action the examinee is asked to perform
  (e.g., answer questions, free-style writing, summarize, plan a sequence of
  actions).
- Modality of the task—the functional channel in which the task is
  performed (e.g., figurative, graphic, symbolical-mathematical, visual-
  linguistic).
- Cognitive functions—whether the task is characterized by a high level
  of input requirements (e.g., reading a detailed contract vs. reading the
  newspaper); a high level of elaboration requirements (solving a mathematical problem vs. putting together a puzzle); or a high level of
  output requirements (a professional lecture vs. a chat with friends).
- Thinking operations—the major thinking operations required by the task
  (e.g., mathematical thinking, deductive thinking, analogical thinking).
- Level of complexity—the amount of information in the task and how
  familiar the examinee is with this information (e.g., walking through a
  familiar city vs. driving through an unfamiliar place).
- Level of abstraction—the extent to which the task is done on mental
  representations, in the mind, or on the physical objects themselves
  (block-building vs. the popular game "Rush Hour").

- Level of efficiency—whether the task demands a high or low level of efficiency (e.g., a computer game vs. reading a book).

Identifying Learning Blockages Using Feuerstein's Model of "Deficient Cognitive Functions"

Pinpointing learning *channels*, an issue that was discussed in the previous section, is just the first step towards bringing about change. The next step, that of identifying learning *blockages*, allows us to penetrate the afore-mentioned "thinking structures" and begin to make change from within. At this point we ask ourselves "what exactly has to be changed in order to expand the learning channels?" After all, this is the main task of the FM: the individual cannot make progress simply by relying on his current learning channels—they may be too restricted.

To this end, the FM seeks to identify and map the learning obstructions, which Feuerstein called *Deficient Cognitive Functions*. Feuerstein argued that beneath the surface of thinking skills there is an entire world of processes that allow or inhibit human learning. He defined those functions as the "cognitive prerequisites essential to learning." The notion of "prerequisites" is a refreshing—even a necessary—innovation in the world of learning. Nor-mally, we focus on skills, asking whether the child is able or unable to read, to perform arithmetical operations, to communicate, to adapt to the society to which he belongs. Feuerstein maintained that, frequently, the lack of such skills stems from an absence of the aforementioned necessary conditions for learning and thinking.

Feuerstein divided the list of functions into three thinking phases: *input, elaboration and output*. Each one of these phases is comprised of different functions that, optimally, are sharp and precise, thereby allowing precise targets to be set in the intervening phase, leading to effective processes of change. Below is the list of Deficient Cognitive Functions as described by Feuerstein:

I. DEFICIENT COGNITIVE FUNCTIONS

Input Level

- Blurred and sweeping perception
- Unplanned, impulsive, and unsystematic exploratory behavior
- Lack of, or impaired, receptive verbal tools which affect discrimina-tion, such as objects, events, relationships, and so on do not have appropriate labels
- Lack of, or impaired, spatial orientation; lack of stable systems of reference impairs establishment of topological and Euclidean organi-zation of space

- Lack of, or impaired, temporal concepts
- Lack of, or impaired, conservation of constancies (size, shape, quantity, orientation) across variation in these factors
- Lack of, or deficient, need for precision and accuracy in data gathering
- Lack of capacity to consider two or more sources of information at once; this is reflected in dealing with data in a piecemeal fashion rather than as a unit of organized facts

The *input process* is responsible for data collection and its transfer to the elaboration phase. The input process should be directed at the task facing the person. Thus, the input process is not only sensory. Input is a thought-driven, planned, and controlled action. In their chapter, Avichay and R. S. Feuerstein describe the following case: "I asked Steve to describe what a square is made up of; for example, how many lines does it have? How long are the lines (are they equal or not)? How many angles is a square made up of? In fact, what is an angle? He was not able to answer any of the questions. Nor did he know the relationship between the different shapes that make up a square or a triangle."

Steve's case illustrates the input phase function, "lack of receptive verbal tools which affect discrimination." This difficulty involves of a lack of geometrical and spatial concepts, and it caused Steve's *blurred and sweeping perception.* In turn, this perception made it hard for Steve to identify even simple shapes.

Elaboration Level

- Inadequacy in the perception of the existence and definition of an actual problem
- Inability to select relevant vs non-relevant cues in defining a problem
- Lack of spontaneous comparable behavior or limitation of its application by a restricted need system
- Narrowness of the psychic field
- Episodic grasp of reality
- Lack of, or impaired, need for pursuing logical evidence
- Lack of, or impaired, interiorization
- Lack of, or impaired, inferential-hypothetical, "iffy" thinking
- Lack of, or impaired, strategies for hypothesis testing
- Lack of, or impaired, ability to define the framework necessary for problem-solving behavior
- Lack of, or impaired, planning behavior

The *elaboration phase* is responsible for transforming the information into coherent knowledge, that is knowledge from which new knowledge can be generated through the process of drawing conclusions, planning, decision making and more. Ginton and Berkowitz report on seventeen-year-old Ian, diagnosed with ASD. Ian was able to successfully perform assigned tasks, but he could not articulate what he did in order to succeed. The therapists understood that he had difficulty in understanding the logic of the task and the logic of the strategies to solve it. This is the elaboration phase cognitive function *"lack of or impaired ability to define the framework necessary for problem-solving behavior"* Ian's difficulty with this elaboration phase function made it hard for him to use a strategy that he had learned in one task and apply it to another one.

Steve, who is discussed in Avichai and R. S. Feuerstein's chapter, found it difficult to connect his inner world to his life experiences. He also had trouble personalizing his e-mails to specific individuals. Thus, he would send messages of similar content and tone to his parents, his brothers and his friends. This represents the elaboration function called *episodic grasp of reality*. This cognitive function expresses a person's difficulty seeing the connection between the whole and its parts. Consequently, Steve did not adapt the content of his e-mail to his addressee; he did not make a connection between his feelings and the expression of those feelings. And, in fact, one of the "building blocks" of that chapter discusses mediation for analysis and synthesis on different levels with an aim to identifying "parts" and connecting them to the "whole."

Lucy, who was also introduced in Avichai and R. S. Feuerstein's chapter, could not seat herself on a chair. She did not know which way to position her body, where to put her bag while she was sitting on the chair, where exactly to put her feet. It thus took Lucy half an hour to sit down instead of a few seconds. This behavior is an expression of the elaboration phase cognitive function pertaining to the ability to plan; to create a sequence of actions with each stage in the sequence leading to the next.

Output Level

- Egocentric communicational modalities
- Difficulties in projecting virtual relationships
- Blocking
- Trial and error responses
- Lack of, or impaired, tools for communicating adequately elaborated responses
- Lack of, or impaired, need for precision and accuracy in communicating one's responses
- Deficiency of visual transport
- Impulsive, acting-out behavior

The *output phase* is responsible for using the conclusions of the elaboration phase in the real world. This process cannot be automatic. In the output phase, one must actively consider how to adapt the conclusions arrived at during processing to the reality before us. Correct functioning at the output phase means, for example, that we will send the same message using different formats to our family or to our colleagues. In Jamet and R. S. Feuerstein's chapter, we read of a common phenomenon among children with ASD: if they come upon an unfamiliar word when asked to read a particular passage aloud, they become "blocked". Feuerstein defined *blocking* as a cognitive function in the output phase (as shown in the list above). According to Feuerstein, blocking is caused by non- systematic and uncontrolled work; when a mistake is made, the person becomes paralyzed for lack of a systematic work strategy. If the child's answer is not accurate, he does not even try to correct it; instead, he freezes. In such a case, the problem does not lie in reading but in the cognitive function of blocking and the failure to deal with this function.

Moving to one of the cases described recurrently in this book, Frei Schreiber presents a child who communicated exclusively through gestures and a medley of unintelligible sounds. The therapist decided to adopt a paradoxical approach and responded to her client using the same incomprehensible language. Grasping the absurdity of her own behavior, the child burst into laughter. Her original communication pattern stemmed from a defective function at the output phase called *egocentric communication*. This function expresses a misunderstanding of the gap between one person and the "other" who listens to him and is in his environment. The speaker, in this case the child, does not take into account the gaps in understanding between herself and the listener. Making her aware of her own behavior helped her to see how she was being perceived by others.

This introduction aims to introduce the reader to the various cognitive functions mentioned in this volume and to the theoretical groundwork that forms the common ground for the various disciplines described in this book. Although they address different aspects of functioning and personality, all the Feuerstein therapists use the same form of analysis and intervention.

The Main Applications of the Feuerstein Method

Feuerstein developed the four major applications that are mentioned in this introduction and to which individual chapters are devoted. The first application is known as *Feuerstein Instrumental Enrichment* (FIE). FIE is divided into one program suitable for medium- and high-functioning individuals (FIE-S) and another program for low-functioning individuals (FIE-B). This program contains a total of 25 different instruments that deal with different cognitive, emotional and social functions. Jamet and R. S. Feuerstein's chapter discusses the implementation of particular instruments for individuals with ASD.

The second application is the *Learning Propensity Assessment Device (LPAD)*. (Feuerstein, R., Falik, L., & Feuerstein, R.S   1998. This assessment is intended to identify the examinee's learning potential, and the optimal mediation and intervention required in order to realize his/her potential. The LPAD has one version that assesses low-functioning individuals, LPAD-B, (Feuerstein, R.S., Feuerstein, R., & Falik, L. (2009).) (described in Ginton and Berkovitz's chapters) and one version that assesses high functioning individuals (described in Paz's chapter).

The third application is the *Mediated Learning Experience (MLE)*. MLE, discussed throughout the book, is the optimal therapeutic interaction to produce structural changes in individuals with ASD—and, in fact, in anyone.

The fourth application is called *Shaping a Modifying Environment (SME)*. How can an environment be transformed into one that encourages change processes? An environment can be a family, a classroom, a clinic, a school, a factory, an office, or any organizational environment. Nakav and R. S. Feuerstein's chapter deals with the transformation of the therapeutic staff into a catalyst for change; the transformation of the therapeutic staff into a kind of "whole" whose total sum exceeds its parts, and how this environment accelerates processes of change in a person in need of treatment, education, and rehabilitation.

It has been noted that the FM can be fairly labor-intensive. It is critical that we have a partner with whom to work together, so that the work that carried out by the Feuerstein therapist can be continued in other environments such as the school and home. The method is under no circumstances a "fix" that occurs by bringing the child for weekly treatments but rather a process of change that occurs by creating optimal learning environments. Finding partners, whether they are family, members of the educational team or other persons who are a regular part of the child's life, is critical in order to ensure that the method can be implemented in a manner that can create change within the child.

We are also aware that there are often many complex issues that may impact a child's wellbeing. At times these issues may need to be addressed with urgency and so take priority over some of the cognitive challenges that we would want to work on. The Feuerstein mediators frequently work together with medical professionals and social workers to safeguard the overall wellbeing of the child. When we met four-year-old Jacob, he was an very picky eater. Our speech and occupational therapist, who observed that he was extremely underweight, worked intensively with a dietician and family members to ensure that Jacob was receiving the necessary nutrition.

The FM requires that a Feuerstein-trained mediator who is able to adapt their skills to each child work as part of a team in order to assist the child to become an active learner. This often requires considerable investment on the part of the mediator, who needs to adapt themselves and constantly update their learning goals for the child. Finding the right mediator for the child and their family members can be challenging.

We are aware that not all the Instrumental Enrichment (FIE) tools are appropriate for every child. Some tools require cognitive skills that may need to be taught before the child can attempt the Instrumental Enrichment (FIE) tool.

We do not promise quick results or claim that a child will reach a specific goal. Instead, we enter into a learning process together with the child that can equip them with tools to potentially progress beyond their current manifest abilities. Some children may even need to learn to adopt skills that can help them adjust to a learning environment so that they are in a state that they can begin to accept the mediation that will be necessary to help them learn. This indeed can be a long process.

It is part of the Feuerstein mediator's job to ensure that family members are kept well informed as to how the child's learning process is developing and how they can adapt to their child's changing abilities. At times, parents and other members of the team may have other events occurring in their lives that may make it difficult for them to focus on their child's learning process. The mediator must ensure that they are sensitive to these changing situations and adapt accordingly. Many families are fearful of being disappointed and may have been exposed to various schemes that had promised outcomes that did not materialize. This may also impact their ability to believe in optimistic outcomes that augment their child's learning process.

Feuerstein mediators have found that one of the best ways to help family members become part of our team is to initially demonstrate some of the early changes that we have observed, however big or small, and so assist them to believe in their child's ability to change. Some families are understandably hesitant or nervous to accept these changes, and it is critical that we understand the process that they are experiencing and work together so that can have a clear understanding of the method and how it can impact their child's learning abilities.

Conclusion

As the FM has been discussed in depth in many articles and books, the interested reader is invited to turn for greater detail to these comprehensive publications. The present chapter aims to clarify the basic concepts of this wide-ranging theory, link it to the various chapters of this book, and demonstrate its coherence—particularly with respect to its influence on the therapeutic processes described.

The FM has been widely implemented. The most prominent application relates to the field of education. The cognitive mediation program, "FIE," has been implemented in schools around the world and translated into many languages. The early childhood program developed by Feuerstein and Feuerstein, known as the Feuerstein Instrument Enrichment-Basic (FIE-B), has been implemented in kindergartens and lower grades in many countries. The same is true of the LPAD. The digital version of the LPAD (LPAD-D), developed by the editor of this book, facilitates its use among growing numbers worldwide.

Other applications for the FM in the clinical field include delaying the progress of dementia, as well as cognitive rehabilitation after head injuries, treating those with chromosomal disorders such as Down Syndrome, Williams Syndrome, Fragile X Syndrome, and more.

The FM, with its ability to significantly modify individuals' learning, thinking, and functioning, has been implemented as a comprehensive educational concept in schools for special education and housing arrangements for people with special needs, as well as in preparation for the employment and marriage of those with special needs. Moreover, there are interesting applications in the field of mental health. It should be mentioned that the FM has also been applied with individuals with learning disabilities and visual impairments. We conclude by noting that this is only a partial list of the extensive applications of the FM and instruments.

References

Feuerstein, R., P. Klein, & A. Tannenbaum (Eds.), Mediated learning experience: Theoretical, psychosocial, and learning implications. Tel Aviv and London: Freund, 1991.

Feuerstein, R., Falik, L., & Feuerstein, R.S , "The Learning Potential Assessment Device: An Alternative Approach to the Assessment of Learning Potential", in Advances in Cross-Cultural Assessment, eds. Ronald J. Samuda, Reuven Feuerstein, Alan S. Kaufman, John E. Lewis, Robert J. Sternberg & Associates, CA, U.S.A., Sage Publications, Inc., 1998.

Feuerstein, R., Feuerstein, R. S., Falik, L., & Rand, Y. *Creating and Enhancing Cognitive Modifiability: The Feuerstein Instrumental Enrichment Program.* Jerusalem: ICELP Press, 2006.

Feuerstein, R. & Spire, A. *La pédagogic à visage humain.* Paris: Le Bord de l'Eau, 2006.

Klein, Penina. *A Smarter Child.* Ramat Gan: Bar Ilan University Press, 2020–1985 (Hebrew).

Feuerstein, R., Falik, L., Rand, Y., & Feuerstein, R.S. (2002). The dynamic assessment of cognitive modifiability. Jerusalem: ICELP Press.

Feuerstein, R.S., Feuerstein, R., & Falik, L. (2005). The Feuerstein programs for early assessment and intervention: The LPAD-Basic and the IE-Basic. In Oon-Seng Tan and A. Seok-Hoon Seng (Eds.), Enhancing cognitive functions. Singapore: McGraw Hill Asia.

Feuerstein, R.S., Feuerstein, R., & Falik, L. (2009). Learning potential assessment device - Basic: Examiner's Manual (2nd revised edition). Jerusalem: ICELP.

Feuerstein, R., Rand, Y. and Feuerstein, R.S. (2006) You Love Me!! ... Don't Accept me as I am: Helping the Low Functioning Person Excel. Jerusalem, Israel: ICELP.

Feuerstein, R., Falik, L., & Feuerstein R. S. (2010). Beyond smarter: Mediated learning and the brain's capacity for change. New York: Teachers College Press

Feuerstein, R., Falik, L., Feuerstein, R.S., & Bohacs, K. (2012). A think-aloud and talk-aloud approach to building language. New York: Teachers College Press.

Chapter 1

Autism and its Changes

Reuven Feuerstein, Louis H. Falik and Refael S. Feuerstein

There has been an epidemic increase in the number of individuals diagnosed with autism, and an accompanying interest in the causes, treatment and prognosis of the condition. Newschaffer et al. (2007) report that in the 1960s and 1970s the incidence was approximately 1 in 1000 in the general population, but that in the 1990s the incidence dramatically increased Morbidity and Mortality Weekly Report, 2009), going as high as an eight-fold increase. Recent research indicates that as many as 3 percent of children in the US may be affected (Christensen et al., 2019). The causes for this increase are a matter of intense speculation, ranging from true increases in the incidence of autism to changes in reporting, unclear and inaccurate diagnostic criteria, environmental and nutritional causes, public awareness, and a strong push for early detection.

The Feuerstein Alternative

In light of this phenomenon—and the many parents who have come to us for help—we have developed an alternative point of view. This view is rooted in our theory of Structural Cognitive Modifiability (SCM; see Introduction to the Theory and Feuerstein, 1990), and the application of our methods based on the provision of mediated learning experience (MLE; Feuerstein, Klein, & Tanenbaum, 1991). Thus, we have used our accumulated experience and practice with children diagnosed as having an autistic spectrum disorder to encourage a different and flexible response to treatment.

The designation of "autistic spectrum" has gained popularity in recent years. It has even replaced the term "autism" in the DSM-5 (the *Diagnostic and Statistical Manual for Mental Disorders* that is the officially recognized categorization of psychiatric disorders used in the US). This term offers a wider view of the behaviors observed and formerly more rigidly labeled as "autistic."

Nonetheless, we believe that it would be more accurate to label, describe and treat the behaviors included in the "autistic spectrum" as *social/ developmental communication disorders,* either within the frameworks of existing treatment interventions (by adding dimensions to them) or as a

DOI: 10.4324/9781003451136-2

fully independent modality of treatment. This change of formulation is of course due to the basic assumptions, theory and applications of the Feuerstein Method (FM). We will expand on this relabeling in much of what follows in this book. At the same time, we will continue to refer to the accepted definition as ASD, in order to relate to the existing practice. We employ a reframing of the concept and meaning of *autism*.

Our perspective is that within human nature and development there is a natural range of social response potentials, some of which are defined by culture and some of which are a consequence of a lack of responding. This potential range of social interaction reflects developmental learning experience, or the exposure to stimulation. Some individuals function at the higher end of the social response spectrum and some at the lower end. At the upper end, we label this "creativity," "eccentricity," and other, generally positive, descriptions. At the lower end, we observe impairments in responding realistically, efficiently, and reciprocally to the environment. One can say that these individuals have not (in our view, "as yet") acquired the social skills needed to respond as the environment expects. Considered in this way, we can readily see the potential to be modified and adapted to normalized interactions.

Thus, we advocate a new perspective and seek alternative treatments. We do not deny the existence of what might be described as "full blown" autism, and variations of intensity and behavior that characterize the spectrum. Our concern, however, is with all of those who may manifest some "autistiform" symptoms and have been inaccurately diagnosed as autistic, with all the accompanying assumptions about cognitive potential and behavioral limitations.

Nonetheless, there is no denying typical communication difficulties, even if they do not necessarily lead to a rigid definition of ASD. Thus, we move in this book between two poles: one that opposes a more or less rigid definition of "autism" based on certain symptoms, and another that relates to these characteristic symptoms and offers them the unique answer of the FM. In the following chapters, we will elaborate on how these limitations affect families, services and responses to individuals who are so diagnosed.

Six Themes to Guide this Consideration

We will discuss six themes that characterize the cognitive/social mediation approach to assessing and treating those who are considered autistic:

1   The implications of the tendency to diagnose children very early (often and increasingly in infancy and within the first two years of life) if they show signs of "autistic-like behaviors."

2   Behavioral differences frequently attributed to the autistic condition but that may indicate desirable characteristics.
3   Looking for and exploiting "islets of normalcy" in the full range of behavioral functioning.
4   Implications of observations, interventions and potential for modifiability in light of findings regarding neural plasticity.
5   Institutional responses and resistances to existing and changing definitions.
6   Mediating cognitive functions for children who have received various diagnoses, among them being on the "autistic spectrum."

We will see that many different "special needs" children may respond to cognitive modifiability in ways that transcend the diagnosis. The final point will be addressed in two ways: by considering popular approaches to dealing with children showing autism and autistic spectrum behavior, and then comparing them to our approach, focusing on treating autistic behavior based on our theory of cognitive modifiability and the application of mediated learning experience.

Throughout this book, we will be raising critical questions and answering them with examples from our clinical experience. At the same time, we will present the conceptual frameworks that has guided our work with the identified autistic population of children and adults. While our approach may, to some extent, challenge conventional opinion and practice, we believe that it is critical for the welfare of many individuals who have the potential to live more promising and productive lives.

A Brief History of Autism

Autism and its various behavioral manifestations, as reflected in the diagnostic term "autistic spectrum disorders" (ASD), is currently considered to reflect some degree of neurophysiological condition—although the specific neurological parameters await discovery. But this was not always so. In this chapter, we will review the history of this development and its consequences.

The psychiatric focus emerged in 1910 with Eugen Bleuler's labeling aspects of schizophrenic behavior as "autistic," describing a withdrawal into fantasies, and distancing from the outer world (Kuhn & Cahn, 2004). Previous to this, Itard's work with the *Wild Boy of Aveyron,* the feral child Victor, described autistic-like behavior but did not label it as such, or attempt to differentiate it from the more general cultural deprivation issues about which he hypothesized. Jean Marc Gaspard tried to teach Victor to develop social relationships and language, but was largely unsuccessful, and became somewhat pessimistic about Victor's potential to overcome his developmental disabilities (Wolff, 2004). This pessimism pervaded later perspectives on the potential of very low-functioning, non-socialized individuals to overcome their disabilities.

The modern view of autism can be traced to Hans Asperger,[1] who, in a 1938 lecture, attributed various asocial behaviors he was studying to Bleuler's designation and description. This conceptualization later merged into the pattern of behaviors associated with his name—Asperger Syndrome—which subsequently came to describe milder levels of autistic symptomology. Asperger Syndrome has been dropped from the most current revision of the DSM-5 categorization of psychiatric disorders.

Considerably more widespread awareness was triggered by Leo Kanner's introduction of the term *early infantile autism* (Kanner, 1943). This notion was followed up and brought to a broader public by Bernard Rimland in 1964, and then popularized by Bruno Bettelheim's widely read books, notably *The Empty Fortress: Infantile Autism and the Birth of the Self* (1967).

The developing diagnostic terminology stemming from these various authors was widely adopted, and led to formulations that were quite negative toward mothers—including maternal deprivation, the "refrigerator mother," the "schizophrenogenic mother"—all of which placed the blame for the child's condition on characteristics or treatment by their mothers. It has been pointed out that in spite of more modern thinking, many of Kanner's descriptions continue to be hallmarks of the "autistic condition" (Happe, Ronald & Plomin, 2006), a number of which found their way into earlier editions of the DSM, and became the diagnostic guidelines used by psychologists, psychiatrists, pediatricians, and social workers. These include social withdrawal, insistence on sameness and repetitive and self-stimulating behaviors. Rimland, however, questioned the etiology of the condition, and later attacked Bettelheim's theory and conclusions (particularly those blaming the parents). Thus, he can be considered a pioneer of the later developing environmental and neurological findings. He also was supportive of the exploration of nutritional factors, such as ingestion of yeast, gluten, and casein which have become *popularly* associated with causation and treatment. In this sense, he was far ahead of his time.

Another strand of research into causes of autistic-like behavior that has historical importance is that of the maternal deprivation studies of René Spitz (1946) and John Bowlby (1952), who described infants raised in orphanages who showed failure to thrive physically and affective impairments—leading to *anaclitic depression, marasmus,* and long-term expressions of social detachment, in spite of later exposure to positive environments. The work of Skodak (1938) and Skodak and Skeels (1945, 1949) identified and then followed into second and third generations the effects on infants and young children who were either "maternally/ affectively deprived, or given sustained contact with caregivers who acted as "maternal substitutes." In brief, the authors found that environmental factors influence emotional (and physical) development. This sheds light on the complexity of the potential causes of autistic-like functioning. Nonetheless, it does not invalidate the recent neurological hypotheses, and may in fact deepen them from the perspective of the contribution of inter- relationships to the condition.

Questions regarding causes have revolved around genetics because of evidence of heritability. But at present there is little real evidence of the role of genetic factors with regard to causation. Further findings on neurophysiological factors are likely to emerge from future research There are clearly language acquisition and social dissociation factors at play, but again with little predictive or etiological evidence (cf., Skoyles, 2008). More recent thinking, somewhat distinct but not disconnected from neurological factors, focuses on various environmental factors.

There are many confusing and contradictory indicators in the origins of autistic behavior. Among them are the children who appear to develop normally and then at the age of three or four begin to show autistic symptomatology. Others are reactions to various aspects of diet, or the relationship to fevers and other physical conditions.

We conclude this brief historical review with the observation that, ultimately, DNA studies and other neuroscience research on the human potential for neural plasticity are likely to bridge the differences between the nature and nurture theories, and greatly clarify autism's origins. Genetic explanations, too, may yet be discovered that shed light on the puzzle of ASD. Fortunately, however, we do not have to wait until this clarity is achieved to deal more effectively with individuals functioning on the autistic spectrum. As this book unfolds, the reader will discover many such ways to do so.

Note

1 Hans Asperger was a Nazi physician who was an important part of the euthanasia project which murdered disabled people in Germany.

References

Bettelheim, Bruno. *The Empty Fortress: Infantile Autism and the Birth of the Self.* New York: Free Press, 1967.

Bowlby, John. "Maternal Care and Mental Health." *Journal of Consulting Psychology* 16, 3(1952): 232.

Feuerstein, R. "The Theory of Structural Cognitive Modifiability". In B. Presseisen (ed.), *Learning and Thinking Styles: Classroom Interaction*. Washington, DC: National Education Association, 1990.

Feuerstein, R., P. Klein, & A. Tannenbaum (eds.), *Mediated learning experience: Theoretical, psychosocial, and learning implications*. Tel Aviv and London: Freund, 1991.

Happe, F., A. Ronald, & R. Plomin. "Time to Give Up on a Single Explanation for Autism." *Nature Neuroscience* 9, 10(2006): 1218–1220.

Kanner, L. "Autistic Disturbances of Affective Contact." *Nervous Child* 2 (1943): 217–250.

Kuhn, R. & , C. H. Cahn. "Eugen Bleuler's concepts of psychopathology." *History of Psychiatry* 15 (3, 2004): 361–366.

Morbidity and Mortality Weekly Report. Atlanta, GA: Centers for Disease Control and Prevention, 2009.

Newschaffer, C. J. (2007). "The Epidemiology of Autism Spectrum Disorders." *Annual Review of Public Health* 28 (2007): 235–258.

Skodak, M. "The Mental Development of Adopted Children whose True Mothers are Feeble-Minded." *Child Development* 9 (1938): 303–308.

Skodak, M. & H. M. Skeels. "A follow-up study of children in adoptive homes." *The Pedagogical Seminary and Journal of Genetic Psychology* 66 (1945): 21–58.

Skodak, M. & H. M. Skeels. "A Final Follow-up Study of One Hundred Adopted Children." *The Pedagogical Seminary and Journal of Genetic Psychology* 75, 1 (1949): 85–125.

Skoyles, J. R. "No New Neurobiology Yet for Autism." *Archives of Neurology* 65, 1(2008): 155.

Spitz, R. A. "Hospitalism: A Follow-up Report on an Investigation Described in Volume I, 1945." *The Psychoanalytic Study of the Child* 2 (1946): 113–117.

Wolff, S. "Autism: explaining the enigma." *The Journal of Child Psychology and Psychiatry* 45 1 (2004): 172–173.

Chapter 2

Searching for Islets of Normalcy

Shoshana Levin Fox[1]

Little Jodi sits alone on the carpet, rocking back and forth, seemingly oblivious to the world around her. She does not make eye contact with her parents. She has no language. When tense, she flaps her hands in front of her eyes as if to blot out the world. Jodi, a fictionalized example, is presenting with classically autistic symptoms.

Had I been working with Jodi from a conventional model, I would have noted these symptoms, compared her symptoms against a listing of accepted diagnostic criteria, discussed the autism diagnosis with her parents, and recommended special education. What an impoverished, inadequate and flawed way of working that would have been!

Fortunately, for the thousands of children who at first glance appeared to be autistic or who had been diagnosed previously as autistic in settings that used conventional assessment means, we at the Feuerstein Institute eschewed conventional symptom lists and assessment measures. Our work drew inspiration from Reuven Feuerstein's vision and ironclad belief in the capacity of each individual for modifiability. From assessment through treatment phases, we worked from a model that focused on strengths, not symptoms.

"Islets of normalcy" is Feuerstein's key term which enlightened our work with children thought to be autistic. What is an "islet of normalcy"? In the sea of the child's symptoms, these are even the tiniest signs of non-symptomatic behavior that will serve as toeholds on which to begin to build the child's positive development. For those who struggle with the notion of "normalcy," try thinking in terms of islets of competency or islets of ability. I found it most helpful to think of islets of normalcy as "anti-symptoms," behaviors or emotional responses of *any* sort from any developmental realm, which are *not* symptomatic of autism, and which give a glimmer of the child's non-autistic potential.

When working from a conventional, symptom-based model, in sharp contrast to the Feuerstein approach, symptoms come first. And, tragically, given the disastrously elastic symptom criteria of the DSM-5, as documented in this contributor's autism casebook, it is currently far too easy to spot (or to

DOI: 10.4324/9781003451136-3

misinterpret) symptoms that *mistakenly* suggest the current one-size-fits-all autism diagnosis (Levin Fox, 2020). However, identification of "symptoms" is not the end game in the work of child development, education or psychology. Identifying symptoms is only a simplistic beginning. Far more critical in assessing young children is identifying those sparks of relevant functioning, incipient and even latent communicative intent, and the child's hesitant, sometimes fleeting, attempts at reciprocity and relationship. When we are seeking evidence of healthier functioning behind the symptoms, we must actively search for even the smallest "islets of normalcy" in the vast sea of the child's symptoms.

So, from the Feuerstein perspective, when assessing or working with a child who presents as avoidant and/or nonverbal and/or non-communicative and/or stereotypically repetitive, we are vigilantly on the lookout for even the most miniscule evidence of *non*-autistic behavior: the slightest indication of interest in or response to the world of emotions, communication and connection. When a visually avoidant child suddenly gives a flash of eye contact, when a child who rocks or spins incessantly suddenly stops, when a child who appears cut off from feelings suddenly smiles when gently tickled, when a silent child emits even a single sound, word or phrase, when an emotionally detached child shows curiosity in a play material or reaches for mommy's hand—these tiny flashes of asymptomatic potential within must always be noted. Later, primarily through the use of interactive play, these encouraging little sparks can be coaxed into a veritable developmental bonfire!

At the Feuerstein Institute, my colleagues and I witnessed impressive progress in children who had been autism-diagnosed elsewhere, progress which began by identifying even the tiniest islets of normalcy. No matter how miniscule, fleeting or rare an islet of normalcy is within a child's profile, it is always developmentally significant!

When we observe such a small islet, the next question we ask ourselves is: "How can I expand and strengthen this islet?" not in the behavioral modification sense of primarily increasing its frequency, but with the aim of weaving and then firmly establishing this expanded and strengthened islet into the totality of the child's presentation. When islets of rudimentary communication, connection, or purposeful functioning do not yet exist, then our goal is to *create* islets even where they are not yet evident (Levin Fox, 2020), by using creativity, play, music, movement and play-based cognitive tasks to elicit new islets while continuing to expand and strengthen existing ones.

The concept of islets of normalcy is important throughout the course of assisting a child initially considered autistic, but it is perhaps most critical in that first meeting with a child and parents. This is so because most parents arrive at the Institute weighed down by the conventionally determined diagnosis which their child has received (which may or may not be accurate) and burdened by their own assumptions regarding prognosis gleaned from their own reading or from other professionals. In a first session in particular, a positive focus on identifying and creating islets of normalcy has the power to demonstrate the promising Feuerstein paradigm that can positively affect parental attitude, morale, and actions, and which can dramatically impact on the treatment plan, educational placement, and prognosis for the child.

The impact on the child, as the clinician actively, playfully and meaningfully interacts with the child in order to explore, elicit and magnify the miniscule evidence of more normative functioning, is no less dramatic. In my office, children not infrequently began to make eye contact, to communicate in some fashion and to function more meaningfully. While the islets I observed may have been evanescent and fleeting, they were nonetheless present—and they subsequently informed further work with the child, the practical recommendations to the parents and even the child's future educational placement.

Bert and Zach were two such young children. Each child had previously been diagnosed elsewhere as suffering from autism. However, in both cases the clinical focus on islets of normalcy, rather than on each child's very evident symptoms, led to a clear paradigm shift for these two children and for their caregivers. Over the years, there have been many other children for whom our focus on islets of normalcy moved the prognosis away from pathology and toward normative functioning, often dramatically so. The following description of Bert's and Zach's initial sessions illustrates how a clinician can search for, identify and begin to work with islets of normalcy.

Bert

I will never forget Bert's arrival at the Institute for an assessment. It was two o'clock in the afternoon, and I was facing my last session of the day, after a wearying morning working with a number of challenging children. I was feeling tired and admittedly not enthusiastic about the next session as I pulled out the file of this new little boy, only weeks short of his seventh birthday. He had been diagnosed as autistic at the age of two by a well-known Israeli autism specialist. I read through the specialist's report that had been submitted in the referral material. Over the course of several sessions, the specialist had applied the criteria of the DSM-IV, then extant, in addition to observing the child at play and conducting an interview with his foster parents. The specialist's conclusion was unequivocal: Bert was autistic. The report was only too rich with supporting descriptions of the child's lack of speech, his lack of communication, his lack of ability to form relationships, and his impoverished cognitive functioning, which the specialist concluded was typical of "mental retardation." The specialist had recommended that Bert continue in a special educational setting for autistic children, a small class in which he received several hours of therapy per week—but was placed among similarly impaired children, who lacked language, social, communication and play skills. Feeling even wearier after reading this pessimistic report, I braced myself for a challenging, arduous last session, one which would surely require massive energy output to assess such a difficult child. I opened the door of my office to Bert and his foster parents. I was not at all prepared for what ensued.

A bright-eyed and eager little boy, with sparkling blue eyes and fetching blond hair, burst into the room with a warm, enthusiastic smile. For a second or two, he looked at me directly with eyes which expressed anticipation and which communicated a sweet and energetic little soul. Could this be the same child described in the specialist's report? Bert was so present and eager, not at all distant or cut off. There was something absolutely charming about him. My mood lifted. The afternoon was going to be quite different from what I had imagined a few minutes ago, when I had been strongly influenced by the mood, tone and conclusions in the report of a specialist who had only noted his deficits and symptoms in conventional fashion, but apparently had not noticed his strengths.

Bert was one of my earlier clients at the Institute. I have since learned to read referral material from other specialists with respect, but at the same time, always to reserve judgment and to be highly cautious of conclusions and recommendations when previous testing is based on the DSM criteria and/or when it is clear from the report that the specialist, or team of specialists, has not played with the child or otherwise actively and warmly tried to elicit engagement. Even in the face of a stack of reports which all express a negative prognosis of a given child's abilities, I always reserve the right to explore each child's potential and to come to my own conclusions about the accuracy of an autism diagnosis and the child's potential for modifiability.

When working from a model which prizes islets of normalcy, the attitude of the practitioner and the intentionally relaxed atmosphere in the room are critical: "Let the child explore. Don't interfere with a child's initiative and explorations, especially in an initial session." This was a cardinal rule for Reuven Feuerstein whenever he first observed young children in his office. He taught us well. Feuerstein's emphasis on permitting a developmentally impaired child, or so suspected, a free range of behaviors and expression (without compromising safety of course) within an assessment or treatment situation resonated strongly with my background and training in play therapy. The Professor's words echoed in my mind as I sat back and let Bert explore the room as he wished.

A child's initiatives and explorations in a new setting tell us an enormous amount about how a child sees and relates to objects, activities, and people in the setting. Beginning with observation allows us to note where a child's development is challenged or compromised. More importantly, unpressured initial observation allows us to identify evidence of the child's latent strengths. An initial observation, even before warmly and playfully attempting to engage the autism-suspected child, is a wonderful opportunity to identify some islets of normalcy. Later, the practitioner can engage the child and begin to help those islets grow and coalesce into what Feuerstein often quipped could become "developmental continents."

From the Feuerstein perspective, a caution is relevant here: A child's weaknesses, developmental deficits and various difficulties should never be used against a child to confirm a pessimistic fate, as often occurs in conventional circles. Rather, observed challenges should be considered a kind of "base line," not in the sense of behavioral intervention, but in the sense of clarifying the starting point from which we will galvanize our energies to help this child move toward meaningful change: "This is the child's starting point. Now, let's see how we can modify and improve this profile." So the early part of an initial assessment session with a young child suspected of experiencing a developmental difficulty such as autism is always devoted to letting the child move around freely, handle objects, make noise, play at will or even just sit mutely on the floor.

Letting the child lead without structuring the contact by requiring the child to sit at the table and "perform" too early on also helps reduce the child's anxiety. In an atmosphere of implicit support and acceptance of a child's initiatives, the child can feel a bit more in control in the strange setting and in the presence of a total stranger. The less anxious a child feels, the more likely it is that we clinicians will see the child at his or her best and most capable, rather than impeded, impaired or even frozen with fear and anxiety. All too often throughout my career, parents relayed to me the distressing experiences they and their children had experienced in previous assessment procedures elsewhere which had involved, at least partially, observation of the child and parents by a team of professionals— social worker, occupational therapist, speech therapist, psychologist, and perhaps psychiatrist—sometimes with an entire assessment team observing the child within the same room. What child would not freeze with dread in such an inhibiting situation?

A close reading of the child's uninterrupted interface with a new setting, its contents and people can yield rich and important developmental information, in particular, islets of normalcy. I signaled to Bert's foster guardians to relax and remain quiet, and assured them that it was fine if Bert handled the play materials or moved about the room in any way he wished.

As Bert wandered around my office examining the few play materials I had scattered around the room, I noticed that he was explorative, but he did not meaningfully engage or play with any toys. Both aspects were significant: On the one hand, he was curious and had an appropriate sense of exploration in a strange setting. On the other hand, there was no meaningful play with a given object. Some practitioners might be tempted to conclude that his lack of purposeful or symbolic play was an autistic-like symptom. Although a restricted repertoire of play behaviors might indicate an autistic-like feature, there are other possibilities: The child's inner world may be underdeveloped; the child may be lacking experiences of warm, caring play interactions with caregivers; the child may feel inhibited in a strange setting. It is so important to view a particular behavioral facet in context and to spread as widely as possible the net of possible explanations for a behavior. It is critical to use extreme caution and *not* to assume that a particular behavior which "fits" the official autistic criteria necessarily means that the child is autistic. There are multiple meanings to every single developmental behavior—and not all of them point to developmental pathology.

Soon Bert stopped wandering and stood opposite me where I sat at my desk. His pausing to regard me closely was in itself an islet of normalcy, revealing curiosity about the other. In fact, thus far I had already noticed a number of islets of normalcy:

- Bert's energetic and eager burst into the room. Evidence of enthusiasm.
- His initial brief and direct look into my eyes, which communicated energy and emotional presence.
- His curiosity.

On the deficit side of the ledger, Bert was not yet playing with the objects symbolically or with pleasure. I made a note of this as something important to work on—pleasure in play and meaningful symbolic play expression.

As Bert stood there regarding me, I pulled out a picture book. He looked at me. Islets began to accrue.

- Bert moved even closer to view the book. Further interest in the other. Communicative intent. Interest in contact. More curiosity.
- More direct eye contact with the assessor.

I noticed that Bert was drooling slightly. Oral hypotonia likely, I thought. Weakened oral musculature might be influencing his severely delayed and impaired speech development. To this point, Bert had not spoken in my office. His guardians estimated that his spontaneous vocabulary numbered roughly fifty words. There was the possibility that Bert's lack of speech was attributable to weak oral muscle tone, rather than to autism. In his case, oral hypotonia might be good news, with what had been considered autism a secondary result of a primary deficit—often correctible with the appropriate type of speech therapy.

Bert took an interest in the book I showed him. As I pointed to a few pictures without demanding a response, Bert spoke his first words of the session! "Tree." "Dog." "Man." Nearly seven years old, Bert was producing utterances typical of a one-year-old child. Some clinicians might be, and in his case had been, quick to critique such impoverished speech as evidence of possible autism and mental retardation. But I was looking for islets of normalcy and so Bert's few words impressed me as potent with positive relevance:

- Bert had shown interest in the pictures in the book.
- He had identified several objects by name.
- His receptive understanding was clearly greater than his current expressive abilities.
- If he could utter a few words, then he possessed the capacity for speech.
- He had uttered these words in response to my silently pointing to a few pictures. Bert was now engaged in a reciprocal learning activity.

I was intrigued and excited to get these glimpses of the charming child behind those autistic-appearing symptoms which had been only too well documented in the referral report.

Bert did not understand English. So I engaged his long-term foster parents in discussion in English about his background. Bert was the middle child of three. Because his parents suffered from complex emotional difficulties, they could not meet his needs. This had led to his being transferred to foster care. While not an islet of normalcy *per se*, this contextual information supported the understanding that Bert's early years had been characterized by a lack of nurturance, serious developmental under-stimulation, compromised parental capacity for warm and meaningful relationship, and even suspected aggressive discipline toward him.

Bert's devoted foster parents relayed more. They expressed anguish that Bert had been placed by the educational system in a special kindergarten for extremely low-functioning autistic children: "We believe that he is intelligent. He has been living with us for a long while and we see evidence of his intelligence in many ways. Recently he's started to speak." These caring people had independently noted many islets of normalcy!

I had already seen enough islets of normalcy and sparks of purposeful communicative intent to sense that Bert possessed much more potential than the report by the specialist had described. Bert had begun to participate with me in the semi-structured, reciprocal activity of looking at a picture book, so I felt it safe to change the approach from basic observation to active engagement with him. I selected a more structured, cognitive, goal-directed activity.

I invited Bert to join me at the small table where I pulled out a few puzzles suitable for a preschooler. Bert readily focused on these and enjoyed doing them. More islets of normalcy:

- Bert understood and responded to the invitation to sit by the table. Evidence of relevant language comprehension and awareness of a social cue.

- Bert was interested in structured tasks.
- He was capable of task orientation, remaining interested and on task.
- His ability to concentrate and his attention span were more than satisfactory, as I sat by him expressing interest and encouragement.
- The simple puzzles were too easy for him. Evidence of lively intelligence.

Seeing that these puzzles did not challenge him, I pulled out my box of three-dimensional wooden puzzles, unique to the Institute. These consist of an inner puzzle of three to five interlocking pieces, symmetrical or asymmetrical, each set within a frame of a small wooden box, which itself has to be constructed by the learner. These puzzles require motor planning skills and the ability to work three-dimensionally—the inner puzzle must be turned and inserted into the box frame which needs to be constructed around it.

I scattered the pieces of one of the simpler ones on the little table and showed Bert a completed box puzzle. Bert was stymied. He had no idea how to combine these scattered pieces to create a whole.

A more conventional view of cognitive capacity might have surmised that he was "impaired" or "retarded" at this stage because he could not solve this on his own. However, in Feuerstein's dynamic interactive method of assessing and teaching learners of all ages, the critical question is not "Can the child do it or not?" but "What interactive mediation will enable the child to move from 'not knowing' to 'knowing'?" In other words, if I give the child the mental or verbal tools and the strategies to learn, can he internalize these? The question then becomes, not "does he know?" but "can he learn?" I wondered, and so I set out to explore this with Bert.

I decided to model for Bert the construction of this three-dimensional puzzle. I verbalized my actions as I sat by his side and constructed the puzzle that had overwhelmed him: "This circle goes inside the square. Now the square fits inside the diamond. Now I slide them along the table and grasp them all together with my hands, like holding a sandwich. Now they need to fit inside this piece, which looks like a bed. The piece that looks like a window slips over them, and finally this top."

Bert was enthralled. He then readily did the puzzle on his own.

- Bert had watched and listened to my demonstration with rapt attention.
- He readily benefitted from the demonstration and the voiceover description.

Had Bert learned or was he simply imitating without understanding? To test this question, I brought out another three-dimensional wooden puzzle. Bert constructed it with ease.

- Bert was capable of genuine learning, that is, of generalizing what he had learned from previous experience.

Yet something emotionally significant was also happening. Bert was excited and thrilled with the challenge and the fact that he had done the puzzle readily. He cried out eagerly, "More! More!"

- Bert was hungry to learn.
- He possessed intrinsic motivation within a learning process.

That afternoon, Bert successfully completed my entire selection of fifteen such puzzles of increasing difficulty. He did them all—enthusiastically, even joyfully. Occasionally he had difficulty with the more complex puzzles, but with a little support or verbal mediation from me, he happily completed them, exclaiming "more, more" after each one. As he cried "more," Bert flapped his hands with excitement and rocked back and forth in the little chair.

A conventional view of Bert's excited hand-flapping might have considered this flapping as a "clincher," proof positive that Bert was autistic. While it is true that genuinely autistic children are prone to hand-flapping, considered stereotypical behavior, the inverse—that all children who flap their hands are necessarily autistic—is not true. There are other developmental possibilities that can account for a child's hand flapping: excess tension, perhaps, or sensory overload. Consider, too, that virtually all infants at a certain stage of development flap their hands. For most, this passes as the child's nervous system and purposeful coordination mature. Some children, though, get stuck in this infant phase. Certainly the description of Bert's early years by his foster parents supported a hypothesis of lack of parental warmth and positive involvement, factors that could account for Bert getting developmentally "stuck." It was clear that Bert's hand flapping would require therapeutic work to help him regulate the powerful, hypothesized combination of impoverished nurturance, tension and the force of habit.

It was also clear that Bert was unquestionably joyful and excited about being challenged, about learning. His enthusiasm, his ability to learn from a model and to generalize his learning (transcendence, in Feuerstein terms), his attention span and concentration—these were more than islets. They formed a continent! So although his eye contact was iffy at times, although he did not engage in meaningful symbolic play, and although his language usage typified that of a very young toddler, on the other hand, the child that had been obscured by the autistic-like symptoms was coming into focus.

Bert did not want to stop doing these challenging puzzles, but it was now four o'clock in the afternoon and our appointment was ending. Had I focused on his symptoms, I might have been tempted to conclude that Bert was, indeed, highly developmentally impaired, even autistic, and that his special setting was appropriate for his needs. But, above and beyond his symptom presentation, the focus on his many islets of normalcy indicated that here was a child with a wonderful capacity to progress, learn and change.

It was clear to me that my involvement with Bert's progress would be long-term and would require my active involvement and advocacy in facing a system which is symptom- and diagnosis-focused. Bert's foster parents were no longer young, and they would be limited in their ability to interface with the educational system. Yet their everyday impressions of Bert as an aware and intelligent child were correct. At the end of this first appointment I told them so.

Since the mandate of the Institute is not only to assess children and to offer treatment, but also to support and guide parents long-term through the odyssey of the child's development, I made a series of appointments for Bert in order to further assess his abilities, and asked for the foster parents' permission to observe Bert in his special kindergarten. I explained to his caregivers that we had a long but worthwhile developmental journey ahead of us. I did not know then what lay ahead. In fact, it proved to be a journey of many years of involvement and advocacy on Bert's behalf—years that were laden with joy in seeing him change and heartbreak when various support systems failed him as he approached puberty. There is no doubt, however, that Bert's strong islets of normalcy—in particular, his enthusiasm for and delight in learning—helped to catapult him into a richer and more functional childhood than the previous specialist's report could ever have predicted.

Zach

> Three-year-old Zach's first assessment appointment at the Institute was no less dramatic. For Zach, too, the identification of emergent islets of normalcy helped propel him toward years of a more normalized childhood. I had read his referral material which included a specialist's report from a respected clinic, along with parallel reports from other medical and therapeutic practitioners from other settings, all of whom had concluded that Zach was autistic. Most practitioners had labeled him as Pervasive Developmental Disorder (PDD), a poorly configured diagnostic term used at the time by most mental health and child development professionals as a synonym for an autistic condition.

Zach's parents, whose energies had been sapped in raising his older sister with special needs, described Zach as neither talking nor relating. They had only recently received the latest report from a specialist, and they were reeling from shock and smoldering grief that Zach had once again been officially diagnosed as autistic (PDD).

Zach was adorable. He looked like a roly-poly little teddy bear. He had a sturdy build and, I noted, as he entered my office and just barely looked around the room, he had good motor coordination. There were no signs of dysmorphia (facial asymmetry) or other soft signs that might indicate a physiologically-based developmental problem. However, Zach was clearly in deep developmental trouble.

He did not talk, and he was effectively avoiding any eye contact with his parents or with me. He did not approach his parents for comfort or connection. He wandered around my small office with no apparent goal. I opened the toy cupboard. Zach was curious. He began poking around, handling the sundry toys. I decided to limit the number of toys he could pull out of the cupboard. I selected a few, set them on the floor, and closed the cupboard door.

Zach was not pleased. He exploded into a full-fledged tantrum. Like a whale that breeches the surface of the water and then slams its enormous bulk broadside on the waves, Zach slammed himself onto the floor and began screaming. His parents looked distressed. The session did not look promising, and I was feeling stymied by what appeared to be his resolute avoidance of contact and connection. While Zach continued to tantrum, I tried to think of some musical, movement or play strategy that might "catch" Zach's interest and lure him into connection.

It was Zach himself who solved the problem. When he had recovered from his tantrum (without having sought to be cuddled or soothed), Zach suddenly began to push my office furniture around the room—the large chairs for adults, the smaller chairs and table for children, and even my desk! Feeling a bit overwhelmed by the frustrating half hour that had preceded this, I stood behind my desk and just watched. Whatever was he doing? Zach seemed to know. He continued to move the furniture until he had created a little row of chairs, big and small, which led to the summit— the top of my desk! He climbed onto the little chair at the beginning of the line of chairs he had created, walked along them and then reached my desk top with a pleased and proud look on his face.

Zach spoke! Loudly! "One, two, three, jump!" And he did, onto the carpet, landing between his equally surprised parents. He was not finished. He applauded himself, "Yay!" As he applauded, he looked directly at one parent and then the other, inviting them with his now expressive eye contact to applaud him and to share the experience.

Zach had a wonderful time for the duration of that first assessment session. He continued climbing onto the row of chairs, reaching the top of my desk, jumping onto the carpet, then delightedly and with a huge warm smile applauding himself and "inviting" his parents to applaud and appreciate along with him. Zach continued to count and say "jump" each time he leaped off my desk. Sometimes he counted in correct English and sometimes in correct Hebrew.

Once in a while, he made a little pitstop at the mirror hung at child level on my office wall. Before attempting his next climb, he would stand in front of the mirror, looking at himself with bright eyes and a warm smile of self-appreciation, while he spoke generous gibberish or jargon. Zach was conducting a gibberish conversation with himself as he looked in the mirror! As he did so, he gesticulated with wonderfully rich hand gestures, much as a lecturer might use to stress a point. As he delivered several gibberish "lectures" to himself, his tone of voice rose and fell with a kind of conscious musical rhythm that seemed to be indicating gibberish phrases and sentences, none of which were understandable.

Zach was very happy. So were his parents and so was I. Zach's play proved to be a remarkable breakthrough and a powerful display of rich and developmentally varied and significant islets of normalcy.

Zach's initial presentation—of strongly avoidant eye contact, lack of emotional connection, combined with a lack of interpersonal communicative intent as well as speech—at first glance had signaled serious developmental impairment, and a strong candidacy for a diagnosis of autism or its then-used synonym PDD, as the most recent conventional specialist had concluded. But when Zach had recovered from his tantrum and had begun to initiate play in a way that was most meaningful to him, he displayed an enormously rich repertoire of islets of normalcy.

The following is a "replay" of Zach's behavior and an elucidation of the islets that provided an exciting basis for our further work with him. The accumulation of many islets of normalcy began with Zach's foraging through the toy cupboard and continued throughout the session:

- Although not interested in the assessor, Zach was interested in rummaging through the toys. This was an islet of normalcy, reflecting intentionality, purposefulness, and curiosity.
- His ensuing tantrum showed that Zach was not indifferent to his surroundings. He had preferences, a strong will, and strong emotions.
- Although he was not yet speaking, he was certainly able to express frustration, loud and clear. His was not a flat, expressionless, emotionless presentation.
- Zach's relaxed and purposeful body movements as he constructed his jumping route showed no trace of tense stereotypy. The absence of this stereotypy can be considered yet another islet of normalcy.
- Zach's arranging of the furniture was purposeful, goal-directed and meaningful to him.
- As he rearranged the room, he had a lovely excited smile on his face. This was not the rote activity of a cut off child. This represented the normative play activity of an enthusiastic preschooler.

- Zach's jumping off the table indicated that he had correctly assessed a height he could manage. He was attending and relating to at least some of the details of his surroundings.
- Zach's ability to count was replete with islets of normalcy. It showed that he knew numbers and could count meaningfully. Although he had not started speaking, it was clear that he had been listening to and internalizing, at least, the elements of two languages. How much more latent speech lay within him?
- His counting, then jumping, activity reflected a cognitive understanding of sequence and at the same time it reflected anticipation.
- Zach's self-applauding was a lovely display of appropriate gestural communication.
- His attendant looks and smiles to each parent reflected the warmth he felt toward each, as well as a capacity for social referencing, as he invited them to share his pleasure in his accomplishments.

His pauses in front of the mirror were equally rich with islets of normalcy:

- The modulated intonation and rhythm of his gibberish were wonderful indications that Zach possessed normative prosody (the rhythmic underlying music and tonality unique to each language).
- Zach's jargon, though indeed gibberish and undecipherable, really did sound like spoken language. Zach was not at all displaying the monotonic robot-like tones of a child cut off from his feelings.
- Zach smiled and even laughed at himself as he lectured before the mirror. He displayed a sense of humor—a wonderful islet necessary for emotional health.
- Zach punctuated and exaggerated his gibberish speeches with a delightful range of hand motions, pointing, gesticulating and widening his eyes as his voice rose in crescendo to make a point. He truly looked and sounded much like a little university professor making some very important points. He possessed a rich and uncanny repertoire of hand gestures.
- Another significant islet was evident in the fact that, as noted earlier, missing from Zach's "autistic" presentation was any form of stereotypical behavior—hand flapping, rocking, spinning objects, walking in circles. His "speaking with his hands" in front of the mirror was anything but stereotypical. He was pointing and gesticulating, with a delighted and amused expression in his eyes. He appeared to be imitating us adults who take ourselves so seriously when we talk.

The numerous, significant and varied islets of normalcy, cumulatively, indicated that behind Zach's initially worrisome presentation lay an emotionally vibrant child with the capacity for purposeful behavior and, most importantly, a capacity for interpersonal communication: gibberish, language, meaningful gestures, social referencing and a range of normative emotions. Islets of normalcy provided a strong basis for our further work with Zach over the next roughly four years. During this time Zach transformed from a child at risk developmentally to a child who could speak, learn to read and write, and enjoy peers and pretend play.

Conclusion

Bert and Zach, like the hundreds, even thousands, of young children whom my colleagues and I assessed and treated at the Institute over the years, have much to teach us regarding the pitfalls of conventional autism diagnosis and assessment. More pertinently, these children exemplify the developmental leverage that the search for the anti-symptoms, those precious islets of normalcy, offers practitioners and parents. During the assessment process and in the course of treatment, the focus on islets of normalcy in children with suspected or confirmed autism diagnoses—rather than on their symptomatology or pathology—provides a powerful launching pad for a much more promising developmental trajectory.

As the stories of Bert and Zach illustrate, the symptoms, impairments, blocks, difficulties and developmental challenges of each child can appear all too obvious at first glance. Granted, it *is* important to note a child's symptoms—their description, their intensity, their duration and frequency, and certainly their prevalence in the child's profile. We do want to get a clear and rich description about the condition in which a child first presents. However, when working within the Feuerstein model, we are not seeking a description of symptoms in order to clinch a diagnosis, a common goal in psychology today. We are seeking a description of the symptoms in order to help us strategize how best to modify the child's profile.

A clinician working from the Feuerstein perspective is constantly asking him- or herself: "How can I best intervene in order to bring about change in the child's presentation, even in a marginal or microscopic way?" Attending to islets of normalcy provides that springboard toward meaningful intervention.

In a conventional method of assessing a child, the compilation of symptoms leads to a *diagnosis*. In the interactive, dynamic way of assessing and treating a child, the reciprocity embedded in the therapist's initiatives and the emphasis on gleaning evidence of latent potential buried beneath the symptoms lead to an *understanding* of the child's functioning. To creatively mix metaphors, islets of normalcy are like tiny sparks which we want to fan, through interactive play or creative cognitive intervention, so that they will grow to become a warm developmental blaze.

It is important to point out that the positive effect of this paradigm shift, from symptom emphasis to normalcy emphasis, is no less dramatic on a child's parents. As noted, parents of autism-diagnosed or autism-suspected children usually arrived at my office carrying a heavy emotional load. In their previous contacts with other educational, developmental or medical practitioners, they had encountered a strict emphasis by the clinician on the child's symptom presentation which had resulted in a "confirmed diagnosis." Sometimes the parents themselves had misgivings about their child's development and had researched extensive online descriptions of "the common symptoms" of autism. Even without the input of a practitioner working conventionally these parents had suspected, feared or concluded (often incorrectly) that their child suffered from autism.

The outlook and mood of parents who characteristically arrived at my office with that enormous load of pessimism and apprehension so often brightened when they observed a different type of assessment, one which was warm, playful and patient with the child's symptoms and difficulties, one that was respectful of the child's choices, and above all, one in which the therapist pointed out all the strengths, the islets of normalcy, observed in the session. Most parents visibly relaxed. Some wept with relief.

It is important not only to identify and describe the islets of normalcy to parents but also to explain to them the powerful developmental significance of these islets. I typically invested much time explaining to parents how these tiny strands of promising functioning can grow gradually to become strong cords of development. It was so important to explain to parents how this emphasis on modifiability, the watchword of the Feuerstein perspective, and the focus on the identification of islets of normalcy can be used to inform a new vision of their child's potential and prognosis.

Parents were also given positive "homework" to carry out between appointments. To replace the parents' hyperfocus on the child's symptoms, I encouraged them to be on the lookout for their child's islets of normalcy. At the end of each session, it was critical to provide concrete tips and strategies of "how to" strengthen and enlarge the islets of normalcy they observed in their child's daily life. Typically, recommendations included guidelines for speaking amply and richly to even a nonverbal child, "soliloquy" in Feuerstein parlance, as well as helpful ideas for turning isolated behaviors into reciprocal ones, often based on DIR Floortime strategies.

When Bert and Zach arrived at the Institute, each was clearly in serious developmental trouble. A superficial observation of their presenting symptoms could easily have led to a confirmation of their previous diagnoses of autism and PDD respectively.

Bert definitely presented initially as cut-off and avoidant, as well as language- and cognitively-impaired. It would have been all too easy, using formalized criteria, to end that first session arriving at the diagnosis of autism, as other specialists had done. However, as the session wore on, and I moved from the phase of unfettered observation to active involvement with Bert, islets of normalcy accrued. Bert's cognitive functioning with increasingly difficult puzzles along with his overwhelming enthusiasm for learning and his rudimentary speech tipped the balance of presumptions from "incapable" to "capable" to an exciting degree.

Similarly, at first glance, Zach appeared stubbornly avoidant of eye contact, emotional contact and purposefully interactive or symbolic play. Could it be other than an autism diagnosis? Fortunately, his explosive tantrum helped him to release tension so that he then felt free to express a genuine interest in purposeful, active play. Perhaps he sensed a certain atmosphere of freedom and acceptance in my office that I might not object if he playfully rearranged the room. I hope so. Ultimately, it was his self-initiated play that revealed impressive islets of normalcy: cognitive abilities, communicative abilities, and emotional richness that had been obscured by his avoidant presentation. Using islets of normalcy as our basis for understanding his latent abilities, I accompanied Zach for many years on his developmental journey as he went on to enjoy normative speech capabilities, the ability to engage in humor-laden and imaginative symbolic play, peer contact, and the acquisition of reading, writing and basic math skills.

In their teen years, Bert and Zach each encountered unfortunate administrative barriers within the educational system and/or experienced emotional/situational crises, whose combination left their young adulthoods less than happy. Despite this fact, I selected Bert and Zach as prime examples of the impact of the clinical focus on islets of normalcy, because their initial sessions were highly dramatic, with a clear and powerful distinction between superficial symptom presentation and the fine latent developmental abilities evidenced in their islets of normalcy. There is no doubt that the focus on islets of normalcy as a basis for dynamic assessment and ensuing treatment resulted in years of happier and more productive childhoods for each child.

Bert and Zach were not alone. Using the positive outlook of searching for islets of normalcy, so central to the Feuerstein philosophy, and by interactively creating islets even when they were not yet evident, my colleagues and I had the great satisfaction of watching many children who arrived at the Institute having been diagnosed as autistic, PDD, or ASD continue on a path in which our team supported and guided them to near-normative and even normative functioning in the realms of verbal communication, peer relationships and learning.

Finally, consider that even a casual observer can readily see that a child "is not speaking" or "has poor eye contact" or "does not communicate or engage in relationship." To engage solely in a mission of seeking symptoms is to short-change the child's underlying abilities and his or her future capacity to change. Beyond and behind the symptoms, we clinicians are duty bound to seek evidence of the child's latent ability to communicate, play and learn. Once we identify these islets of normalcy, we must work to enlarge, expand, and strengthen them within the child's profile. Slowly we assist these tiny specks of normal functioning to grow and coalesce. As the islets coalesce into continents and the child's strengths grow, the proportional impact of the symptoms diminishes. This is a fact which I have witnessed in so many children as the result of the hard work of the parents, my colleagues and myself began to bear fruit.

Note

1 Chapter Copyright © Shoshana Levin Fox 2019, All Rights Reserved.

References

Feuerstein, R., R. S. Feuerstein, L. H. Falik, & Y. Rand. *Creating and Enhancing Cognitive Modifiability: The Feuerstein Instrumental Enrichment Program.* Jerusalem: ICELP Press, 2006.

Levin Fox, S. *An Autism Casebook for Parents and Practitioners: The Child Behind the Symptoms.* New York: Routledge, Taylor & Francis, 2020.

Chapter 3

The Mediating Clinical Team

The Importance of Teamwork when Treating ASD Individuals Using the Feuerstein Method

Chana Nakav and Refael S. Feuerstein

Background

According to Professor Feuerstein's Mediated Learning Experience theory, intelligence and human functioning develop through interaction with the environment in a process that Feuerstein called the "Mediated Learning Experience" (MLE; see Introduction to the theory). In this inter-personal process, different mediators (in the early years, typically the parents) are responsible for imparting a variety of learning and thinking strategies to the child. For example, parents teach their child to focus his gaze, to imitate words, and that there is a connection between sounds, objects and actions. Mediation develops the child's primary communication modalities that improve over time.

This chapter focuses on the clinical team and how we work together with the child and family members in order to implement an optimal mediated learning experience. We are aware that many of the children who come to the Children's Clinic at the Feuerstein Institute attend other educational establishments. It is critical for us to work together with the educational staff at these institutions. However, an in-depth discussion of this essential collaboration is beyond the scope of this chapter.

Part I: Creating an Effective Therapeutic Environment through Teamwork

Setting Common Goals

Therapeutic work with individuals with communication difficulties can be extremely complicated. From the perspective of the Feuerstein Method (FM), people with ASD are particularly challenging to work with because the central process for creating change and growth (the "learning mechanism") is limited, and sometimes even obstructed. Professor Feuerstein emphasized the crucial importance of the learning mechanism for a person's development. The communication problems we often see in

DOI: 10.4324/9781003451136-4

children with ASD delay the normal learning process, and as a result, functioning in other areas is affected. With the FM, the main task of the therapeutic staff is to develop the child's learning mechanism to a level that will enable the process of rehabilitation. The specific role of the staff member is of less importance—it could be a teacher, speech therapist, or other—but the success of each professional in her/his work relies on the existence of an ability to learn. This is what the team emphasizes in the early stages of treatment.

Cooperation between therapists, family members and others involved in the rehabilitative process is vital. This cooperation goes well beyond divisions of labor or coordination; it concerns working together towards common goals. The first aim is to transform the child into a learner, or, as one of our staff members aptly put it: "I need him to understand that he is a student, and I am a teacher." Another stated: "The main task is that the child sits on the chair." By this she was not simply referring to the physical act of sitting, but to the child's perception of his role in the situation. Sitting on a chair involves focusing, relaxing one's movements, focusing one's gaze on a specific area to which the chair is directed. This goal is shared by the entire therapeutic team, each member using different learning techniques. Next, the staff deciphers the child's condition as a learner, usually by making use of the Dynamic Assessment (see Chapters 3 and 4). Already at this very early stage, during the assessment, the child begins to acquire strategies for effective learning.

Each therapist has specific methods with which she works towards a shared goal: this creates a productive atmosphere of mutual learning. However, there is also overlap, meaning that staff members will support the others when working on the same therapeutic area. For example, if a speech therapist is teaching imitation of language, she might ask other staff members to emphasize this in their sessions with the child. Or, if an occupational therapist is emphasizing the regulation of behavior in order to reduce the client's impulsive behavior, she will direct the rest of the team to focus on this. In this way, an hour a week teaching the ability to learn, plan, mimic, and so on suddenly becomes eight hours. This strategy significantly amplifies the power of the therapy received.

Everyone Can Change

The idea that everyone has the ability to change is the most central issue in the team's work. While teamwork with the FM indeed concerns the creation of common goals, it most intensively involves a profound partnership among the staff regarding how they perceive the clients. Here we touch on a fundamental principle of the FM; the belief that people have an innate capacity to change. Behind every educational or therapeutic approach lies an assumption about humanity. Behavioral approaches (such as Applied Behavior Analysis—ABA) are based on the ideas that people are driven by a desire for pleasure and to escape from grief or suffering. Such approaches do not consider "thinking" the essential component of human functioning, but rather the products of behavior. Other approaches assume that a person's chromosomal make-up determines his level of cognitive, behavioral, and communicative functioning. If this is the underlying assumption, there is no point in treating the person diagnosed with ASD, as it is an inherent part of his physiology. Indeed, the ongoing effort to identify the genes responsible for ASD tends to confirm that the person with ASD cannot depart from this definition. From this point of view, the purpose of intervention is not to simply to improve quality of life, but to fundamentally change one's basic functioning.

The FM argues that every single person has the ability—or the possibility—to change. The change, of depends largely on the efforts made. This approach distinguishes the FM from other methods. The assumption is that the person with ASD (or any other syndrome) *can* be detached from his condition. The team is responsible for realizing the potential for change in each of their clients.

Modifying the Parents' Attitudes—a Central Part of the Therapeutic Effort

Families who choose the FM have often heard for years that they cannot expect any real changes in their child. The working assumption in many therapeutic approaches is highly pessimistic—most assume that the child will remain on the spectrum and progress will be limited. The novel assumption of the FM is that there *is* a possibility for change. There is no guarantee, of course, but we set ambitious goals. Establishing high expectations can be emotionally risky for family members. Nonetheless, this premise, that a person has the ability to change, can powerfully influence how the staff and parents interpret the initial results of the treatment. No one expects dramatic changes after one month of treatment. The changes in the first stages of treatment may be small, even miniscule. And much depends upon interpretation. Take, for instance, the following scenarios:

- A child who, until now, would enter the therapy room, sit on the floor and completely ignore the therapist, now enters the room and sits on the chair facing the therapist without being asked.
- A child who, until now, would look past the therapist with barely any eye contact is now able to make eye contact.
- A child who begins to pay attention to the therapist's instructions after months of showing a complete disregard for them.

Such changes may seem unimportant when considered in the overall context of the individual's low functioning and abilities, but that may not be the case when interpreted on the basis of Feuerstein's SCM (Structural Cognitive Modifiability; see Introduction to the Theory) theory. These changes signify a kind of "oil mark" that attests to the existence of a large underground reservoir—or, as Feuerstein called them, "islets of normalcy" (see Chapter 2). In contrast, if therapists and family members take a static approach, and do not believe in the possibility of change, they may overlook the significance of these changes. When the therapists believe there is such a possibility, and work hard towards this goal, then they and the family members will interpret the first stages of change as meaningful, and as a sign of the child's learning potential.

We have noticed that a child's progress during treatment can often create significant changes in the families' attitude to the child. Consider the following example:

> *Parents brought their newborn daughter to Professor Feuerstein wrapped up in a blanket so that no one would notice that she had Down Syndrome. Their first conversation with the Professor changed their whole approach. He boomed "Congratulations!" in his deep voice. "You need to inform your family and friends that you deserve congratulations. You should share with your community the fact that you have a child with Down Syndrome". This conversation was life-changing for the parents. Contrary to what they heard in the hospital, that their daughter would never achieve much, they were now being told that their daughter had potential and could make significant development. Professor Feuerstein gave them hope for the future: "I expect you to invite me to her wedding, and we will get her married". Following this conversation, the child's mother began investing heavily in her daughter's future and turned her daughter's education into her life project. Today, this young girl is doing well in an integrated school environment.*

And a further example:

> *A four-year-old child diagnosed with ASD arrived at the Institute for an evaluation. His parents had already invested heavily in their son's treatments, to no avail, and now felt a lack of direction and absolute despair due to his very low functioning. Their son displayed severe behavioral problems at home, with frequent outbursts. His parents had heard "he cannot" and "he is not able to" countless times and all the experts recommended that he attend special education kindergarten. During his dynamic assessment at the Institute, his parents were surprised to see that their son could do much more than they thought (with the appropriate mediation). Today, he speaks fluently, reads and is proficient in mathematics.*

It is important to emphasize that the changes themselves are not sufficient to produce a change in the parents' attitudes and behaviors; any changes in the initial stages may be rather limited in scope. Instead, it is the interpretation of these changes that holds real potency in this context. The belief in one's ability to change enables family members to correctly analyze the changes they observe in the child as *meaningful* rather than *meaningless.*

This new approach can prompt caregivers to engage in therapeutic work, turning them into active mediators for the child. In the first stage of this process, families learn to re-examine the "fixed" or "pre-determined" nature of the child's condition and his past prognoses. This first step of questioning and reassessment is essential in changing a caregiver's approach to a child. The next step is to renew their "contract" with the child; to reconnect with the child given the new role they have adopted. The parents see their child in a completely new light, and they move from protecting him to communicating and mediating to him. In short, they change their attitude from accepting the situation to working actively to change the situation.

Professor Feuerstein strongly distinguished between these two basic approaches, the first, one of "passive-accepting" and the second, one of "active-modifying." This description reflects one of the most crucial turning points in shaping parents' attitudes towards their children. The passive-accepting approach assumes that people have fixed and unchangeable traits. A glance at our cultural climate as presented in the points below, indicate that frequently we are pushed to adopt the passive-accepting approach:

- Intelligence tests determining our IQ from a very young age.
- Screening tests for schools and even kindergartens.
- Professional qualification tests required during the hiring process.
- Clinical tests that determine from a young age that a child is on the autistic spectrum or has a developmental/learning disability of one kind or another.

In the keynote speech at a Washington conference convened by the pediatric psychiatrist Stanley Greenspan, Professor Feuerstein dealt with the following question (as he put it): "Early detection—a blessing or a curse?" In his lecture (which was later published as an article—Feuerstein, 1998), Feuerstein characterized early diagnosis as a kind of "self-fulfilling prophecy." Once a parent hears at such an early stage that their child is defined as being on the autistic spectrum, they tend to reduce the amount of speech they engage in with their child because they assume that this effort will not help; that the child does not understand and will never understand. Owing to the lack of sufficient exposure to speech and connection, the young child may present with more pronounced initial signs of autistic traits.

Therefore, Feuerstein called for focusing on the child's learning potential and on the effective ways in which he can be mediated to. The child's diagnosis then becomes a driving force for family members and caregivers to push the child forward, rather than letting him lag behind. It is not enough to accept the child as he is; a vigorous effort must be made to make a tangible difference in the child's communicative and cognitive abilities.

In this vein, let us consider the term "inclusion," which is a buzzword in special education today. This approach accepts the child's abilities as a given and attempts to adapt the educational and employment world to him. In contrast, the FM promotes. Intensive cognitive mediation of the child in order to open up possibilities to him beyond his current capabilities (and to integrate him). As stated above, the FM is based on the premise that people can change, leading to an active effort in all areas with this goal in mind. Parents and caregivers undergo a sort of "struggle" to break out of their confines. Consider an athlete who pushes her body to its limit in order to achieve a better result, or a high school or university student who struggles desperately to understand the presented course material. Our lives are full of struggles, and these efforts are an essential part of our ability to survive and thrive in a challenging world. This is the *determined environment* to which families are exposed in the FM.

Mediation for Intentionality and Reciprocity

One of the most significant changes caregivers undergo while using the FM is gaining the ability to mediate *reciprocity* for their children. Reciprocity is one of the vital parameters necessary for efficient mediation. This form of mediation differs from frontal learning, where the child is taught a skill in a uni-directional manner. Here, rather, a mutual dialogue is created in which the mediator serves as a sort of trigger for the child, modeling the behavior he is to learn. For people with normative communication skills, dialogue can be created through many different channels. It is possible to converse, to present a problem and lead the recipient of the mediation to attempt to solve the problem. It is possible to create an atmosphere at home in which children are challenged by tasks that require thinking and encourage them to participate. All this requires communication skills and assumes that the child feels himself to be a part of the environment, able to absorb, decipher, and respond to its messages. The child with communication problems will have difficulty in all of these areas. Moreover, as the child's parents will not expect this reciprocity from him, they will not make requests of him that demand his cooperation or participation. Busy trying to shape his behavior and respond to his needs, these caregivers are unlikely to encourage him to try and find his own solution to problems.

Feuerstein therapists seek to produce reciprocity at a more complex level, giving the child instructions that require thought and action on his part. One might think of a kind of back and forth, "ping-pong" form of communication with the child. Not infrequently, parents watching this process are shocked by the level of reciprocity that their child is achieving. Often, caregivers are persuaded that they, too, can create such reciprocity, and start to look for ways to do this at home with their child. This focus on reciprocity can serve as a springboard for the development of increasingly complex learning processes. Building reciprocity in the child is not a purely therapeutic achievement. This shift in reciprocity exposes the caregivers to a child who is not a kind of "present-absentee," but a person who can be communicated with and who has an ability respond. There is potential here for profound emotional change, which can lead to renewed bonding within families. Here is one example of such a long and rewarding process:

Case Study: Hope

Hope is a young girl diagnosed with autism and another unknown syndrome. She is low functioning in many areas, including communication. She was brought to the Feuerstein Institute as a newborn, and her parents invested in her treatment heavily over the years. There were periods of progress, but when the treatment was not intense, she regressed. She was unable to focus her gaze and observed things with a blank expression. Following a treatment gap of several years, she returned to the Feuerstein institute at the age of nine. Suddenly, changes started to happen. She started to smile and, for the first time, to make eye contact. She began to enjoy conversation and to burst into laughter. Her parents now saw a child who they could bond with, who would respond to them. All these achievements occurred at a time when her parents were close to despair. After such a long time, they certainly did not expect anything like this to happen. These changes led to a profound change in the parents' attitude and behavior.

Considerations Involved while working with families as Partners in Therapy

As noted above, the FM stresses the families' role in their assisting their child's progress. We strive to change attitudes from passive-acceptance to active-modifying. A crucial part of achieving this goal involves exposing caregivers to Mediated Learning Experience (see Introduction to the Theory). In this way, they observe how professionals mediate to their child and learn how to apply the principles of mediation at home.

Several points must be considered. Before bringing caregivers into the treatment room, we consider the extent to which the child is dependent on his caregiver, and the caregiver's ability to relinquish this The strong relationship — which may be creating this dependence. Often, parents may be over-protective of their child, whom they perceive as vulnerable. The messages they repeatedly receive from professionals, who do not recognize the child's potential to develop, reinforce the parents' perception that they are their child's eternal guardian. This relationship needs to be modified so as to assist the child to function in a more independent manner.

We have observed that the parents' shielding behaviors may be a factor in the child's delayed development. On the one hand, we aspire to make the treatment room a space in which the child discovers and develops independence. On the other hand, as stated, the caregivers need to be present in order to modify their own perspective. Therefore, it is important to consider each case carefully and consider when and how often caregivers should be present in the therapy room. Furthermore, the child's tendency to become distracted must be considered. Once a strong relationship is established with the therapist, the entry and exit of additional people, such as the parents, may interfere with continuity of treatment. If a clinical decision is made for a period of time, not to have the caregiver present in the therapy room, the final 5–10 minutes of each session is dedicated to observation or a discussion with caregivers, so that they can see for themselves the changes their child experienced during the treatment session.

Changing the Home Environment is Critical for Treatment Success ("Bridging" and "Transcendence")

The changes in the attitudes of family members refer to more than renewed bonding with the child, as described in the previous section. After being exposed to the mediation process, family members also learn how to become mediators. This benefit will become clear when we consider one of the most essential mediation parameters: *Mediation for Transcendence* (see Introduction to the Theory). In order to bring about a structural change in the child, he needs to be able to understand instructions in a wide range of diverse environments. The therapeutic environment is quite monotonous, involving the same therapist, the same room, the same hours, with often similar stimuli and activities. The scope of the therapist's mediation is therefore somewhat limited. Even if the child learns to understand the therapist's instructions, how can we ensure that he understands the instructions of parents, teachers, and friends?

Feuerstein argued that the ability to transfer any acquired principle to another situation requires the active creation of connections. If an active effort is not made by the therapist and other mediators to link the functional principle (e.g., "understanding instructions") to other areas of life, the acquired skill will remain isolated, and will have little effect on the child's overall functioning. Since our goal is to improve functioning in all areas of the child's life, it is vital that the skills mediated in the treatment room are also mediated elsewhere. Optimally, this should be done at home, as the home is central to all spheres of life—eating, tidying up, playing, watching television, and so on. In all these situations, family members can mediate the skills learned in the treatment room. For example, if the acquired skill is "following instructions," parents can mediate this skill in many areas: while playing a board game, in preparing and eating food, setting the table, and so forth. This skill is relevant in all areas of life. If the acquired skill is "the ability to understand that language is a means of communication," family members can leverage this skill during a vast range of home-based actions that constitute a possible platform for communication. Of course, the mediator cannot and should not transfer the new skill to all possible fields. Instead, the purpose of the transfer is to create a tendency to use a particular skill, rather than leaving it "isolated" and meaningless. This tendency is acquired through a great deal of mediation aimed not necessarily at acquiring a particular skill, but rather at using accumulated skills and knowledge.

The Uniqueness of the FM Treatment Team's Work—Seeking "Islets of Normalcy"

Many therapeutic and rehabilitative approaches focus on their clients' abilities and direct them to the occupation or course of study that suits their current abilities (this is mostly relevant for those with low-functioning autism, who may be unsuited to normative frameworks). Higher-functioning ASD individuals are often referred to normative employment and academic frameworks.

The FM views learning as the core process in the construction of personality. With the FM, the therapeutic staff does not focus on what the child cannot do, but rather, actively seeks out his existing abilities, even if these are limited in scope and quality ("islets of normalcy"). After identifying these processes, the therapist uses them to impart more complex skill, and also makes an effort to expand, deepen and develop the existing processes in order to bring about the desired change in the child.

Professor Feuerstein described these capabilities as islets because they are surrounded by a wide and deep ocean of difficulties and deficiencies which are usually quite noticeable to the observer. Why did Professor Feuerstein attribute importance to these islets? The FM answers that these islets are important because they teach us about the person's ability to change or learn, however limited in scope that ability may be. Here and there, we can detect open windows that allow communication and learning (see Chapter 4). As Chana tells us:

> I was just starting my work alongside Professor Feuerstein. I arrived at
> his office feeling frustrated due to a particular child's limited abilities

and low functioning. The Professor told me to take a notebook and to write down something; the "normal" I see in the child every day. Needless to say, this notebook remained pretty empty. However, one day I discovered to my surprise that the child displayed a special interest in cars. He observed them; really studied them. I realized that I had found an islet of normalcy, albeit small. From that day on, I focused all of my therapeutic work on cars. We learned about colors, shapes, sizes and types all through the use of cars. Through the mediation for transcendence, we gradually transferred what he had learned to other objects. The child eventually reached the point where Professor Feuerstein was able to assess him using the Raven test, which was unimaginable at the beginning.

For us, these "islets of normalcy" attest the existence of learning ability; they are the products of learning processes. The dynamic assessment tries to identify these existing processes and guides the therapist's work through such openings. The therapists are highly attentive to the learning processes that are already present in the client, as it is through such processes that they begin to rehabilitate deficient or missing functions (e.g. the child's interest in cars was the opening through which he was able to be taught concepts and strategies). Our Feuerstein teamwork frequently calls for a common fighting spirit, and this attitude of determination is enhanced immeasurably when information about "islets of normalcy" is shared between therapists. In this way, one staff member can use the information received from another, greatly improving the quality of the treatment as a whole.

The Therapists' Perspective Influences Clinical Work

While the search for learning processes harnesses the therapists' clinical experience, it depends on other factors as well. The first link in the chain is the therapist's firm conviction that we all have the ability to change. This directs the therapist in her work, on a daily basis. Much like we direct our information-gathering skills to the relevant stimuli when driving in an unfamiliar area (we look for road signs and landmarks so that we do not get lost), so too, the therapists direct their information-gathering skills to identify tiny signs of change that a therapist from a different discipline might ignore or even dismiss as unimportant. The therapist is directed not only to pinpoint small signs of change, but also to take meticulous note of any learning mechanisms. She may work on a certain task with a child and notice that a particular behavior has been internalized better than other behaviors. The therapist is not yet sure that this behavior is more effective, but she will hold onto that hypothesis and investigate further. The very forming of such hypotheses is made possible by the special sensitivity of the Feuerstein therapists—they work on the assumption that significant changes in their clients' intelligence and functioning are to be expected.

Therapists who use the FM are guided by a detailed theory and set of concepts regarding the entire treatment that orients their focus to those micro-changes in highly specific functions. This set of concepts emphasizes the conditions of human functioning (see Introduction to the Theory). The basic premise of the FM is that, by improving cognitive abilities, one can improve overall human functioning. For example, one can enhance communication skills by teaching the *role* of communication, and not necessarily by increasing communication skills through reward and punishment. This is because one's understanding of the concept of communication is partly related to one's ability to understand the role of symbols as conveyors of meaning, the meaning of sequences (e.g., a question is followed by a response), and the concept of cause and effect. These cognitive functions and operations must be mediated by the therapists in order to facilitate the acquisition of higher functions. Initially the therapist plans her intervention based on which cognitive functions are missing or insufficiently developed.

The second link in the chain is the goal (or the skill that the therapist plans to impart to the child). The set of concepts included in the "cognitive map" enables the mediator to understand which cognitive functions characterize the skill they wish to mediate. In other words, what are the cognitive functions required to teach the child writing or reading? What is the level of abstraction required for teaching writing versus reading? What is the complexity level of the skill? Is the child ready for the level of complexity/abstraction required to acquire the skill? If not, what does he need to be taught first to prepare him to acquire that skill?

The third link in the chain is the mediator (whether teacher, family member or therapist). How should she mediate the required skill or cognitive function to the child? What is the form of mediation required that will enable the recipient to absorb and respond to the mediation given? Should mediation be given from more of a distance, or is a lot of assistance necessary? Does the mediator need to take the child's hand and help him to perform a writing task, or can she simply instruct the child, waiting patiently until the task is carried out? Should mediation be authoritative, with set limits aimed at gaining the child's cooperation, or will a softer, more accepting approach be more helpful?

These three links in the chain are supported by a detailed conceptual system and shared "language" that relates to the overall observations of the therapist. This has several implications:

- The conceptual system allows the therapist to sharply formulate her observations; to analyze the client's behaviors and focus on those that are most relevant to planning her therapeutic work with the client.
- It allows the therapist to impart meaning and psychological significance to the child's behaviors. For example, a therapist may notice

a significant reduction in the amount of energy she needs to invest in order for a skill to become internalized. In Feuerstein theory, this is referred to as *Mediation for Intentionality*. Intention modifies the teacher's interactive style, and way in which she addresses the child so that they are ready for and open to the goal of the mediational interaction (Feuerstein et al., 2006). This mediation gradually takes the child out of his comfort zone and develops his ability to adapt to different situations and different mediators. After some time, the need for mediation for intentionality will decline.

- The shared language is not unique to a specific discipline, but a generic one that enables efficient communication and cooperation between staff members. All therapists working with the Feuerstein Method share the same unique conceptual platform that deals with the child's learning mechanisms. Each therapist targets different aspects of functioning, but all endeavor to bring about change. The mechanisms of change in one child may be similar or identical to those of another child. As such, the information that one therapist brings to a discussion about effective learning processes may have a decisive influence on the work of another therapist.

The therapists' focus on the processes of change enables not only a common discourse, but mutual learning and the establishment of common goals, the purpose of which is to empower the child to become an effective learner.

The Determination of the Professional Staff

The FM is based on the fundamental belief in a person's ability to change. Consider a therapist who has successfully used a particular method to teach a certain skill for many years. A new child enters her room, and she uses the tried- and-true method—but this time, with no success. The therapist will try again, in a slightly different way, but to no avail. The therapist may at some point conclude that the child cannot acquire the skill in question. The Feuerstein practitioner, who knows that the burden of proof is on her, approaches this scenario differently. She is motivated by the basic belief system that the person before her has the ability to change—even if such change will only emerge after immense effort. Of course, there may be failures along the way and slow progress, but the therapist will do absolutely everything in her power before giving up. If a Feuerstein therapist does not succeed, she will never say, "this person is not treatable," but instead, "I could not do it." Much more than simple semantics, this attitude conveys the constitutive identity of the Feuerstein team.

Part II: Teamwork and The Role of the Cognitive Dynamic Assessment (LPAD)

A. The Cognitive Dynamic Assessment (LPAD) Identifies the Open Windows through which Effective Mediation can be Provided:

CHANA NAKAV: Sean came to our clinic when he was three years old. It's fair to say that he was fully self-absorbed and unaware of the world around him. He would not have thought of asking questions such as "How are you? How do you feel today?", nor did he respond in any way to feedback (even positive). I even remember seeing him with his mother at the local health clinic. She was simply helpless. He was banging his head against the wall so much that I was really concerned for him. The goal of the cognitive dynamic assessment was to find "open windows" through which it would be possible to communicate with him. After much effort, I noticed that when a certain topic was meaningful to him, it was possible to create a kind of connection. The process of searching for open windows took a long time, but with the belief in the ability to change, the assessor did not despair. The real change occurred when the child realized for the first time that communication was taking him out of his existential isolation. It was as if he did not previously understand the meaning of communication, or how it could relate to him.

The multidisciplinary teamwork involved in LPAD assessment is of great significance, especially for clients on the autistic spectrum. The LPAD focuses on the main obstacles that prevent the client from developing (these barriers will also appear during treatment). Solving this riddle is therefore a vital step before beginning treatment. Detecting and defining the "open windows" prior to starting treatment saves many hours of frustration and dramatically enhances treatment efficiency.

B. The LPAD's Universal Language: The Cognitive Functions

In today's professional world, each field has its own unique tests and evaluations, which is usually aimed at the professionals from that field. Occupational therapy diagnoses are for them. diagnoses that speech and language clinicians are designed for, and so on. However, the LPAD is able to guide all FM clinicians, whatever their discipline (occupational therapists, psychologists, teachers and so on). How is this possible?

The first answer, noted above, is found in the universality of the LPAD. In the Feuerstein method, all professionals from all disciplines aim to use the 'open window' to the patient's personality. Additionally, the LPAD uses FM concepts to provide a general "road map" for the therapists; the cognitive functions, normal and defective in the client. These cognitive functions are relevant to every human function and every action, therefore they are relevant to language, behavior, motivation, academic abilities, and so on. More than half a century ago, Professor Feuerstein clarified this, explaining that any complex skill, such as reading, speaking, playing, writing and understanding emotions, is based on the existence of more basic cognitive functions which allow these complex operations to occur. For example, information-gathering processes are necessary for each of the various skills mentioned above. Of course, the information gathering required in reading (in which precision is vital) is not the same information gathering required in playing a game of "catch," but the action of gathering information is the precursor to successfully carrying out these and most other tasks. Even eating requires information gathering, time management and the ability to understand and follow instructions. Every human action requires the existence of the cognitive functions that are relevant to that action.

Feuerstein defined the various functions that are involved in each stage of thinking: input, elaboration, and output (see Introduction to the Theory). At the elaboration phase, we process the information that was gathered at the input phase and turn it into knowledge. We organize it, make connections to prior knowledge, draw conclusions, and so on. At the output phase, we organize the knowledge and prepare for implementation, ensuring that it matches the context in which the action will take place. For example, I may be angry with my parents because I disagree with something they said (elaboration phase), but I will contain my anger and turn the emotional hurricane into an appropriate response. The output phase takes context into account: etiquette, respect for parents, and so forth, shaping the form of the output to fit the social context. It is possible that a similar situation, with a friend rather than parents, may evoke a harsher response.

The cognitive functions are universal to all of the disciplines involved in human behavior, and thus in advancing the child. One of the most important cognitive functions in the elaboration phase is known as "an episodic perception of reality." This is defined as a difficulty in seeing the whole picture, or the difficulty in seeing that the whole is greater than the sum of its parts. For example, Brendan, aged ten years old, has trouble holding an organized conversation. He jumps from subject to subject, each sentence is not necessarily related to the next, and it is difficult to follow his logic. Brendan's speech is influenced by a deficient cognitive function— an episodic grasp of reality. Brendan has neither the inclination nor the ability to seek and produce a complete picture. He perceives his life as fragmented and lacking in connection between the various components.

A speech pathologist must stimulate a tendency and ability in him to create longer sequences with connections between each part of the puzzle. Categories or concepts are the "glue" between the pieces. For example, if I want to tell a story about a chain of events, I can decide that the "conceptual glue" is a cause-and- effect relationship (at first, I spoke rudely to my friend—therefore— he was angry with me—therefore—we did not talk to each other for a few days—therefore—we both felt bad—therefore—we wanted to make up—therefore—we reconciled). Instead of cause and effect, I could choose time as the "conceptual glue" (last week on Sunday—we fought—on Monday—we no longer spoke to each other—on Tuesday—we both felt bad—on Wednesday—we decided to reconcile). Of course, the two concepts can be combined.

An occupational therapist will encounter difficulty with Brendan's perception. Brendan has trouble writing—even copying letters and words is difficult for him. Often, the occupational therapist will work on input-output copying skills ("you see the word, now try copying it"), and break the letters into parts to make it easier for him, but she may neglect the elaboration phase. The therapist using the FM will furnish Brendan with a strategy that will enable him to use the relevant terms and concepts in order to copy the letter, (e.g., line, diagonal, right, left, circle). He will understand how to organize the letter using its components, instead of simply perceiving it. The occupational therapist will be mediating for Brendan the same cognitive function as the speech therapist; how to use concepts to organize reality.

Brendan's teacher will have to deal with his episodic way of working. His acute difficulty in seeing the connection between the whole and its parts will make it hard for him to see the link between what he learned and the task ahead. This difficulty is also expressed in his ability to see a complex task as consisting of smaller tasks that make up the whole. In order to treat Brendan's episodic functioning, the FM therapist may use the "Analytic Perception" instrument (part of the Feuerstein Instrumental Enrichment—FIE; see Chapter 7). The FIE is a set of instruments designed to develop a learner's cognitive structures, leading to more efficient learning and problem solving (Feuerstein et al., 2006). The "Analytic Perception" instrument introduces the idea of analysis into the child's cognitive repertoire through perceptual processes dealing with the relationship between the parts and the whole. It is important to note that the FIE tools are meant to affect a range of areas involved in rehabilitation, not just the specific skill being targeted.

The entire FM staff mobilizes in order to work on the same deficient cognitive function, the one that acts as the central barrier to the development of the individual receiving mediation. In Brendan's case, the occupational therapist, teacher, speech pathologist, and the cognitive clinician using the FIE all focused on his episodic manner, thus significantly increasing the likelihood that he would improve.

The LPAD Enables the Therapist to Understand the Root of the Problem

Conventional assessment tools usually produce extended lists of functional difficulties in the field that is being assessed (e.g., reading or writing).

When the child is functioning on a low level, the result may be a long list (sometimes too long) of therapeutic goals. This list can be confusing and frustrating to the professional. The order of priorities between the many different therapeutic purposes is often unclear, and a clinician may feel overwhelmed, not knowing where to start. The LPAD, by contrast, aims to identify, among other things, the primary cause of this long list of difficulties. The same cognitive problem may explain numerous functional difficulties. In Brendan's case, we saw how one cognitive function—an episodic perception of reality—explained many functional difficulties in a variety of fields.

We further illustrate this point by discussing another deficient cognitive function—"egocentric thinking" (from the output phase). Someone with this deficient function will correctly process the data, but when expressing or using it, he will not take the environment into account. This function manifests itself in a wide range of fields. In the area of social skills, we see it when someone speaks in a way that is clear only to him, without taking into account that others around him do not understand him. When it comes to cognitive motor functioning, such as drawing, the person will "doodle" without trying to complete the task he was asked to do (assuming that he knows how to do so).

The advantage in seeking the root cause of deficient functioning is in concentrating efforts on one strategic goal that can improve a variety of areas. Addressing a strategic goal rather than many secondary goals also makes for more efficient use of limited time resources. As mentioned earlier, seeking the root of the problem permits the integration of a diverse professional staff, thus maximizing therapeutic results. This is the advantage of the LPAD.

The LPAD Acts as a Guiding Light Throughout what may be a Lengthy Treatment Process

Treating ASD clients is challenging, owing not only to the numerous goals that tend to be part of the treatment plan, but also to the difficulty of achieving real changes. There are legitimate reasons why there are very different opinions about how to treat someone with ASD (see Chapter 3). There are approaches that call for inclusion, which propose not to adapt the student to the normative classroom but to adapt the classroom to suit him. When it comes to dealing with the integration of people with disabilities, this approach is certainly a worthy one. But the question that arises is whether this method, which replaces approaches such as normalization, is not the product of a sense of deadlock when it comes to creating real change in a person with developmental disabilities. In other words, it is assumed that the individual with ASD (or any other mental disability) will remain forever as he is today, and that the only way to integrate the disabled person into a normative society is through inclusion.

The Mediating Team

Other approaches follow the principles of behaviorism—such as ABA. This approach is not proposed for implementation in regular schools with so-called normative children but appears to be a last resort for those children who cannot be educated in a mainstream manner.

The FM offers a middle ground; a cognitive educational system aimed at making a lasting difference in the functioning of the person with ASD. This method has the ability to identify the most strategic goals (discussed in the previous section), and to draw a road map that guides all members of the therapeutic team. The LPAD offers the unique advantage of not only identifying strategic goals; it also explores the very possibility of changing the child.

It is important to note that in the FM, the clinical team engages in an ongoing assessment of its own therapeutic successes and failures; it is constantly examining its progress toward the goals that the LPAD set. Often, the therapeutic team will adapt therapy goals, owing to the difficulty in bringing about real change in a person with ASD.

The LPAD Assesses the Extent to which Significant Structural Change is Possible

Until now, we have used the term "strategic goals" to describe one of the important products of the LPAD. At this point, we will turn to a discussion of how the FM defines these strategies. Earlier in the book, we described the SCM theory; that there is a possibility of dramatic change not only in a person's functioning and skills, but in his thinking structures. These structures (or "schema" in Piaget's language) were defined by Piaget (1962, 1970). The cognitive structure is a kind of mental fusion of past experiences, information and actions with a common denominator that organizes them together. Our thinking structures affect how we perceive, process, interpret, and apply information. For example, a person with a cognitive structure of low self-esteem will interpret his successes as failures, providing justifications and explanations why this is the case.

In contrast to the ABA approach, which focuses on the two main components of behavior antecedent and consequence, the FM perceives behavior as the result of cognitive structure. The ABA method often focuses on specific behaviors. The FM will try to understand the cognitive structure involved that makes a person interpret a stimulus in a way that generates a violent/non-violent reaction. ABA measures, treats and evaluates a child's behaviors. Therapy sessions may use basic conditioning with an immediate reward or punishment to encourage or discourage specific behaviors. Treatment goals are very specific to each child and situation.

In the DIR method (Developmental Individual Differences Relationship, also known as "Floor Time"), parents are advised to "get by" or cope with the child's severe behavior or outbursts in high-stimulus, unfamiliar environments. A protected and appropriate space is created around the child instead of deciphering the structures of thought that are causing the child to interpret the normative environment in such a distorted way.

Feuerstein's theory holds the fundamental belief that cognitive structures can be changed. The purpose of the LPAD is to identify islands of normalcy and the cognitive structures that cause deficient cognitive function. The LPAD assessor needs to identify the type, quality and intensity of mediation that assisted the child to make change during the assessment.

A crucial measure of structural change is the ability to transfer what has been learned to new areas of activity. Haya Ginton (see Chapter 6) tells of a child whose main interest was beverage cans. After the attempt to tell him a story from a photo album did not work, the assessor counted five cans with the child (she returned to the child's main interest). Following that, the child spontaneously returned to the book and pointed to a page with five fish. The idea of counting "five" did not remain in the field of the object being studied, but rather became an abstract concept that could be adapted to other contexts too. A second measure of structural change is increased efficiency of the implementation of the acquired strategy. If the strategy has been internalized, it is expected that its operation will be more efficient. A third measure is the ability to anticipate, and to plan in advance the action that has been internalized.

In summary, the LPAD identifies goals for structural change (or strategic objectives) in individuals with ASD, and all staff members work together to bring about this change.

C. The LPAD Assesses the Individual's Ability to Overcome Psychological Obstacles, and Increases their Motivation to Cooperate

Although cognitive-sment assessment focuses mainly on the potential acquisition of cognitive skills, it also deals with non-intellectual skills, that is, with emotional-motivational skills. Significant obstacles blocking a child's progress may include anxiety, fear of failure or even success, and dependence on the parent or therapist. The LPAD aims to evaluate and make structural changes in these areas too. The assessor strives to mediate in a way that reduces anxiety, increases enjoyment/success, and heightens independence.

The chapter on Introduction to the Theory discusses all the mediation criteria that are designed to make the individual an independent and effective learner. The criteria do not focus on cognitive abilities per se, but on personality, emotional and motivational abilities, such as Mediation for a Feeling of Competence. This type of mediation aims to bring a person to a relatively accurate assessment of their abilities and functioning. An improvement in the person's self-competence may release many of their emotional barriers, as it gives them an unbiased picture of their abilities. For example, someone who is in the initial stages of acquiring a skill, say, swimming, bike riding, or reading, will understand that there will be necessary difficulties along the way, which do not need to overshadow their true abilities. Such understanding can lead to greater motivation when learning new, more complex skills.

Mediation of Challenge (the search for novelty and complexity) is designed to bring the child to a situation in which he will not be deterred by a task that he is not prepared for. Through this mediation, the assessor prepares the child by articulating the expected difficulty of the task, instead of simply asking him to carry it out—"Do you know how difficult this task is, how complicated it is?" Such preparation enables the therapist to provide *Mediation for a Feeling of Competence,* as it is more meaningful to succeed at a task that one knew in advance was rather challenging.

Notably, the structural goals presented in the previous section and the motivational goals we are now discussing lack specific content. They constitute a broad goal that crosses the various treatments. The different types of mediation will be used by all therapists, each in their own manner, whatever their area of expertise, enabling cohesive teamwork that greatly increases the effectiveness of the various treatments.

The LPAD Increases Staff and Parents' Motivation Once They See that the Possibility for Change Exists

While the LPAD is not considered therapy, it has therapeutic qualities in different contexts. For the moment, we shall put that idea aside. It is important to note here, though, two essential elements that can often be significant obstacles when working with a child. I am referring to two additional criteria that have not yet been mentioned. The first is *Mediation for the Search of an Optimistic Alternative.* When some parents or therapists adopt the ASD diagnosis (or any other similar definition), they may predict the future of the person being treated and thus believe that they are unlikely to achieve long-term goals. Sometimes, the optimistic therapist will say to the pessimistic parent: "but look what he can do!" and the parent will answer: "but look what he *cannot* do." They are both right, the crucial difference being perspective and attitude. This is a delicate point, particularly if the client's case is complex. However, the parents and therapists' attitude is of vital importance. Attitude can have immense influence on the treatment plan and the degree of investment of those involved. A delicate balance needs to be struck between hope and optimism as a driving force, and impetus for action.

The second parameter is *Mediation of the Awareness of the Human Being as a Changing Entity.* Here the general optimism discussed above is more specific and focused. Do all those involved in the treatment believe that everyone can change? Or do they believe that people are born with a specific genetic determination that cannot be changed? This may seem like a simple question, but the answer has life-changing implications. Feuerstein's article on early detection insisted on the paralyzing power of definition. Parents, whose children are diagnosed at a very young age as "on the spectrum" may reduce, sometimes unconsciously, the intensity of verbal stimulation they provide to the child. "Why frustrate him *and* us?", "There is no point to these efforts." So the parents talk less to the child and consequently the child speaks less (one might call this "manufactured autism").

The LPAD employs both these types of mediation, *Mediation for the Search of an Optimistic Alternative* and *Mediation of the Awareness of the Human Being as a Changing Entity.* For the first time in their lives, the parents see the changes that can occur in their child—and this parental change in attitude can be critical to their child's advancement.

When considering the therapeutic process as a whole, the LPAD is a highly efficient search for mechanisms of change. Its speed makes it a powerful means of mediating for optimism and for the awareness that a person is a changing being. While we do not expect a complete turnaround in attitude on this issue, we do seek to crack the prevailing wall of pessimism. If the clinical team members take an optimistic approach and perceive the child as capable of change, it is likely that the parents and the child himself will adopt this attitude. This, in turn, makes it likely that a change for the good will take place in the quality of intervention, both at home and in school.

References

Feuerstein, R., R. S. Feuerstein, L. H. Falik, & Y. Rand.. *Creating and enhancing cognitive modifiability: The Feuerstein Instrumental Enrichment program.* Jerusalem: ICELP Press, 2006.

Feuerstein, R., S. Gross, B. Brodsky Cohen, S. Levin, A. Rathner, T. Stevens, T. Brill, & L. Falik. Early detection: Blessing or curse. In S. Greenspan (ed.), *Approaches to developmental and learning disorders in infants and children*, pp. 253–280. Bethesda, MD: ICDL, 1998.

Piaget, J. *Play, Dreams, Imitations.* New York: W.W. Norton, 1962.

Piaget, J. *Structuralism.* Translated and edited by C. Maschler. New York: Basic Books, 1970.

Chapter 4

The Dynamic Assessment of Young and Cognitively Low-Functioning ASD Individuals

Haya Ginton and Orit Atara Berkovich

Part I: Goals and Rationale

This chapter discusses how dynamic assessment (DA), specifically the Learning Propensity Assessment Device (LPAD), is vital for assessing young and cognitively low-functioning individuals diagnosed on the autism spectrum. Based on four central principles (described below), the LPAD (Feuerstein, Feuerstein, & Falik, 2009) assesses this population in a way that exposes their potential for change and outlines the therapeutic approach necessary to realize that potential.

The Importance of Distinguishing between Manifest Functioning and Potential Functioning

For methodological reasons, standard (or static) intelligence tests do not distinguish between an individual's functional and potential ability. These tests have a predictive goal, that is, constant, unchanging characteristics. In fact, distinguishing between manifest and potential functioning can even impair the predictability of these tests. Feuerstein, Feuerstein, Falik, & Rand (2006) argued that for people with normative functioning, a lack of distinction between functional and potential ability will have a marginal effect on the test's results. In contrast, for individuals with low cognitive functioning, there is tremendous benefit to making this distinction, and it is highly significant for planning intervention or for treatment recommendations.

DA seeks out the hidden ability that exists beyond the manifest functional ability. This is done by analyzing the individual's successes and failures according to two parameters. The first concerns the task characteristics—what Feuerstein called the "cognitive map"—including the content and the modes through which it is presented to the individual, the mental operations involved in solving the task, and the cognitive functions required to activate them: abstraction, complexity level, and learning style. The second parameter refers to the temporary conditions that may affect the efficiency of thinking processes such as fatigue, anxiety or fear of

DOI: 10.4324/9781003451136-5

failure. Through intervention, the LPAD assessor can create a change in one or all of these parameters.

When it comes to ASD individuals, the gap between manifest and hidden abilities becomes highly relevant. As this population lacks the normative tools by which their hidden abilities can be revealed, in the absence of the DA approach, their test results may well be misinterpreted and be used to recommend ineffective interventions. The dynamic, informed use of the LPAD and structured mediation enables us to look for ways to break through the communication barrier and see the individual's true ability.

Case Study: Heather

> *Nine-year-old Heather exhibited communication difficulties from a very young age. She did not speak at all, and her hand was almost always in her mouth (this was accompanied by a great deal of salivation). Heather was home-schooled, and her parents described her functioning in all areas as very low. During her assessment, each time an object was presented to her, she put it to her mouth and then threw it on the floor. Heather wandered through the room and stopped in the corner, climbed onto a low table, and curled up. She was not completely disengaged, however, as she maintained partial eye contact with me (the assessor) and with her parents, who were present in the room, and she smiled in response when they talked to her from afar. I approached Heather and showed her a 3D wooden puzzle, demonstrating what to do (from afar) while verbalizing the process. Heather was attentive, and since she could not reach the puzzle, she could only watch what was going on while waiting to receive it. When I finally gave her the puzzle, she spontaneously put it to her mouth and then threw the pieces on the floor. I gave them back to her and thus began a slow process where we assembled the puzzle together for the first time. I took her hand and directed it to manipulate the puzzle. We repeated the process several times, and gradually, her movements became more deliberate and coordinated with my movements. In this way, "joint attention" was created until the task was completed. After a while, when I presented the puzzle to Heather, she put the pieces in the right order, one on top of the other, without placing each piece inside the other, as requested. To ensure this was no coincidence, I gave her the pieces again, and she arranged the parts in exactly the same order. She no longer threw the pieces on the floor or put them in her mouth. The resulting connection made it easier for me and Heather to change our position in the room, and she returned to sit at the table for further activity.*

Static psychometric assessment (whose objectives and characteristics were already mentioned) would have ended once Heather had thrown the puzzle pieces on the floor, and the relevant conclusions would have been made. In this case, the dynamic assessor noted that, despite her position in the corner of the room, Heather was aware of what was going in the rest of the room. This was Heather's sign that we could continue. From there on, precise preservation of a sequence of mediated actions led to the exposure of hidden abilities. It appeared that Heather had the ability to attain even more precise perception, to remember a sequence of actions. In other words, it seemed that her communication could be improved through appropriate mediation.

The LPAD Looks for "Islets of Normalcy" in a Sea of Abnormal Behaviors

Despite Heather's progress during her assessment, she continued to throw objects and put her hands in her mouth in her normal environment. Her therapeutic journey would be a protracted one, and it would be a long while before a real change in behavior was seen. Nonetheless, this event reinforced for us that initial impressions do not necessarily predict ability. Moreover, we succeeded in revealing behaviors in Heather that were very different from those she normally presented, even if they were transient and irregular. As previously mentioned, standard tests do not look for these events. In order to ensure their predictive validity, these tests only look at typical behaviors, ignoring and treating as insignificant, the fleeting ones.

Professor Feuerstein introduced the term "islets of normalcy" (Feuerstein, Feuerstein, Falik, & Rand, 2002, p. 352) as a starting point for assessing individuals with low cognitive functioning, with particular reference to those defined as on the autistic spectrum (see Chapter 4). Firstly, the dynamic assessor must move away from the "sterile" interaction that characterizes the standard tests and from the tendency to link an individual's behavior to a diagnosis, whether it is autism or any other diagnosis that includes low cognitive function. She is tasked with creating a dynamic interaction, establishing ongoing communication, and imparting meaning to the few normative behaviors the examinee shows. She is to treat these behaviors as reflective of his personality. Secondly, the assessor must focus her efforts on identifying normative behaviors in the individual, even if they are of short duration and irregularly presented. Feuerstein argued that, if the assessor does not direct herself to search for these "islets of normalcy," she probably will not discover them even if they occur right before her eyes.

In Heather's case, her effort to maintain eye contact despite her physical disengagement was an "islet of normalcy" from which the aforementioned process began. First, I signaled to her that I could see she was looking at me and listening. Next, I reinforced her effort to make eye contact by encouraging her to focus her gaze on me and the puzzle for an extended period of time. Our steady eye contact probably stimulated in her a positive attitude towards me, which later enabled me to take her hand and work with her without resistance until a pattern of action with a normative meaning emerged. This mediated interaction made a normative action that was initially random and transient, relatively prominent and stable.

Jastak explained the aforesaid process thusly: "...the peaks in the examinee's performance are indicative of his potential whereas the summed and averaged scores, namely, the global index, are representative only of the individual's manifest level of performance, since this index wipes out the saliency of the peaks. The peaks of performance must therefore be viewed as extremely important hints of the existence of a capacity that does not become generally manifest because of the individual's inefficiency in using it" (Feuerstein et al., 2002, pp. 42–43).

The LPAD Uncovers the Functional Potential Following a Process of Intervention

In this section, we argue that the mediated intervention that takes place during dynamic assessment with the LPAD allows one to penetrate beneath concrete thinking abilities, where no mental processes are involved, to reveal abstract thinking abilities in both children and adults with low cognitive functioning. This is the purpose of the LPAD: uncovering the ability to change.

Concrete thinking is both state-dependent and stimulus- dependent. The examinee who presents with a concrete way of thinking responds to events and objects in a passive manner. Even when a stimulus is encountered, its effects disappear since he lacks the cognitive tools to preserve his encounter with the event or object. As an example, a young child at the end of a long busy day in pre-school is unable to share what exactly he did during the day. This is also the case for learning processes: the low-functioning individual will learn a new skill in a particular context, but when he is required to apply what was learned in another situation and/or at another time, it is as if the learning never occurred. This person will need re-exposure to the relevant skill in order to present what he learned.

Abstract thinking occurs when one is no longer dependent on the physical presence of the stimulus because one has created a mental image of the object or event through input and elaboration processes. These processes involve the following: At the input stage; clear perception and an effective concept system and object permanence; At the elaboration phase; the ability to identify and compare spontaneously, the selection of relevant stimuli, the provision of logical proof and. The ability to create mental images provides us with constancy and the capacity to internalize learning processes; additionally, it extends our mental field beyond the perceived information. The LPAD demonstrates that, with the correct intervention, even low-functioning individuals can manage to solve abstract problems.

Case Study: Ian

> *Ian, aged 17, was diagnosed at the age of four with communication problems. His parents reported that until four he displayed typical development, even at a higher level than his twin brother. Since his diagnosis, Ian attended special education schools. His teachers could not provide any indication of Ian's future based on his current abilities, although he was about to graduate from school. His parents, too, did not dare to express any belief or hope for change. He lived in an environment that no longer presented him with expectations and challenges, but rather tried to solve specific behavioral problems. Over the years, Ian learned to read and write, though he did not reach the level at which these capabilities could be the basis for expanding knowledge and developing higher thinking abilities. Ian's communication skills were limited. He made an effort to answer the questions he was asked, sometimes displaying echolalia while giving an answer. During the LPAD assessment, Ian did not initiate communication, and verbally expressed his needs and feelings in a limited way. Despite the fact that Ian was diagnosed as having low cognitive functioning, it was decided to present him with a more challenging test to identify his ability to change. He received some brief preparation before the test (Organization of Dots), where he was asked to identify the corners of a square and a triangle and to connect them into the correct shape. Ian's visual perception proved to be good, and he solved the simple problems. He had a hard time explaining his actions, which raised the concern that when the task complexity increased, he would no longer be able to work independently. Accordingly, he was given mediation which focused mainly on providing logical proof of his decisions. Our request for logical proof raised his awareness that he had strategies that helped him, and indeed when he came to the more complex problems, it was clear that his impressive success was due to his use of strategies. Ian was then asked to solve a number of problems from Raven's Coloured Matrices (A, AB, B). Here too, he struggled to offer logical proof for his choices using the relevant terms and concepts. At first, his answers indicated concrete thinking based on visual perception, and he found it difficult to transfer strategies from one problem to another. A breakthrough came when he was asked to solve figural analogies taken from Raven's Variations Test (more complex problems based on the Raven Matrices). Here Ian began to spontaneously share the logical reasoning behind his answers, something which requires a reasonable level of abstract thinking. In this way, Ian learned not to give answers for which he had no logical proof.*

Although Ian's final test results were good, they did not provide us with the information we were looking for. It was important for us to understand the impact of the intervention and how it could be reduced so that Ian would reach maximum independence in problem-solving. Intervening through mediated interactions during the LPAD assessment did allow us to break through Ian's tendency toward concrete thinking; he reached abstract thinking in the area of problem-solving. This is where the LPAD diverges from static assessments: the latter assume learning ability is geared toward a final outcome while the LPAD seeks to track the learning process following intervention. In this respect, we might say that measuring IQ without taking into consideration the ability to change is like measuring the size of an iceberg by its visible part on the surface, without taking into account its total volume.

The Search for an Individual's Modifiability is Based on the Idea that a Diagnosis Indicates a State rather than a Trait

Professor Feuerstein had a mantra: "No diagnosis, however accurate, reflects all that a child is." This refrain characterizes the Feuerstein Method. Beyond diagnosis, there is a whole world of abilities that the dynamic assessor is tasked to seek out. In this view, a diagnosis is more a temporary state rather than a fixed trait.

Feuerstein's claim concerning cognitive structural change following mediated learning (Structural Cognitive Modifiability; see Introduction to the Theory) has received impressive confirmation in recent years following the scientific world's acceptance of the notion of brain plasticity. It thus seems that two processes of human development (neurological and socio-cultural) are in continual dialogue, each influencing the other. When one teaches a blind person to use his other senses to get information and help him overcome his biological limitations, his brain structure changes. Mediated learning is an important element in influencing the flexibility and plasticity of the brain. Following this theoretical assumption, we can say that when it comes to people, we are talking about systems with a tendency to change. That is why we prefer to describe the individual as a cluster of states rather than as built from traits. The difference between the two is that states are flexible and open to change from the environment and intervention, while traits are fixed, rigid, and unchangeable. The LPAD is based on these assumptions; it assumes that we can modify the individual, and it searches for the best way to do this.

Moving to my assessment of seventeen-year-old Ian, two issues guided me:

First and foremost was Ian's diagnosis. I did not know him when he was diagnosed at age four with communication problems. The fact that until this age he developed normally, even surpassing his twin brother, raised questions: Did his parents accept the diagnosis as fact? Did the assessor's recommendations reflect the approach that a diagnosis is a fixed trait? And what was done to change his situation? Did the absence of proper and timely intervention make this situation permanent? Neither Ian's parents nor his teacher could answer these questions.

The second issue concerns the process of my assessment. I decided to give Ian tasks that were at a higher level of complexity and abstraction than what he was used to, because there would be no benefit to the assessment if I gave him tasks that he could easily handle. We would reach the same conclusions that previous assessors made over the years. There was a need to create a situation in which we could break through Ian's behaviors that had become hardened and which strengthened the idea that his diagnosis was fixed, in order to discover his modifiability. This would transform his diagnosis into a state—something that can be changed.

As an assessor, I needed to work intensely with Ian. Although he did not object to the interaction, he initially found it difficult to benefit from the mediated learning intervention. I had to adapt my mediation frequently to move Ian out of his passive learning mode. He did not use the right tools to gather information, and, when it was gathered, he did not know how to use the information to solve simple figural analogies. When the path to active learning was found, however, Ian began to succeed. The fact that he succeeded in solving the more complex problems on his own attests to the modifiability we seek during the process.

In conclusion, the four parameters described above, which show how the LPAD is highly appropriate for people with communication difficulties, are in fact relevant to anyone exposed to the LPAD assessment. Feuerstein, Feuerstein, Falik and Rand (2006) specifically refer to the special-needs population, including individuals defined as autistic, and offer a modified version of LPAD, the LPAD-Basic which retains the central parameters of dynamic assessment but differs in its goals. Assuming that children with low cognitive functioning are blocked from receiving mediation from their environment, intervention in the context of the LPAD aims to penetrate their resistance and create the conditions for Mediated Learning Experience, enabling new learning and thinking processes. Rather than seeking to identify hidden cognitive structures, the LPAD assessor seeks to identify the extent to which an individual has the ability to change as well as the intervention methods required to reveal his hidden potential.

Part II: Intervention during Dynamic Assessment

Introduction

Earlier, we emphasized intervention as an integral part of the dynamic assessment process, the same process by which we discover the hidden abilities of an individual with low cognitive functioning that we wish to develop and expand. In this section, which offers a more in-depth discussion of the interaction, we argue that LPAD assessment interventions contribute significantly to exposing an individual's ability to change or learn. This is particularly true for those with communication difficulties.

Many assessment tools now available for use with individuals who have communication difficulties feature an intervention component as a key part of the diagnostic process. For example, Kerry Shulman (2002) presents a wide range of tools for assessing the child with suspected autism. However, while such tools involve mediated interactions with the child, the interventions in these tests are preplanned. Accordingly, they do not take into account the unique states of the individual. A related problem concerns the analysis of the test results, which does not take into account the quality of the intervention. In these diagnostic tools the principle of norms is preserved, and the assessor (and intervention) remains a fixed object rather than a flexible subject in the interaction.

The LPAD, which does not refer to norms, offers a fundamentally different viewpoint. While norms are the outcome of comparing the child's results to the general population, the LPAD assessment compares the child to himself. Thus, we create models of learning situations and examine how the intervention affects the changes that were observed. We then compare the child's functioning from before intervention (pre-test) with his functioning after the intervention (post-test).

It is important to remember that, generally speaking, parents turn to the LPAD after a diagnosis has already been made. Experts have already recommended a therapeutic and educational course that typically places the diagnosis at the center and does not take into account the child's potential to change. Parents who are not satisfied with the diagnosis, or even oppose it, seek additional samples of behavior, usually to learn about other approaches to diagnosing and treating their children's problems.

Case Study: Dylan

Eleven-year-old Dylan is the only child in a single-parent family.

His mother turned to us for assistance in finding the most suitable educational framework for him. Dylan was diagnosed at age four at one of the child development institutes with a communication disorder and hyperactivity. Immediately after receiving the diagnosis, he was sent to special education frameworks for children with communication disorders and began to receive medication. Dylan's mother, who recognized the need to help Dylan develop socially and communicatively, was concerned about the negative effects of the medicine and the negative impact that the special educational framework was having on his cognitive development. She decided to home-school him for a limited period of time, in the hope that when she discovered higher learning abilities, he would be able to reintegrate into a regular framework with the therapeutic support he needs. Two years later, when she approached the system, they refused to acknowledge Dylan's change and forced the mother (while threatening to take legal action) to agree to continue sending him to special education frameworks. Dylan was placed in a framework amongst teenage boys with communication problems and low cognitive functioning. As soon as our assessment with Dylan began, it was clear that he was a "gifted under-achiever" who lacked experience in formal learning. On one hand, he had acquired knowledge in many fields, through direct exposure, but on the other hand, he lacked the tools to expand and deepen his cognitive abilities. He solved the simpler tests without any difficulty. He hardly needed our intervention to solve problems that required sharp and clear visual perception. However, since we were also going to present him with higher abstraction tests, we provided intervention focused on building a set of problem-solving strategies: he was asked to prove why his solution was correct, to explain how he came to the solution, and when he made a mistake, to explain how to correct it. Thus, a list of strategies was developed that would be of use to him later in the assessment. The results of the assessment, which included a battery of tests designed for adults, requiring high verbal, figural and mathematical abstraction levels, were particularly impressive. With these results and recommendations at their side, Dylan's assessor came to the educational placement committee that was imposed on his mother by court order and succeeded in convincing the committee members that Dylan belonged in a normative setting.

Dylan's case clearly demonstrates the power of mediated learning/intervention in exposing a person's potential. In the LPAD approach, the potential abilities of an individual are placed at center stage, and the rigid diagnosis is shifted to the background.

Dynamic assessment has three characteristics which contribute to understanding the meaning of intervention in the creation of change in individuals with communication difficulties and low cognitive functioning: 1) the test's structure; 2) the "learning process"; and 3) identifying goals for intervention. We will now discuss these features.

Test Structure

LPAD instruments are built in a way that invites intervention. Below, we discuss four aspects of the test's structure that reflect the positive place of intervention during assessment (for more detail, see Feuerstein, Feuerstein, Falik, & Rand 2006 and Feuerstein, Feuerstein, & Falik, 2009):

1   The *Cognitive Map* (see Introduction to the Theory) presents the structure of the LPAD test using the following seven parameters: content, modality, cognitive functions, mental operations, complexity and novelty, abstraction level and efficiency level. The first task acts as a starting point for manipulating the parameters as needed for intervention. In the following tasks, one can leave several parameters constant while changing others (e.g., keeping the modality of the initial

task but changing the level of complexity). The goal of manipulating the task is to find the best type of tasks for the intervention/mediation.

2   The *Principle of Variations*. The LPAD instruments include a number of tests designed to work on the assessed individual's logical reasoning. In the *Principle of Variations*—unlike in conventional tests, in which the tasks are unrelated to each other—each task in the assessment differs *slightly* from the previous one. The similarity between the tasks in the Principle of Variation stimulates the development of a process of change in the examinee. Moreover, this feature makes the instrument very sensitive to any changes that take place in the context of the assessment.

Case Study: Mark

Mark is two years old and was born with Down Syndrome. This lively and curious child was given a colorful puzzle consisting of a board with round holes painted in seven colors, and seven circles to match accordingly. His mother told me that he did not know the names of the colors yet. We built the task according to the principle of variations: first we wanted to make sure that Mark understood the connection between the board and the circles. We found that he was very focused on the circles and the way they rotated but ignored the board. Through mutual play, Mark learned that there was a connection between the two, and he began trying to place the circles in the holes. Here we learned that his fine motor skills were still limited. Mark's alertness and curiosity made him try again and again until his coordination began to improve, but he did not succeed in the main objective of the puzzle: matching the colors. We took advantage of his alertness and curiosity in favor of learning. Thus, I took all the circles into my hands, and asked Mark to point to the color he wanted (he was not yet verbal). When I presented him with the circle he had asked for, he was then asked to point to the hole where he would put the circle. In this way he experienced, for the first time, a situation where he needed to match items in a structured and planned manner. In order to strengthen this basic mental activity, we switched roles and now he had to give me the circles at my request. Here a welcome change was observed: the deliberate reference to color as a matching criterion.

Although this was not a formal test, here too, the dense network principle guided us in building the learning process. Mark's complex task was broken down into subtasks, where each step added one dimension that was based on the previous step. In this way, Mark could not fail. Using the cognitive map parameters also guided our building of the stages so that the learning process was appropriate for him.

1   *LPAD tests consist of three phases: pretest-intervention-post test.* This structure allows us to compare the individual's functioning before and

after mediation as well as assess the intervention parameters he needed in order to produce a meaningful learning process. Thus, we can identify the delta between the two stages of the test and capture the examinee's potential both quantitatively and qualitatively. Additionally, we can identify interventions that produced changes and those that were less effective.

Case Study: Robert

Robert is a ten-year-old boy with normal intelligence and a long history of academic failure. He developed behaviors that caused further regression until it got to the point where integration into a special education class for children with communication problems was recommended. During my intervention with Robert, I presented him (among other tests) with Feuerstein's dynamic version of Rey's Complex Figure Design. His first copying attempt showed an episodic grasp of reality, and he did not take into account the spatial relationship between the forms. Furthermore, he compressed many unrelated items together and added items that were not in the original figure. In the first recall stage, Robert drew separately the few items he remembered. After this stage, the assessor analyzed his performance and reached the following conclusions:

In the face of complex and meaningless visual stimuli, Robert needed to make a considerable effort on the copying task due to his difficulty with organization and planning, and the result indicated that he is "pulled in" by the stimuli with no real control over the situation.

Despite the poor result, the presentation of the parts he remembered attested to an effort to follow some sort of logical procedure.

His grapho-motor skills were good and did not constitute an obstacle in organization and planning.

From previous tests given to Robert, we knew that he had a good vocabulary that could be useful to him in the learning process.

It is important to address emotional responses when faced with a complex task, mainly of wanting to succeed in the face of fear of failure. We need to pay special attention here to Robert's feeling of competence. If we succeed in imparting strategies for the planning and development of internal representations, emotional responses are likely to moderate.

The intervention process started with precise scanning and verbal analysis of each shape using the correct terms: space, size, shape, direction, and so on. Robert felt confident, since this particular task enlisted his good verbal ability. We began the intervention copy stage with intensive intervention to reassure Robert that he was not going to make a mistake. We offered Robert organizational strategies and ensured that he understood the logic behind them. We helped him free himself from episodicity and encouraged him to seek connections, spatial relationships, common characteristics, and so forth. Gradually, it was possible to slightly reduce the intensity of the intervention while he copied the shape, until Robert requested to continue alone, expressing comfort and satisfaction with the result. We verbalized the process together with him and praised him for his progress. As can be seen in Figure 2, the second copy and recall stages (without intervention) showed impressive improvement compared to the first stage."

Rey's Complex Figure Design

Rey's Complex Figure Design

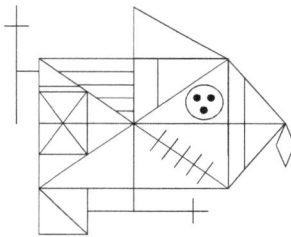

Copy 1   Recall 1

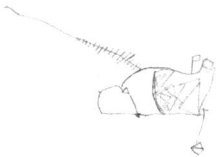   

Copy 2   Recall 2

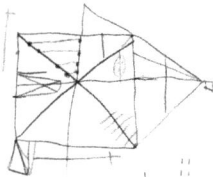   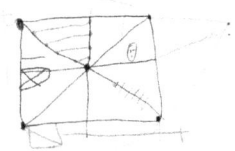

Figure 4.1 Reys Complex Figure Design.

In standardized tests that use the Rey–Osterrieth complex figure test, the test may have ended after the first recall stage. The results would have indicated serious difficulties in a number of areas that could explain Robert's poor school performance, and the likely recommendations would have been special education and lowered expectations. But our intervention and its results provided us with more in-depth information that led us to other conclusions. First, we saw that our assumption about feelings of competence was correct. When we gave Robert tools for self-monitoring and helped him to understand his mistakes and correct them using proper planning, he felt confident that he could succeed. Secondly, the starting point of the intervention made use of Robert's verbal skills, in which he felt sure of his abilities, thus creating openness to mediation and motivation for change. The last and most important conclusion is that one should not lower expectations but rather demand that the individual aim high, toward a normative framework, while providing the assistance he needs in order to develop cognitively and socially.

1   *Analysis of errors.* Intervention in the LPAD is based on the individual's abilities (as we saw in Robert's case), which constitute the starting point, as well as on an analysis of his errors, which constitute the assessor's goals. The assessor systematically analyzes the examinee's errors during the assessment. On the multiple-choice tasks, the incorrect answers are distractions. Choosing one of them may indicate one or more deficient cognitive functions. The Tri-Modal Analogies test includes simple analogies that appear in three modalities: pictorial, verbal and figural; the individual must choose the most suitable option out of 6 possible distractions. In the example page (Figure 4.2), choosing option 5 indicates the possibility that no attempt was made to relate to the data and to process it. Choosing options 3 and 4 could suggest that data collection was superficial and inaccurate, and therefore there was also failure at the processing stage. Choosing option 2 may mean that information processing has occurred, but the logical operation was wrong: instead of analogy, the individual used logical multiplication. Choosing option 6 could indicate impulsivity, or the individual did not take all the data into account. The analysis of errors throughout the test can identify patterns of repetitive errors that will in turn become the target of intervention/change.

Trimodal Analogies B

A

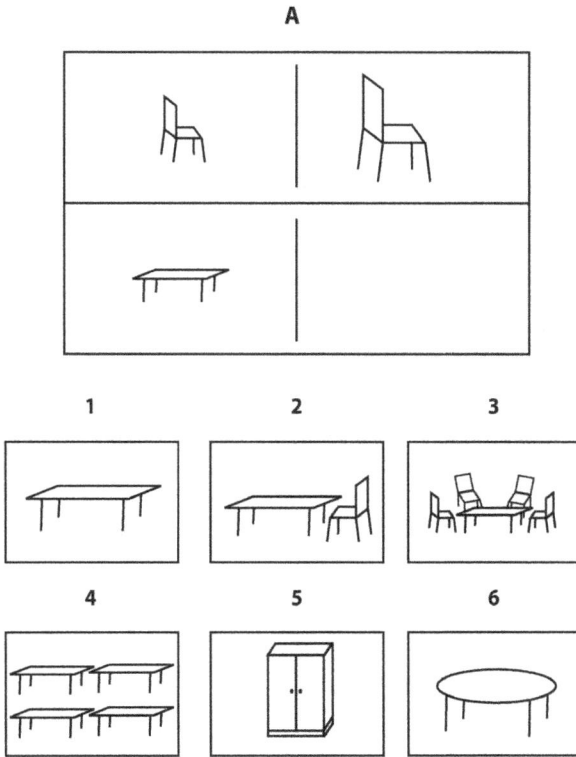

Figure 4.2 Trimodal Analogies from the LPAD Handbook.
Source: © Feuerstein™ Publishing House Ltd

The "Process"

The second characteristic of the LPAD refers to its learning-process-oriented structure. The LPAD allows for the formation of varied intervention situations, which can be adapted according to the purpose of the assessment. Some of the tests include several subtasks which are similar in content and modality. However, each subtask consists of elements that the individual is already familiar with and some new elements that build on what he already knows (as noted above). The LPAD process therefore has two functions. The first is to facilitate the individual's data collection process (because the content and modality remain constant), enabling him instead to focus efforts on problem-solving, that is, to activate the cognitive functions for elaboration. The second function is to crystallize the strategies acquired during intervention. The new elements in each task prevent the individual from working automatically and force him to use the strategies he has learned in a meta-cognitive approach until they are crystalized. In this way, even individuals who really struggle can achieve success. This kind of structure enables the assessor to intervene in two ways:

1   Since she has in-depth knowledge of each test's cognitive requirements, she consistently prepares the individual for the next task. This is the case whether the individual succeeds at the task or struggles with it. If he succeeds, the individual will usually be required to logically explain his choice; if he struggles, the cognitive functions required to correct the error must be activated. With the former, the request to provide a logical argument reinforces the individual's meta-cognitive awareness of using strategies that may later become habit.
2   The second way the assessor intervenes relates to changes in the examinee's motivation level, which can lead to a change in his behavior/approach when faced with a problem. Initially, he will perceive the need to solve a problem as threatening, which may lead to resistance and even detachment. Gradually, however, he will develop a tendency to seek out challenges, believing that the tools he has acquired for solving one problem will also help him solve other problems, even if they are more complex.

The LPAD intervention process is unique in that the assessor- client relationship becomes similar to a teacher-student relationship; problems are solved as a team. When the assessor's involvement in the task is very high, the examinee receives the impression that the task is important; difficult, but definitely solvable. Gradually, the assessor will be able to distance herself and give the client responsibility for solving the problem. When an individual achieves success after working on a problem, he will feel the desire to repeat the experience. Such repetition has a functional value in that it forms behavioral patterns of success and increases one's aspiration for achievement. Motivation at this stage often becomes intrinsic, and less dependent on the assessor.

In assessment situations, a change in the interest or motivation of the examinee is the result of the client's ongoing activity over time, even after the assessor no longer gives instructions or ceases to be actively involved. This change in motivation is achieved by providing meaning, encouragement, and assurance that the client will continue to experience success. Even if he makes a mistake, the overall process of change is what really matters. In contrast to static tests, in which feedback is very limited and must be given in a way that does not differentiate between individuals, feedback during the LPAD is provided constantly, and continuous intervention, sometimes even beyond the task itself, is vital.

Below, we describe a situation in which intervention was made possible by the test's process:

Case Study: Lisa

Lisa, aged 10, had experienced constant failure in studies from an early age, alongside difficulties in social adjustment, without a satisfactory explanation. e gave Lisa the "Organization of Dots" instrument from the FIE battery. Lisa solved the first three or four rows of the learning page almost automatically, and she did not allow the assessor to intervene. She requested that she be allowed to solve them by herself. The test procedure requires intervention even at the early stages, where the individual is able to solve the problems alone and with ease. Intervention is given at the beginning of the test in order to encourage the individual to self-reflect (what made me succeed?), to create openness to mediation (Intentionality and Reciprocity), and to lay the groundwork for more complex tasks. Despite the importance of intervention even in situations of success, we allowed Lisa to continue solving the problem alone. This continued until she reached a problem where there was a big jump in complexity, and then she made a mistake. She intended to erase the answer and try again, however, we stopped her and asked her to define the nature of her mistake and explain how she was going to correct it. The intervention was aimed high, and she was required to provide logical proof of her proposed solution. Lisa learned that the intervention provided her with tools for self-monitoring, which would prevent mistakes and strengthen her ability to deal with more complex tasks independently. This significant turning point affected the rest of the evaluation, which brought her to experience many successes. A wonderful learning process was created, and we revealed a smart girl with learning potential that had not yet been expressed. Lisa learned that dealing with a test in which the level of complexity increases from one task to the next does not necessarily lead to failure, provided that she is willing to accept intervention that will help her expand the range of strategies she can use, and understand what she has learned in every task in order to help her cope with the next. Later, Lisa was able to solve most of the problems on her own, despite their increased complexity; moreover, the need for active intervention by the assessor was reduced. A positive process of self-mediation began. Her performance on the other LPAD tests also reflected her higher abilities. Nonetheless, her school achievements prior to the LPAD assessment did not reflect these abilities.

In the above case study, task complexity increased to the point that the examinee could no longer use strategies that were familiar to her—a tendency that may have caused Lisa's low academic achievements. Here, a window of opportunity was created for intervention that allowed her to expand her abilities in preparation for more complex tasks. Lisa's success following intervention produced motivation and a general change in her approach to problem-solving. If it were not for the assessor's insistence on providing intervention, we might not have revealed Lisa's high cognitive potential.

Intervention Goals

The third characteristic of the LPAD is identifying the goals for intervention and mediation during the assessment. This is critical for examinees with poor communication because it enables us to distinguish between two types of children. The first type is the child who comes to an assessment with communication difficulties, bound by his sensitivities to outside stimuli and limited activities and blocked from being able to benefit from intervention or understand the world around him. The second type of child, following intervention, reveals curiosity, asks questions, "invites" the adult to mediate, and learns how to learn.

Feuerstein described children with autism or communication difficulties as children who do not respond to their parents' or others' attempts to interact or mediate. Despite their communication difficulties, these children are open to direct exposure from the environment but derive limited benefit from it. In the absence of mediation, they do not know how to integrate new information into their psychological repertoire, and thus they are blocked from the learning that will enable them to continue to develop cognitively on their own (Feuerstein, Feuerstein, & Falik, 2009). In addition, the difficulty these children experience in relating emotionally to their surroundings leaves them isolated. In their case, the assessor tries to penetrate the resistance to mediation, identify islets of normalcy, initiate Mediated Learning Experience, and facilitate a learning process.

Greenspan and Wieder (2006) presented an approach that is relevant for assessors of children with communication difficulties. Children who begin to respond to their environment as a result of intervention sometimes show excessive or even strange behavior. Yet, this change is positive, and as clinicians we must seek interventions that moderate the behavior and make it as normative as possible.

Intervention, then, is at the heart of the LPAD. Indeed, the instruments are often chosen primarily to create openness to mediation rather than to identify cognitive abilities. More specifically, they are geared to identify the learning processes created by the intervention rather than those formed through direct exposure.

Feuerstein suggested selecting LPAD instruments according to the following three criteria:

1   For individuals at a particularly low level of functioning, choose modalities that address the input and output phases over the elaboration phase (e.g., use of light, sounds, music, rhythm).
2   These individuals' limited exposure to complex content should be taken into consideration. In order to create openness to mediation, it is important to choose content that is familiar to the client.

3   Because the assessment situation is usually new to these individuals and they are not able to follow the rules of conduct during the assessment, the assessor must use special intervention methods in order to obtain a response that reflects the individual's learning ability.

We would like to discuss four main areas of intervention that assist us to form our goals: body awareness, activity space, communication, and specific behaviors that generate learning. Importantly, any distinction we make between these areas during assessment is arbitrary and artificial. It is done only to help the individual make sense of the wide range of interactions he has with his surroundings, which naturally appear, disappear, develop, and change.

Body Awareness

Body awareness develops from a very early age, from when a baby starts moving its head from side to side, and it detects that a change in motion leads to a change in his view. The young child gradually gains the understanding that moving his body gives him different perspectives on his environment. This discovery opens up a whole world of insights for him. He begins to discover that his hands, and then his legs, are an extension of his body that allows him to influence the environment: he can grasp objects, move objects around, put things in, take things out, push and pull, walk, and later use tools and materials.

The DSM-5 refers to body awareness specifically in relation to limited or repetitive patterns of activity. It refers to over-reactivity or under-reactivity to sensory input according to predefined severity levels. The LPAD attributes special importance to the development of body awareness, which supports, especially during infancy, the development of normal input. A delay in the development of body awareness may reduce the child's information-gathering skills when learning, gaining experience and communicating. Thus, therapeutic intervention regarding body awareness when a child is at risk is absolutely essential (see Chapter 9).

Children with communication difficulties often use arms and legs mainly as a way of self-stimulation, or for defense purposes (hitting, pushing or escape). For a child whose verbal communication is limited or non-existent, an effort will be made to expose him to broader, more meaningful practices with his body, which cannot be expected spontaneously, but can be produced through deliberate intervention.

Case Study: Megan

Megan, a nine-year-old girl diagnosed with autism, did not speak. At the beginning of the first session, she found some finger puppets inside a toy box. She took them and put them on her fingers. Megan's mother drew my attention to the fact that each time she placed the dolls on her fingers, she did it in exactly the same order (not necessarily in finger order). My intervention attempts ended in failure. She resisted all my efforts to create a dramatic game with the dolls and ended the interaction between us when she abandoned the dolls and found a new game to play alone. In our next session, while making sure to use content that was familiar to her, I tried to create learning situations through other means using play, sounds, songs and dance movements. It was possible to see "islets of normalcy" in her responses to the intervention, but these came and went without forming a stable process of change. At our third and final meeting, I suggested to Megan that we listen to a variety of songs she liked, including a song about fingers. Megan went to the closet, took the puppets and put them on my fingers and hers, and we continued to listen to the song and do the movements together.

In the progress made during this assessment, we discovered an islet of latent potential in Megan, albeit one surrounded by a sea of objection to interaction. This single event followed a number of planned mediated interactions aimed at communicating by hand signals as an alternative to verbal communication. We therefore attributed the event to learning that occurred following intense intervention and believed that this activity could be expanded until it became part of Megan's behavioral repertoire. Furthermore, the intervention that led to the finger puppet joint activity showed an understanding of meaning, an understanding of the logical connection between events and objects, and it was important to continue to explore these abilities in Megan, to bring them to the surface, to encourage them and to expand them in a variety of contexts and modes.

We have seen individuals with communication difficulties and low body awareness whose movements are limited to very specific functions that have been learned through conditioning. Thus, we found individuals with physiologically normal motor development avoiding motor interactions. Substantial intervention is required to help them give or take objects from an adult or child, hold an object for a long time, or initiate motor manipulation of objects. Holding an object for a period of time and trying to see how it works are, in fact, the basis for exploratory behavior in young children. Lack of sufficient capacity or motivation prevents the child from gathering information about the object or exploring and understanding cause- and-effect relationships. Understanding such relationships is a prerequisite for reducing episodic thinking and the development of abstract thinking.

Case Study: Heidi

Nine-year-old Heidi was diagnosed from an early age as functioning at a low cognitive level and was later diagnosed with autism. Heidi's hand-use was very limited, even ineffective, and she needed help with every routine action, although physically she was able to do more. Heidi enjoyed just a few activities, one of which was ball games, and yet she was unable to hold the ball long enough to direct it, and it would fall out of her hands. We assumed that Heidi had not yet developed the awareness of the ability to influence the environment through her hands. We found that she was fond of listening to and watching songs on the computer. Heidi did not have the communication skills required to express her enjoyment of listening to songs in this way, but we saw that she was able to get up easily from the floor alone (which usually requires special intervention) when she heard the songs and sat in front of the computer. In a process of intensive intervention, we mediated to her how to continue listening to a song if we paused it (she had to press the spacebar on the keyboard). She succeeded in repeating this action even when the intervention had stopped.

In the intervention process, we did not mediate to Heidi the motor action of pressing a button, and we did not teach her to move her hands. Rather, we mediated to her the connection between her desire for something to happen and the action required. Here, too, we discovered a potential in Heidi to develop an awareness of the use of her hands, which stems from the understanding of a cause–effect relationship.

Constructing the Activity Space

The idea of "activity space"—the area in which an action takes place—emerged from the field of occupational therapy, which views it as the basis for the development of complex actions in the future. The body's voluntary movements usually determine the area of activity. An individual's movement changes the way he sees the world and provides him with different perspectives on his environment (Smith, 1998), thus accelerating cognitive and social development processes. A baby who begins to crawl can already draw a mental map of the space in which he operates, let alone when he is sitting, standing, or walking. The spatial mental map created by the young child is actually an expression of the meaning of the action. He "runs away" and hides from his mother who calls him, as a fun game, or he runs to his father to be lifted up after not seeing him all day. The child learns to divide his space, or to break out of it when he wants to reach an object that is outside the boundaries of the space he created. Sometimes the object seems too far away, and then we will see him turn to someone else—perhaps crying in order to receive help. Babies who show difficulty in creating an activity space for themselves will struggle to reach an object that interests them, even if they are very active. We see young children who "lose their way" while trying to reach the object, and we observe them crawling or walking seemingly without purpose.

In defining autism, the DSM refers to social development and points to different degrees of severity regarding a person's lack of social skills: from a significant reduction in social interactions to limited initiation, to short-term social interactions, with no significant mutual dialogue. The DSM does not specifically address the way in which a person diagnosed with autism builds his activity space or creates a space that helps him to develop communication skills.

The LPAD deals at length with the building of an activity space because of its contribution to the individual's overall development, the implications of which are very broad. These implications range from its contribution to the development of spatial perception, to reading and writing, to understanding spatial relations, to the ability to understand reality from different points of view, and to understand another's perspective. Building activity space as a goal of intervention is based on the following questions:

1   Is the space suitable to the task characteristics? How does the individual build his activity space to suit the characteristics of the task? In other words, how does he organize the toys, where does he build/paint, how does he copy a pattern?
2   Does the individual change his activity space when the task or goal changes?
3   Does the individual tend to start working in a large space and gradually reduce it, or vice versa?
4   Does the individual take into account the presence of another person in his activity space (does he move aside, give up space, sit on, face or move away from the person)?
5   Does the individual have the ability to refer to more than one space at a time?

Heidi (the nine-year-old girl we met earlier), entered the therapy room and stood at the door. I suggested that she play ball with me, which we know she particularly enjoys. It was obvious she very much wanted to play. With a happy expression on her face, she started to move towards me in a "dance-like" manner, moving back and forth, until she sat opposite me at a suitable distance so that we could play. Later during the assessment, while we sat on the floor (her preferred place to sit), I suggested to Heidi that I read her a story. Without physical intervention, she changed her sitting position so that she could see the pictures: she moved from sitting to lying on her stomach, raised her head, and followed the story.

Heidi's apparently purposeless back-and-forth movements are a typical characteristic of children diagnosed on the autistic spectrum. In static testing situations, this behavior is not analyzed in order to change it; it is simply considered another criterion fitting the diagnosis. If we had not let

Heidi take her time to sit down, the ball game might not have happened, or we would have sat her down ourselves, thereby missing out on the important information that was received about how she built her activity space. In a post-assessment analysis (while watching the recording of the session), I explained Heidi's movements as her attempt to construct a mental map of her activity space, making use of one fixed point in the space—the assessor sitting motionless with the ball in her hand, encouraging her to come closer. That is, we created a point of reference for her in the space, to which she could direct herself, even if it took her a long time. This is an important point to remember when recommending how to mediate building the activity space of an ASD individual.

Heidi's teachers described her as extremely passive and in need of constant physical guidance to move from place to place. When they had no choice, they admitted, they simply moved her themselves. Here was a rare opportunity for Heidi to determine her activity space herself, and we saw that she was capable of doing so. Moreover, it seemed that her successful attempt to sit independently gave her the motivation to change and build another activity space that would be more appropriate for reading the book.

Another aspect of how the activity space is built relates to its reduction and expansion. Reducing it too much does not allow the entry of another person into the space, thereby diminishing possibilities for sharing and communicating. Expanding it too much, by contrast, prevents the possibility of focusing on a specific experience—and, here too, sharing with others is almost impossible. When Megan, who we met earlier, entered the room, she would take an object, examine it briefly, and sort it according to her level of interest. She kept the interesting objects next to her and threw the less interesting ones on the floor. When she began to play, we realized that her activity space was very limited; she played the game exactly where she found the object. Thus, she stood in the closet playing with the hand puppets inside the box, and specifically concentrated on arranging the objects in a certain order that remained unchanged. Each object was moved and returned exactly to the place from which it was taken. Megan's use of her activity space left us no room for intervention. Any attempt to change the activity space ended with anger, violent behavior and tears. In the following sessions, by which time she knew and trusted me, I was able to help her expand her activity space so that we could play together.

Case Study: Michael

Michael, a twelve-year-old boy diagnosed with autism, was known to have high cognitive abilities, but he did not speak. We presented him with a number of LPAD tests, including high- level abstraction tests, which are normally performed at a table. Michael got up from the chair after a short while and began to walk around the room. After attempts to persuade him to

> *return to the chair did not help, the assessor followed him from place to place and presented the problems from the test manual. He pointed to all the correct answers, including those problems that require very high levels of abstraction. He did this while constantly changing his position in the room: by the window, on the floor, even sitting on the table.*

Michael's impressive thinking skills contrasted sharply with his inability to adapt to the normative spatial demands of the task, or, as Feuerstein described it, a lack of proper social conduct in assessment situations. Megan and Michael built different types of activity spaces, both of which made it difficult for the assessor to intervene during assessment. Neither of the types of activity allowed for normative communication with the environment: one was very limited, and the other was amorphous, in a constant state of flux. In contrast, Heidi, who presented with many communication difficulties, succeeded on her own, albeit after a long time and with a great deal of effort, to build a suitable activity space that facilitated the intervention process.

Part III: Communication

Diagnosis or distinction? Evaluating children with communication difficulties

When a child and his family are referred to us for assessment, frequently the child has already been tested and 'diagnosed.' Parents have been given a 'name' for the child's condition, as well as a prognosis and suggested treatment methods that emerge from the diagnosis. An autism diagnosis is usually based on a standard assessment, which is mostly static in nature, and the tester must be as neutral as possible so that his conclusions can draw upon standard criteria, for example, those appearing in the DSM. Such a diagnosis enables the system to provide parents with professional and financial support.

Dynamic assessment (DA) of communication issues can identify developmental difficulties and is not blind to difficulties and deviations from the norm. It is unique, however, in that it raises the question of the reason for the communication problem; whether it stems from primary language impairment, hearing impairment at a young age, or syndromes and various diseases that can affect the communication of the child and/or adult with low cognitive functioning. DA is not satisfied with the definition given to parents, but rather asks who is 'the child behind the diagnosis' with the assumption that there is no child like any other, even if two children have the same diagnosis. DA generally advocates that 'every child must have a suit tailored to him and only to him'. The Feuerstein assessor follows the child's inclinations, his difficulties, his talents, his family and his educational framework.

Case Study: Alex

Ten-year-old Alex entered the room in a flurry of excitement.

> *His mother and sister said goodbye and immediately closed the door behind him, so the assessor had no chance to invite them in. The reason for their rapid disappearance was immediately apparent. Alex began to try to destroy everything he could reach. In less than sixty seconds, the room became absolute chaos. All this time, Alex did not look in the assessor's direction and seemed unaware of her presence in the room. Suddenly he stopped at the flowerpot on the windowsill, looked in the assessor's direction, turned it over and put the soil into his mouth, keeping his eyes on her. He asked with his eyes, 'What are you going to do now? How will you oppose me?' The assessor must have done the last thing Alex would have thought of: she went over to him, looked at him directly, and put the soil into her mouth too. Alex's expression was unmistakable; he did not expect this at all, and he prolonged eye contact, apparently with astonishment. Then the assessor burst out laughing, and Alex too was drawn into the laughter for a moment. At that moment the assessor sat down at the table and motioned with her eyes for Alex to join. After he sat down, she took out a train game and Alex managed to play for four consecutive minutes—the longest Alex had ever sat willingly with anyone.*

Alex's prolonged eye contact with the assessor was a cue that an opportunity for change had presented itself. She understood Alex's provocation as an invitation to make contact with him. It took a great deal of investment for her to discover a situation in which Alex was able to create a normative connection (the shared laughter). The investment was based on the assumption that Alex in fact wanted to play and was seeking to share his enjoyment with another person.

Evaluating a child with communication difficulties in a new situation, with all its many components, must be understood as different from a regular encounter. One needs to take into account the range of circumstances the child has experienced from the time he woke up in the morning and until he entered the room, the wider circumstances regarding the family in which he grew up and the educational framework in which he studies. Observation can tell us about how he plays and communicates in the present.

DA, by contrast, shows us how an assessor's intervention can bring about a change in the child. But how does one begin assessing a child with communication difficulties? There is no manual in the world that can provide a ready-made answer to this question. The answer to this must come from the child. We must stop and observe him - either with his parents in the waiting room or by noticing what draws his attention, or by simply asking him or his parents what he likes. This will help us answer the question of how to break through the wall that the child has built around himself in order to avoid normative communication. Only when the child agrees to let us into his world, —will we be able to make a change. This wall can be penetrated through a very narrow slit, which must be discovered carefully and sensitively, so that we can expand it through intervention.

It is remarkable how quickly children notice that they are in situation that is different from the one they are used to, and that the assessor is not there to 'diagnose' them. This is in contrast to the parents, who often, at the start of the assessment, shift in their seats uncomfortably. They do not understand why the assessment has not yet started, sometimes half an hour or more into the meeting. However, when the child shows change or performs differently than what they are expecting, the 'wasted' time at the beginning of the meeting begins to take on powerful meaning.

Case Study: Madeline

> Six-year-old Madeline functioned like a two-year-old with respect to communication abilities. She displayed impaired speech with no eye contact. At the beginning of our session, she took objects (toy furniture) out of a box and arranged them according to her own logic. This was incomprehensible to the assessor, who encouraged her to sort the furniture according to the different rooms in a house, to no avail. Madeline did not respond to the assessor's communication efforts and continued with her activity. We can say that, at this stage, the assessor focused on Madeline's difficulty rather than the girl in front of her.
>
> But things began to change when the assessor changed her approach to that of the Feuerstein Method. She left the room, returned with little dolls and began to play with them and the mini furniture on the table. Madeline tried to snatch all the dolls, so the assessor held them out to her, but kept one back. She said, 'this is the little baby; the dolls you have are his family, and they will take care of him'. Madeline agreed and began to look after the baby using the other dolls. The game shifted from simply taking items out of a box (which is developmentally characteristic of the second year of life) to a symbolic game. As the game progressed, Madeline began to show more initiative, expressed her feelings and thoughts, and the game gradually became a socio-dramatic game with characteristics that corresponded to her age. The mother and grandmother who were in the room asked to record what was going on and said that no one would believe what had just happened if they had not seen it with their own eyes.

Within an hour and a half of the meeting it appeared that, Madeline 'grew up' by four years. The many errors that accompanied her speech at the beginning of the session were reduced, her sentences were more complete and detailed, and her behavior was dramatically more mature.

In situations where the assessor fails to establish a relationship with the child during assessment, they may conclude that the child is 'not cooperating', thus providing further evidence of the presumed autism diagnosis. The burden of proof, however, should not fall on the child but on the adult. Dynamic assessment encourages the assessor to enter the child's world; this is the only place where the child will allow an encounter with another person. In the above example, the assessor's suggestion to add dolls to the game allowed her to reach Madeline in her own place, where Madeline felt comfortable. In this context, the assessor was given the opportunity to introduce new elements, to create a change and to examine its character, strength and quality. Notably, even when joint attention was created, Madeline dictated the rate of change according to her ability to adapt to the new situation.

It is important to emphasize that the essence of the change that occurs during the assessment is not the result of learning new behavior, but rather the exposure of learning abilities that already exist in the child, but for one reason or another have not yet been expressed. In the cases described above, the assessor created the optimal conditions for normative behavior that did not currently exist in the child's behavioral repertoire but existed in potential.

In conclusion, the purpose of dynamic assessment should be 'distinction,' as opposed to diagnosis. The diagnosis given at the end of a static assessment only reflects the superficial visible presentation of behaviors and is usually shallow and limited. This is because the behavioral repertoire of a child with communication difficulties is likely to be extremely limited, with superficial expression. In contrast, dynamic assessment is a process that starts with diagnosis but turns into a treatment session, in which the assessor makes a distinction between the child's clinical definition and his personality: what does he think, what does he feel, what is meaningful to him, what frightens him or moves him? The behavioral aspects will be temporarily marginalized, and the child's motivation for change will be the center of discussion.

Dynamic assessment for children who have been diagnosed with autism, or adults with low cognitive level, takes into account all the standard communication functions, but it does so without the use of a clear formula. In particularly complex cases, the assessor will focus on one specific functional aspect which has been identified as an 'opening' through which the child can share with the assessor. This could be humor, playing with a train set, coloring, and so on. Whatever it is, the assessor's goal is to find this 'opening,' which can be exceptionally small, and expand on it. One must take into account the chaotic manner in which the child thinks and communicates with his surroundings, leading him to allow another person to enter only where he feels safe, in a familiar and pleasant place. Once allowed to enter, we must tread carefully. Sometimes, we will expand the same activity, sometimes we will take it in a different direction, and sometimes we will try to add a new element. There is no one formula; it all depends on the person who is in front of us. The assessor's role is to let the child tell his story.

A process in which there is no search for the invisible will remain confined to externalized behaviors, which can be modified by behavioral methods. To expose the conditions that increase the motivation for internal change requires that the assessor make an effort to discover who the person is behind the diagnosis.

Part IV: Behaviors that Generate Learning

In this section, which continues our presentation of the goals of intervention, we will address two features that are foundational to the learning process: curiosity and exploratory behavior, and motivational-affective factors. These features tend to be deficient or missing in individuals with communication difficulties or low cognitive functioning.

Learning processes can occur in two ways: through direct exposure and through a mediator. In the direct exposure model, our control as adults or mediators on the learning process is only partial. We cannot control the range of stimuli to which the child is exposed, and we cannot confidently understand or analyze the learning process that took place on the basis of the child's response. When the learning process takes place through a mediator, the adult has more control over the process, and she can analyze behaviors and draw conclusions more easily. The mediator creates an optimal environment for the child that will ensure a learning process and has a goal in sight. The mediator is aware of the mediational interactions she has created, and based on the learner's responses, she can speculate about the optimal means of mediation necessary for the formation of a learning process. Yet, one should not conclude from this that direct exposure does not contribute to learning. Rather, the opposite is true: we aspire for the child to demonstrate independence and learn from direct exposure. We believe that when mediated learning experience is successful, the child eventually self-mediates even in situations of direct exposure. LPAD assessment distinguishes between these two learning methods. In the remainder of this chapter, we will examine a variety of behaviors that generate learning and consider how interventions encourage or accelerate them.

Our intervention model emphasizes the theoretical difference between curiosity and exploratory behavior, although, in reality, these two behavioral aspects appear simultaneously. This distinction rests on Feuerstein's model of mental action (see Introduction to the Theory, and Feuerstein, Feuerstein, Falik and Rand, 2002), a model that will help us analyze other behaviors. Feuerstein described three phases of mental operation: input, elaboration and output. Distinguishing between the phases allows us to analyze behaviors and identify targets for intervention. The input phase is characterized by information gathering, which is driven by the individual's cognitive functions: scanning, spatial perception, use of verbal concepts, accuracy in data collection, and so on. This step prepares the way for a response. The elaboration phase is characterized by the use of the information collected at the input phase. Cognitive functions at this phase include comparison, the search for logical proof, reasoning, understanding the nature of the problem, and hypothetical thinking. The output phase reflects the manner in which one expresses the results of the thinking process. Among the main deficient cognitive functions in this phase are egocentric language, impulsivity, and trial and error (as opposed to searching for ways to solve a problem). To this we add motivational and affective factors, which affect the entire process and the nature of the interaction during intervention. These last two factors create learning behavior, and, for the ASD population, sometimes form the focal point of the assessment.

Curiosity and Exploratory Behavior

Curiosity can be understood as the interest that we display in the objects in our environment and our manipulations while interacting with these objects. This is an example of the use of the cognitive functions model. In order to develop the child's curiosity, we focused on the input and output phases and leave aside the elaboration phase, but still creating a change in the elaboration phase. This demonstrates the principle that, sometimes, handling input and output is sufficient to produce a change in the elaboration. The individual who perceives the stimulus responds in one of two ways: either impulsively, moving quickly to the next object, or repeatedly manipulates the object without planning or intent, until it becomes automatic.

Case Study: Elizabeth

> *I met Elizabeth for the first time when she was twelve years old. She has Down Syndrome, and her general development was delayed. Elizabeth only started walking at the age of 10. She did not speak and showed very limited interest in her surroundings. Although no clear autism diagnosis was reported, her behavior met most of the criteria mentioned in the literature. In our initial meetings, every attempt made to interact with her was met with resistance. Her only points of interest were objects she could spin while she lay on the floor, focusing her gaze on the rotating object (as if mesmerized by it). She could lie like this for a long time, only stopping when the object was taken away.*

This is an extreme example of how curiosity is expressed by object choice and according to the specific needs of the child. For Elizabeth, the variety of objects in the environment that aroused curiosity in her was limited to those that could be rotated. The curiosity of other children is stimulated by the environment, but they may show only very brief interest. This was the case for Megan, who we met above. Upon entering my room for our first session, Megan scanned every object in sight, and, within minutes, every one of them was lying on the floor.

The aforementioned situations can be described as "input- output." Thus, elaboration had no effect on the mental thought/ action. After intervention, however, we saw significant change. The purpose of the intervention is to build/stimulate/activate the elaboration phase of the thinking process so that the initial curiosity supports meaningful action. In Elizabeth's case, we chose to short- circuit the automatic manipulation by providing alternatives to the rotating object. After discovering that eating was another significant occupation for Elizabeth, we introduced this activity. We thus intervened in the process of arranging and dividing up the food, and we directed how she placed the food in her mouth. During the assessment, we found islets of exploratory behavior regarding the food, with partial responsiveness to our intervention. In fact, we created the exploratory behavior—an intermediate stage between input and output which required the reinforcement of elaboration functions: choosing between two foods, creating an even eating rate, separating between courses, cutting large pieces of food into smaller ones, and so on. The resulting change led us to recommend this intervention as a basis for continued treatment.

Megan's intervention turned out to be particularly challenging. After she threw all the objects on the floor, a change occurred and she began to sort the objects into those that did or did not interest her, the latter which she threw down again. As previously mentioned, she began to arrange finger puppets in her own special way. All of this indicates active elaboration; however, she was unable to produce significant and comprehensible output. Since direct intervention led to resistance, we resorted to indirect intervention. In the next session, we chose to play her songs on the computer, something she particularly enjoyed. When we came to a song about fingers, she went to the closet and took out the finger puppets, which she had played with in the first session, and put them on her fingers. This was a dramatic change: Megan went from being wholly self- and object-oriented to showing significant exploratory interest. Thus, she made a connection between the game of the previous session and the music she heard, and even expressed this by inviting me to play with her.

Case Study: Tom

Tom, an eight-year-old boy, was diagnosed with communication problems and autism. He could not talk, but he found a way to express his needs, desires and feelings through gestures. Tom's curiosity was very limited: he

continuously looked only for beverage cans, which prevented him from any
meaningful communication with his surroundings. Despite this, we were able
to interest him in a book containing repetitive elements and the numbers 1 to
5 (with which he appeared to be familiar). After we were unable to discover
how he collected data and solved problems, we tried to connect with him
through his preoccupation of beverage cans. Instead of giving him cans, we
showed him pictures of cans on the computer. Tom pointed to the cans one by
one, as if counting them. After pointing to five cans, he brought the clinician
the book we had read a short while before, pointing to the picture of five fish
we had counted while reading the story.

Tom's case further shows how, through intervention, exploratory behavior can emerge from curiosity. Using the information Tom's parents gave us about his excessive interest in beverage cans, we were able to demonstrate that such interest stimulated cognitive abilities that normally remained unexpressed due to Tom's impaired linguistic ability.

To summarize, curiosity is the foundation of exploratory behavior. Intervention to discover and stimulate exploratory behavior requires us to distinguish between curiosity that prompts repetitive behavior, limited in terms of areas of interest, and curiosity that prompts short-term interactions with a large variety of objects. In both cases, there is an investment of effort only in the input and output phases. Intervention aims to prompt exploratory behavior by awakening elaborating cognitive functions: comparison between objects (Elizabeth) and the discovery of connections between objects (Tom and Megan).

Greenspan & Wieder (2006) discussed a further point of importance for children with communication difficulties. They claimed that in order to achieve exploratory behavior—that is, to develop elaboration functions, and even to reach abstract thinking—intervention concerning the child's ability to respond emotionally to his surroundings is required. Feuerstein agreed with this idea; he saw this ability as an important condition for openness to mediation in those diagnosed with autism.

Motivational-Affective Factors

Alongside the goal to create cognitive change in the ASD individual, it is also crucial to consider motivational-affective objectives. Feuerstein defined motivation as the degree of effort one is willing to invest in any given task, and the extent to which one uses one's newly acquired cognitive abilities (Feuerstein, Feuerstein, Falik, & Rand, 2002). Affective factors, which are emotional factors that influence learning, can be positive or negative.

The relationship between the assessor and the examinee can strongly influence the results of the assessment and constitutes a goal of intervention—features which are unique to dynamic assessment. In interacting with the examinee, the assessor strives to create the following process: first, the examinee will act from extrinsic motivation—a desire to please the assessor or someone significant in the room. Next, the examinee and assessor will interact around a task. By the end, the examinee will act from intrinsic motivation: he will work on his own, cope with problem-solving, experience success, and need less intervention. We will discuss this inner motivation shortly.

In static tests, the tester makes an effort to remain neutral, in line with the test's formal requirements. Individuals with communication difficulties may perceive the tester's neutral responses as boring, or even as threatening and anxiety- provoking. Additionally, examinees in static tests tend to have little understanding of the test situation, including why they are taking the test.

Among the many tasks of the dynamic assessor, intervention to change motivational-affective factors is perhaps the most challenging. This is all the more so when it comes to individuals labelled as autistic, whose affective abilities are low—in many cases lower than their manifest cognitive abilities. According to Feuerstein, Feuerstein, Falik and Rand (2002), "motivation" includes the following behavioral characteristics, which the assessor must identify and select as the goals of mediation/intervention:

- Intrinsic/extrinsic motivation
- Need for mastery
- Fear of failure
- Pleasure in success
- The need for control
- Frustration vs. tolerance
- The need to work independently
- Self-image
- Degree of egocentricity
- Search for complexity and willingness to accept novelty
- Reaction to criticism

Even after identifying these factors, it will take patience and investment on the assessor's part to create a positive interpersonal process. Initially, this process will be marked by resistances such as a lack of curiosity and a lack of exploratory behavior. Feuerstein (in Feuerstein, Feuerstein, Falik, & Rand, 2002) argued that in order to develop the curiosity that leads to exploration, one needs to be exposed to the concept of novelty. Thus, one discovers something with which one is not familiar, and one wishes to explore it. The concept of novelty relies on cognitive functions such as the ability to make comparisons, analytic thinking, and the ability to understand changing relationships within a fixed framework/structure.

An individual who reacts negatively to new tasks may have a history of negative experiences. Repeated failure can create a generalized negative attitude to wards everything that is new. The following case study describes an intervention process for changing motivational factors. This child's motivation began at a low level but developed into intrinsic motivation with a high level of functioning:

Case Study: Adam

> Adam, aged five years, six months, was diagnosed with autism and language problems and started attending a special kindergarten for children with communication problems. The kindergarten did not meet the parents' expectations, so they sought other ways to help him, eventually bringing Adam to the FI for a consultation. We presented Adam with a variety of LPAD-B instruments (LPAD Basic is an LPAD adaptation aimed at the early childhood years and/or for people with low cognitive functioning). Among the instruments presented was the "Visual Transport" test. This test is designed to create a process in which the child learns how to transfer a given model from place to place first by copying and then from memory. The model undergoes several transformations in terms of complexity: from very simple (Figure 4.3), to most complex in terms of the size of the matrix, and the number of positions the child must remember. The test pages are not particularly attractive to young children. Adam, as an obedient child, did not object, but also did not express any special interest. After Adam solved the first task on his own, we provided intensive intervention in order to generate interest in the next task and the one after that. Here is an excerpt from our conversation that took place during the test:

ASSESSOR: That's great, you solved it by yourself, and it's really not easy. Yesterday, we had a boy here who did not succeed so well. How would you teach him to succeed on this task?

ADAM: Look, here and here.

ASSESSOR: But he will not understand, because you said it very quickly, and he also does not understand what 'here and here' means. Can you explain better?

(Adam is silent and seems puzzled, but he begins to show interest).

ASSESSOR: Maybe instead of 'here and here,' you can give the squares names, and then it will be easier for the other child to understand.

Adam then enlisted himself in the task with full force. We saw that he understood spatial concepts, but these did not come to him spontaneously. He later learned to name the squares according to their position in the matrix (top right to bottom left) and we practiced an imaginary dialogue between him and the "other child." Gradually, with ongoing encouragement, he began using the spatial concepts, in part to ease the visual load that accrues when level of complexity increased. Despite the learning process that Adam demonstrated, he displayed a temporary decline in motivation. In order to boost his motivation, the assessor involved Adam's father, who was present in the room. Thus, she asked him to solve a difficult problem, and asked Adam to "teach Dad" how to deal with the difficult task. Adam's father, who took on the "student" role and gave Adam the "teacher" role, asked him questions until Adam said, "Let me, I will do it myself." During this test, which took a long time, Adam revealed outstanding ability. His sense of competence continued to increase, and when we got to the very complex tasks, he commented "Wow, it's hard"—but did not flinch. Moreover, he solved the problems without any difficulty. When we reviewed the assessment with Adam, we compared the simple beginning of the test with the complex ending so that he could see the change that had occurred. Adam's father told him that when he saw the complex task, he was afraid Adam would not cope with it, but now he felt surprised and proud.

Visual Transport

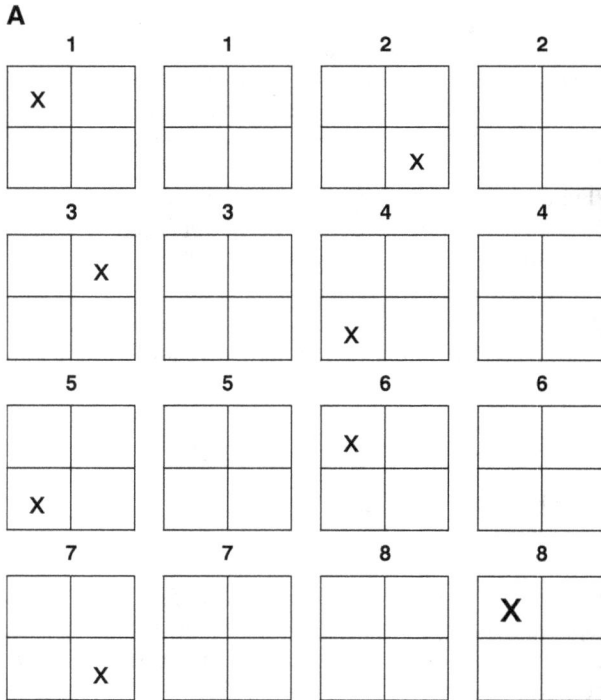

Figure 4.3 Visual Transport Instrument from LPAD-Basic.

Alongside the learning process that took place during the assessment, a highly significant change also occurred in Adam's motivation. We used a number of intervention goals in order to shift his motivation from extrinsic to intrinsic:

- By means of strategic intervention, we succeeded in shifting interest from the unattractive task to an interesting dialogue, with the task itself in the background (reduced egocentricity). Intervention was needed to "awaken" an existing set of concepts (right-left, up-down). This was an action in which Adam had little interest, but his motivation increased in the context of helping someone he cared about.
- The interaction was one of a mediator and mediatee rather than of an assessor and individual. A mediator will do everything in his power to facilitate the success of the mediate, and this message was conveyed to the mediatee. In other words, the mediator was interested in the task and saw success in the task as important to them both. This is what we call *mediation for reciprocity* (see introduction to book). The idea is as follows: If the mediator is so interested, perhaps the child will feel it is worthwhile to dare overcome the fear of failure.
- Involving Adam's father in solving the task helped build Adam's curiosity; if it interests Dad, then it must interest me, too. This is the principle of shaping the social environment in order to accelerate processes of change (see introduction to the book).
- The role reversal, where the child was given the teacher role, stimulated curiosity in the child, who for many years had taken a passive position in treatment. Here, he was given a sense of control.
- The intervention took place against a background of success rather than failure. He was able to enjoy success, and thus experience a shift to a more positive approach to problem- solving.
- Adam felt a sense of success despite the increase in complexity level— thus demonstrating a willingness to accept novelty and challenge. This is what the theory calls *mediation for the search for complexity and novelty.*

Intrinsic motivation develops from two important processes: first, the individual begins to understand the factors that help to determine his success in solving the task and transfers strategies from one task to another. This is what the theory calls *mediation for transcendence*, which leads to cognitive structural change that allows transfer (see Introduction). Second, the individual begins to enjoy problem-solving situations instead of experiencing them as threatening. This is the product of *mediation of challenge.*

As Adam received a diagnosis relating to communications problems, we began the intervention from a standpoint that is difficult for children diagnosed with ASD—the ability to understand the other's point of view.

Adam's success in these areas raised the question: Perhaps the diagnosis was no longer appropriate? Perhaps his manifest language difficulties did indeed reflect communication difficulties. Nonetheless, when we circumvented these language difficulties, we discovered abilities that had not yet been observed. Was it now appropriate to think of entirely different ways to intervene?

At this point, we reiterate that dynamic assessment not only allows for intervention to take place, it is an integral part of it. Thus, one is incomplete without the other. Analysis of the results takes into account the nature of the intervention, its intensity, and the degree of its impact on the change achieved.

We conclude with an important point: Despite the dramatic change that occurred in such a short time in Adam, we did not assume that we had finished creating a meaningful change, and that all his problems were solved. Instead, we had created a *sample* of change as a result of deliberate intervention which enabled us to advise Adam's parents, caregivers and teachers how, specifically, to realize his potential.

References

Feuerstein, R., R. S. Feuerstein, L. H. Falik, & Y. Rand. *The Dynamic Assessment of Cognitive Modifiability: The Learning Propensity Assessment Device: Theory, Instruments, and Techniques.* Jerusalem: ICELP Press, 2002.

Feuerstein, R., R. S. Feuerstein, L. H. Falik, & Y. Rand. *Creating and enhancing cognitive modifiability: The Feuerstein Instrumental Enrichment program.* Jerusalem: ICELP Press, 2006.

Feuerstein, R. S., R. Feuerstein, & L. Falik. *LPAD: Learning Propensity Assessment Device Standard − Manual for the mediator* (3rd revised ed,). Jerusalem: ICELP, 2009.

Greenspan, S. I. & S. Wieder. *Engaging Autism: Using the Floor Time Approach to Help Children Relate, Communicate and Think.* Boston, MA: Da Capo Press, 2006.

Shulman, K. "Tools and Methods for Diagnosing Pervasive Developmental Disorders (PDD) and Autism in Very Young Children." In S. Lowinger & P. Klein (eds.). *Connections: New Directions in the Assessment and Treatment of Children with Communication Disorders.* pp. 9–20. Kiryat Bialik: Ach Publishing House, 2002.

Chapter 5

LPAD With ASD Children and Adults Mild to Moderate Levels

Monica Paz

The LPAD as the Optimal Method for Assessing the Learning Propensity of Individuals Diagnosed as ASD

The LPAD is a system for evaluating modifiability, that is, learning potential. This assessment device is more than a test: rather, it is an assessment which incorporates teaching mediation from the assessor and is adapted to the examinee's particular needs. An analysis of the evaluative interaction makes it possible to detect strong and weak features of cognitive functioning in all three phases of thinking, that is, input—elaboration—output (see Introduction to the Theory), as well as to determine effective remedial methods.

The LPAD seeks to create the optimal conditions to reveal the examinee's true potential and learning propensity. Of course, optimal conditions vary from individual to individual. The LPAD assessor, unlike the administrator of static tests, has a great deal of flexibility regarding presentation of tests and instructions, time allowance, and, most especially, in the interaction she has with the examinee. This interaction includes giving personalized feedback, mediation, time for self-reflection and the possibility of reconsidering responses if they were incorrect. The autistic examinee who, by definition, has communication and social interaction issues, has much to gain from this personalized approach. Conversely, the standardized testing situation, which, frequently allows for no flexibility, may lead to total non-compliance on the part of the examinee. The assessor, too, has much to gain from the LPAD: she can assess from the outset which techniques and mediational strategies are required in order to forge a relationship with the client.

a small number of moderate-to-high-functioning autistic people possess extraordinary talents in specific spheres, a phenomenon known as "autistic savantism." Thus, it becomes all the more crucial that we understand exactly *how* to create these optimal conditions and how to enable our client to reveal and/or achieve his highest possible performance. Moreover, the examinee's family and teachers may not have been exposed to the extent of the person's potential, since some cognitive abilities may only emerge under certain conditions. Put simply, it is possible that because of

DOI: 10.4324/9781003451136-6

low manifest performance, no one believed that the client was capable of more, and thus he was never challenged with higher-level tasks. Perhaps the tasks were not presented in a way that aroused the client's interest and motivation, or under mediational conditions that would stimulate success.

Learning Profiles Emerging through LPAD

In our work over many decades, we have noted some significant differences in the learning profiles of individuals with communication disorders as compared to those who suffer from other disorders. These specific characteristics require our special attention and demand differential treatment and mediational strategies during the assessment.

The LPAD assessment aims to reveal which cognitive functions (prerequisites for learning; see Introduction to the Theory) impair adequate performance, and thus become targets for modifiability. We try to modify them *within* the assessment process to witness *samples of change* which will then serve as our blueprint for further intervention following the assessment. These deficient functions can be analyzed according to the three phases of the mental act: input phase, elaboration phase and output phase. Although in practice the phases are highly integrated, this division might help to define the common areas of difficulty in the autistic population and facilitate the development of targeted intervention strategies.

The additional dimension, the affective-motivational factor— which affects all three phases of the mental act—also warrants our attention and has yielded interesting insights.

Almost without exception, clients on the spectrum present with some sort of difficulty in accessing the cognitive functions required for correct/efficient functioning of the input phase of the mental act, the phase responsible primarily for gathering data for evaluating or solving problems. Since it has been documented that many of the symptoms of autism result from an underlying disability in the child perceive the world through his senses, it makes sense that difficulties would appear at the input phase.

Blurred and sweeping perception occurs when stimuli are perceived either incompletely or with a paucity of detail, lack of clarity and/ or imprecise definitions of their borders. This can be observed in many examinees from the moment they enter the testing room. For example,

Case Study: Peter

Peter, age 12, arrived at the door of my room with his father.

> *As I got up to greet them, he rushed straight past me and into the room, touched some objects lying on the shelves, and then settled himself into my chair—at which point he began swiveling around, totally delighted with*

himself. He then looked up to see what was next. Being drawn to the array of games and ornaments in the room, Peter seemed not to have noticed the adult waiting to greet him at the entrance to the room.

While this behavior is not uncommon among younger children, older people tend to display a fairly high level of anxiety, which also expresses itself in a sweeping level of perception. The LPAD assessor should carefully observe how examinees enter the room. Do their eyes dart around as they hesitantly enter? Do they survey the new environment and avoid eye contact with the assessor until they feel more comfortable? And when, exactly, does that sense of comfort show itself? It is crucial to observe how clients collect information from the environment before the actual assessment begins.

Once the assessment starts and the examinee is faced with specific tasks, the assessor determines whether he is generally able to collect information in a focused and precise manner. We seek to understand whether he has the capacity for precise focusing. What are the conditions that bring about this change? What types of tasks appear to engage him? What kind of instructions lead him to become focused?

Unplanned, impulsive and unsystematic exploratory behavior manifests itself in gathering incomplete data. We noted how many of our clients would respond before collecting all the information required. This impulsivity often seems to stem from anxiety and irritability—not enjoying the task and therefore wanting to finish with it as quickly as possible.

Case Study: Danny

> *Danny, age 13, was not particularly happy during the assessment. He had his parents sitting on either side encouraging him, but also making it clear that he had to cooperate. He would look briefly at the task and respond quickly almost so as to "get it over with." Later on, as the tasks became more challenging, a remarkable change was noted. The irritability and restlessness disappeared entirely. Danny became totally engaged in the task, weighing up all the sources of information carefully and systematically in order to reach the correct solution.*

Clients' impulsivity often appears to be related to the type of task presented. When the task sparks his interest and he feels challenged, a significant reduction in impulsivity is almost always observed.

Lack of or impaired receptive verbal tools necessary to receive, store, elaborate and express information. This lack also affects discrimination, that is, objects, events or relationships that do not have appropriate labels. This is a phenomenon that occurs across the board, as difficulty with language usage is a defining characteristic of a communication disorder. It is important to determine to what extent the client shows an understanding of the task at hand even when he cannot verbally express this comprehension.

Case Study: Sunny

> *Sunny, age 9, could not think of one word that expresses "red, blue, green, yellow." The moment he heard the word "color," he used it thereafter spontaneously.*

Many clients display evidence of superordinate concepts present at a receptive level. This ability can be revealed though mediational questions. Subsequently, a list can be supplied to help them use the terminology, which will, in turn, help them distinguish between different variables as they collect information.

In general, clients reveal far higher functioning at the elaboration phase than at the input phase. The elaboration phase plays a central role in the act of thinking, unlike the peripheral one played by the input and output phases. By and large, once input has been remediated, that is, the client has slowed down his search and correctly labels the incoming stimuli, intact processing becomes evident.

As mentioned, once given the opportunity to enlist capacities for performing higher-level cognitive operations such as analogies, seriations and permutations, and challenged to use representational thought, clients generally show a significant change in behavior. Many become highly focused, engaging in a task with such absorption that even minimal mediation is rejected.

Case Study: Jenny

> *Jenny, a sixteen-year-old girl, was somewhat agitated and anxious to get started. During her performance on Variations 2, which is a test that examines different skills in abstract thinking designed by Feuerstein, a little post-mediation was provided to help sharpen her impaired verbal tools. Jenny was resistant to this; becoming annoyed, she would declare: "I understand! I understand!*

Case Study: Peter

> *On a task from Raven's Standard Progressive Matrices, a test devised by J.C. Raven to examine differential abstraction skills, Peter was now more focused, sitting and concentrating well. He rejected mediation, making it clear that he wanted to solve the tasks on his own.*

The *episodic grasp of reality* describes a lack of orientation in the client to seek and project relationships, and to summarize events. Objects or events are

VARIATIONS 2   POST

A-4

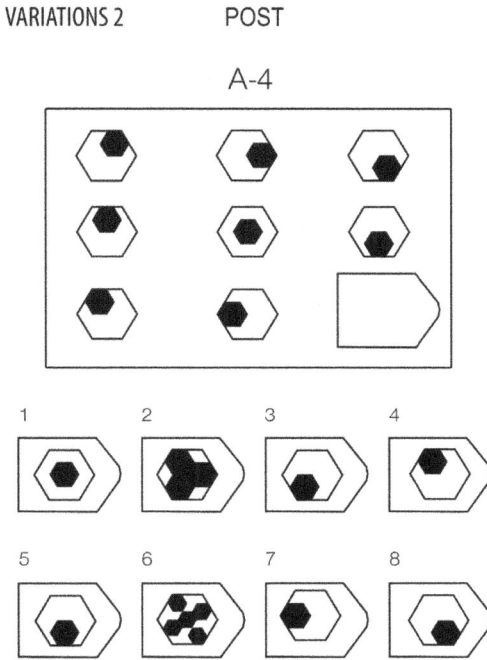

Figure 5.1 Variations 2: A4.

viewed as unique and isolated, without any relationship to what preceded or might follow it. Interestingly, although many younger and more severely autistic children seem to have an episodic grasp of reality, this does not always seem to be the case with higher functioning clients. An episodic grasp of reality often becomes apparent when we request that the client copy the Rey Complex Figure. This well- known test devised by Andre Rey, is administered in a dynamic way, in keeping with the test-intervention/ mediation-test approach of the LPAD. Clients who do not relate to the larger "whole" shape but rather tend to copy each detail in a somewhat isolated fashion, without understanding their connection to the larger whole or the relationships to each other, can be said to have an episodic grasp of reality. Generally speaking, higher-functioning indivi-duals seem to relate somewhat to the whole shape and appear to under-stand the continuity of the major dissecting lines. Although most people benefit from strategies that help them remember and relate to more detail, their starting point is not severely episodic.

This finding strengthens our assumption that it is not in the elaboration phase of the mental act that those on the spectrum have most difficulty, but rather at the input and output phases. In our experience there was only one youngster whose grasp of reality was quite episodic; David, who began life as severely autistic but thanks to major and even heroic efforts of the parents achieved moderate-to-high levels of intelligence. He stood out among some children who had moved from low to moderate functioning but had been treated at the Feuerstein Institute with the Feuerstein Method. It would seem that receiving the right mediation can help children overcome an episodic grasp of reality.

Rey's Complex Figure Design

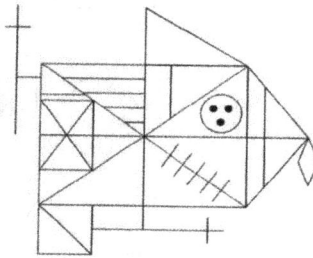

Rey's Complex Figure Design

David, First Copy (Age 9)

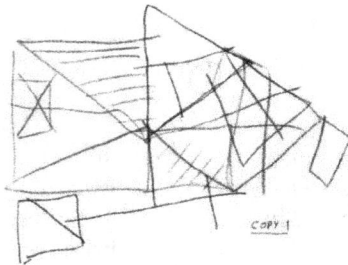

David, First Memory (Age 9)

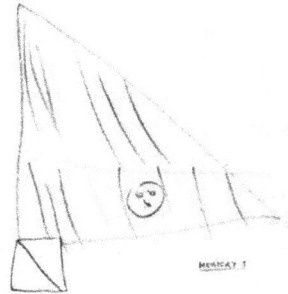

David, First Copy (Age 12)

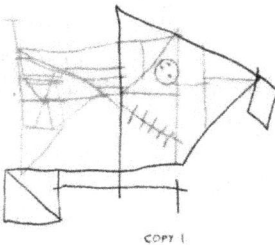

David, First Memory (Age 12)

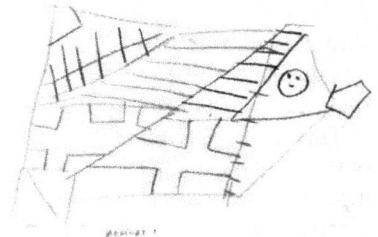

Figure 5.2 Rey's Complex Figure Design.

Naturally, performance in the output phase can be extremely challenging for people with communication issues. This phase involves the adequate communication of elaborated responses.

Egocentric Communicational Modalities refer to the way an individual perceives the other in an interaction, and whether he has the need to spell out in a clear way what he has to relate.

Lack of, or impaired, need for *precision and accuracy* in communicating responses is another deficiency that requires our attention.

The request from an outside source (in this case, the assessor) for clear verbal explanations can be met by frustration or simply annoyance. Here we can analyze the client's responses, or tendency toward egocentric communications, as a function of a lack in either the *need* or the *capacity* for socially accepted responses, for providing logical evidence, and for clear verbal expression (Rand, 1991).

If we observe the client pointing to the information requested, that is, showing us the correct answer, we are observing his understanding of the material as well as his willingness to respond to the request with his limited tools. By contrast, if the request is met with an irritated sigh, we learn that he does not have the *need* or ability to convey this information. When one wishes to express a response but lacks the verbal tools to do so, frustration can result. Providing the necessary tools (i.e., a list of suitable words) can help when the client has developed the *need* to communicate his responses in a socially acceptable fashion.

An analysis of affective-motivational factors reveals an interesting combination of emotions found among the autistic population in their approach to learning tasks. On the one hand, when they are faced with tasks in which they are interested and which offer them a challenge, we see intrinsic motivation. Many ASD individuals display intellectual curiosity and a strong need to master a task. At the same time, they generally show low frustration tolerance. Parents who bring these children to treatment often seem edgy or anxious: they are anticipating that the child's failure will lead to an emotional outburst. In such cases, there appears to be far more frustration with failure than joy in success.

Streamlining the LPAD to Match the Needs and Learning Profiles of ASD Individuals

In the light of these findings, how does the assessor create the optimal testing conditions for clients to reveal their potential?

First and foremost, we can help the client relax, focus, and reduce anxiety (and impulsivity) by creating a warm, undemanding environment. Letting a more agitated client "let off steam" and validating what is on his mind can leave him more open to participation. Clients must feel safe; hence, a child should be accompanied to the assessment by a familiar and supportive figure.

As noted, the ASD client's elaboration processes are generally quite good. Thus, the assessor's role is to help him achieve higher- level tasks by remediating deficient functions at the input phase. For example, one would prepare him for such tasks by encouraging focusing, as well as systematic and non-impulsive information collection. Following such encouragement, he is likely to be able to solve more complex tasks, where he can shine and reveal his potential. It is important to keep the mediation short, uncluttered and focused, so as not to frustrate or inhibit the client, who ultimately prefers to function independently.

We can help the client communicate his answers by providing him with accurate terminology and by modelling well-phrased answers.

We keep mediation to a minimum during the assessment, since we mediate in order to create a sample of change. However, it is important to mention that *after the entire assessment,* during intervention, helping the client improve his capacity to communicate can move beyond modelling. After modelling, we can proceed to help the client improve the level of his speech by introducing thinking/cognition into the process. Since we are now equipped with the knowledge (as a result of the assessment) that our client has mastered analogical thought, we can use this capacity (the understanding of analogies) to bridge to understanding idioms of speech. In other words, we can help the client to go beyond literal speech, to understand nuances and idioms. It is important not to shy away from helping the autistic client's speech become more abstract.

Summary

In sum, many children and adults on the spectrum appear to have a profile of $I - E + O -$, referring to someone who possesses good elaboration-E capabilities but has difficulty with the systematic collection of data (input) I and difficulties in conveying his response effectively (output O). (See R. S. Feuerstein, 2017.) In such cases, input and output processes are not a priority; the main focus is the internal world. Thus, during the assessment, it is of utmost importance to correct input functions, which will allow the client to reveal his elaborational capacity. Peak performances are indications of learning potential and should be highlighted when building an intervention program. It is after the assessment that the hard work of remediating input and output processes to improve learning skills and habits, and to bring changes to the manifest levels of daily functioning, begins.

Precautions During the Assessment Procedure

Despite the related trends observed when analyzing the profiles of the autistic population, it is crucial that we see each new client as an individual and not as part of a diagnosed group. As similar as the findings outlined above are, many differences emerge among people, and *openness and alertness* can lead us to discover new information. It is important to "think out of the box" when faced with someone who comes with a diagnosis. Being extremely sensitive to the particular needs of the individual being assessed can help him blossom within the assessment session and reveal many more *islets of normalcy* (see Chapter 4) than have been previously acknowledged. In the Feuerstein Method, we try to focus as much as possible on the islets of normative functioning within a sea of abnormal behaviors.

This approach is especially important when we are dealing with mild cases of autism. Here, our initial impressions are of prime importance. If, as the client enters the room, he makes eye contact with the assessor and engages willingly—perhaps even deriving pleasure from the interaction— we are already witness to many islets of normalcy. We might even have to question the diagnosis at hand.

Attention must be paid to other variables that may have prompted a mistaken diagnosis such as ADD, depression, OCD, excessive anxiety, or premature diagnosis. Many of these conditions, outlined above, can induce communication issues, which then become secondary symptoms rather than evidence for a primary diagnosis. Importantly, financial concerns and the promise of governmental aid may have caused ASD to be the preferred or even desired condition, and many children may have acquired this label too easily. Additionally, the wealth of readily available information on the internet, which includes diagnostic checklists, has allowed parents to self-diagnose their children, another diagnostic hazard. (Feuerstein et al., 1979).

We end this chapter with a critical point: balance is the key. While appreciating the knowledge that we have acquired in our extensive work with these populations, we stress the need for a fresh outlook and an open mind when assessing an individual who has been labeled "autistic."

Reference

Feuerstein, R., Y. Rand, and M. B. Hoffman. *The Dynamic Assessment of Retarded Performers: The Learning Potential Assessment Device: Theory, Instruments, and Techniques.* Baltimore, MD: University Park Press, 1979.

Chapter 6

Communication Skill-Building with ASD Children

Rina Frei Schreiber

Parents and Caregivers as Part of the Therapy Process

Introduction

Using the Feuerstein Method (FM), we aim to combine the theories of Professor Feuerstein with the traditional toolkit of a speech therapist in order to provide the children we treat with an optimal therapy experience. When assessing a child, the emphasis is placed on a positive search for the communication capacities of the child—that is, identifying any skills that he can use to express himself. A dynamic assessment method is adopted, thus enabling us to take an active interventionist approach while using speech therapy assessment tools. The therapists assess which forms of mediation are most helpful in assisting the children to learn and adopt new communication skills. As such, it is important to understand their learning profile and observe which deficiencies were underlying previous learning difficulties. During the dynamic assessment process, we explore the child's learning potential so that it is clear both to the child and his caregivers that the therapy process can be meaningful for them.

At the Feuerstein Institute, the speech therapists implement the theories of Feuerstein's Mediated Learning Experience (MLE; see Introduction to the Theory) together with other members of our multidisciplinary team (teachers, psychologists, occupational therapists). Together, we seek out "islets of normalcy" (see chapter 2)—the skills that are the child's forte. These islets of normalcy are then harnessed to create a strong base for treatment, to identify learning mechanisms, and to formulate mediation so that it is best fitted for the child to maximize the effectiveness of the intervention, making it part of the mediated learning experience.

To ensure that the speech therapy provided at the Feuerstein Institute is part of the MLE experience, the clinician/mediator, while carrying out any task, must first have a well-defined *intention*. In other words, we begin by asking ourselves the crucial question: What do we want the child to see,

DOI: 10.4324/9781003451136-7

feel, and hear? *Intentionality* involves transforming both the stimuli and the mediator in order to achieve mediational goals. The stimuli should be made more attractive and salient by changing their loudness, duration and frequency—and so changing the state of the child, making him more prepared to attend. The mediator thus animates the intention and changes herself depending on the child's level of engagement. Stimuli are presented and mediators behave in ways that are maximally effective for each individual child. This creates the ideal setting for learning.

Specifically, we seek to present stimuli in a manner that will generate a *reciprocal response* from the child. Interactions based on intentionality and reciprocity can create in children an awareness of the learning process and the principles that underlie it. Activities are also presented in a way that has *meaning and value* for the children we are working with. Thus, the stimuli must be worth attending to in relation to other things around them. All tasks are presented such that their *meaning and value* are clear to the child. After all, there has to be a reason for anyone to pay attention to one thing over another. The clinician communicates to the child the importance and relevance of a task. This is designed to create in the child the desire to *search* for meaning, to *internalize* it and so ensure structural change—all the while working towards independent modes of functioning and strengthening his confidence to attempt the presented activities.

In many cases, one of our primary goals is to work together with parents and other caregivers to help further a child's communication skills. We are aware that a child participates in our program for a limited time, and much of the subsequent progress will depend on the parents, teachers and others who are in the child's environment. Whenever possible, we encourage parents and caregivers to be present in the therapy room so that we can explain what we are doing and why we are doing it, as well as how they can carry out similar activities at home or in the child's educational setting.

MLE is the scaffold for our therapy strategy: it creates an infrastructure for the therapy process and is the medium through which we impart information. The clinician is always clear as to the communicative goal of a presented activity, but also as to how she wants the child to perceive the stimuli she presents. Thus, she transforms an activity such that it is optimally suited to the needs of the child. Of course, this will vary from child to child. For one child, the clinician will need to slow down her speech rate; another will need the therapist to talk more quietly. A slower speech rate gives a child time to observe how the speaker is articulating and forming sounds and words, to understand what the speaker is saying, and to plan a response. Allowing a child to choose activities ahead of time and involving him in the decision as to how long the activity should last or how many pages/repetitions of a book/ task should be carried out grants him a certain degree of autonomy. In doing so, the clinician is mediating for feelings of competence and intentionality by making sure the stimuli are appropriate—thereby ensuring a successful outcome and at the same time demonstrating to the child that we respect their opinions and decisions. The message conveyed is that the child should feel positive about attempting a task that he has chosen, and that he may participate for as long as he chooses to do so.

Case Study: Nathan

> *Seven-year-old Nathan was sensitive to his communication difficulties and found it hard to participate in any activity that challenged him; more often than not, he would simply refuse to participate in an activity. Taking this sensitivity into account, the speech therapist first explained to Nathan how the assessment was structured, increasing incrementally in difficulty and so mediating for challenge so that Nathan would be prepared to search for novelty and complexity within a task. Then, he was shown how to signal as soon as he felt a task was difficult. When he did so, the clinician reminded him of the tools that they had learned that would equip him to carry out the task. Nathan was also given the choice of how many pages of the assessment he wished to complete during a given therapy session; together, he and the therapist would place a marker on the page at which he chose to stop. The therapist thus gave Nathan autonomy over his learning process. He appreciated that his opinions were valued and that he knew what to expect during the assessment. This resulted in an increased willingness to attempt more novel and complex tasks and so embrace the challenges presented.*

Working with ASD children, regardless of where they fall on the spectrum, is always challenging for a speech therapist, since communication is commonly one of the most difficult skills the children struggle with, and often they are well aware of their difficulties in social communication. So, when a speech therapist arrives on the scene, children are quick to discern that we are targeting a skill that is one of their principal challenges. This is an undertaking we have learned to embrace as we employ a "social/ cognitive" approach at the Feuerstein Institute. By combining classic speech therapy tools with the Feuerstein approach, we work together with the child, family and other professionals in endeavoring to expand and develop the child's communication repertoire.

Ensuring the Child has an Understanding of the Assessment/ Therapy Situation

Generally speaking, children who arrive for Feuerstein treatment are not strangers to the testing situation. Many will have been tested multiple times before walking through this particular door. As in other approaches, accurate assessment is pivotal to treatment. Yet, as we have learned throughout this volume, the Feuerstein assessment differs fundamentally from other testing situations. We recall that dynamic assessment forms a critical basis for the initial course of treatment: thus, we observe *how* the child is learning and observe exactly which type of mediation is most effective in assisting him to develop communication skills. In this way, the speech therapist can then adapt the clinical style to best suit the child.

When first meeting a child with ASD in a clinical setting, we bear in mind that children frequently find the unfamiliar clinic environment uncomfortable—making any type of communication assessment during a first speech therapy meeting less than reflective of the child's optimal abilities. In fact, when entering an unfamiliar setting, children with ASD may "switch off", as they are busy trying to tolerate, absorb and learn about the *new situation.*

When preparing to meet a child, the speech therapist should obtain his full medical, physical and developmental history. In addition, the clinicians should also have information regarding the toys, games, books, and activities that the child enjoys so as to help him feel as comfortable as possible during the first meeting. Thus, we can engage the child in an activity that they will like and reduce some of their anxiety towards the assessment situation. It is likely that this will help the child be more ready and willing to communicate. Studies have demonstrated that when children experience anxiety, their communication skills become more restricted (Chang, Quan and Wood, 2012; Wood 2006).

Communication problems are multi-determined. Issues such as a hearing loss, oral or verbal dyspraxia, emotional and social issues, breath control, diet and feeding concerns and specific language or articulation difficulties may be co-occurring. It is critical that children with hearing impairments are identified and properly aided by the relevant professionals. While noting individual symptoms, the clinician will take a neurodevelopmental approach that observes the learning processes, thus analyzing the underlying causes of communication and feeding difficulties.

The clinician models a healthy communication environment. She does so, for example, by consistently explaining the meaning of tasks and by sharing information with the child. Prior to assessment or treatment, the child needs to be told that he is visiting someone who wants to work on his communication skills. This can be frightening because, as we have noted, children can be acutely aware of their communication difficulties. They may have even given up on speech entirely to avoid the immense anxiety they experience or the enormous effort it takes for them to communicate.

Another practice to help a child feel more relaxed is to first approach him and his caregivers in the waiting area and start a conversation there. This gives the child time to become accustomed to the clinician's voice, physical appearance and general manner of communication. We generally invite a parent or caregiver to be present during an assessment so that the child will feel calm having a familiar person around. On occasion, a child is only willing to address his parent or familiar caregiver. When this is the case, the clinician must be careful to be minimally intrusive in the verbal interaction, aiming to slowly join the child and family's circle of communication. While the speech therapist may be a "professional communication expert," parents have unmatched knowledge of their children. The Feuerstein method recognizes this precious knowledge and leverages it in the treatment process. The clinician listens and interprets what the parent is saying so as to maximize the clinical benefit for the child. Which types of mediation are best suited to the child? How do others in the child's environment respond to him? What a parent or caregiver may see as an obstacle to learning, the Feuerstein clinician will interpret as a deficient cognitive function so that they can then work out what learning is necessary to help the child overcome this difficulty.

The Feuerstein dynamic communication assessment is often carried out after a Learning Propensity Assessment Device (LPAD; see Chapters 4 and 5). The LPAD provides the speech therapist with a vast amount of qualitive information as a guide to assess communication skills.

We begin with observation. At this stage, observation is not made in order to report to the parents the level of their child's communication skills. Rather, our initial observational objectives are to understand the processes that the child is marshalling to communicate. In this way, we can pinpoint where he is experiencing difficulty and then figure out ways to help him learn and adopt new skills that will help him to communicate. We seek to identify the child's strengths in multiple modalities (e.g., auditory, visual, motor). Later, these strengths will be used to support the learning of communication skills. Thus, assessors identify islets of normalcy in order to recognize the learning systems that support existing skills. These systems can then be employed for future learning.

Assessment may be a lengthy process, spanning several sessions. This time can be maximized by the clinician, who will observe how the child's communication shifts as his familiarity with the therapy setting increases. In this way, the clinician incorporates the principles of the LPAD into the communication assessment.

This period is also an opportunity to glimpse the child in different moods. Parents feel awkward if their child has a tantrum in the therapy room. The therapist can explain to the parent that such behavior is a valuable aspect of the assessment. No one lives in a static environment, children least of all. By revealing his range of responses, the child discloses essential information that can help the therapist plan a therapy program.

Attention to person and task (Mediating for Intentionality) and Joint attention (interpersonal engagement)

The speech therapist must be exceptionally alert to any communicative attempt of the child. Crying or rejection of a task can demonstrate a child's intention to communicate. Even a gentle tap on the table or a nearly inaudible noise could be an attempt at communication. The slightest movement or sound may have called for tremendous effort from the child to behave in a reciprocal manner, and so it is critical that we are alert to these attempts and respond to them accordingly. Often tiny spikes of success can demonstrate a person's potential and arouse latent infrastructures.

Some children arrive for assessment with no language whatsoever. They need to develop prelinguistic behaviors that serve as the basis for language acquisition. These basic skills include attention to the communication attempts of others, joint attention, using other forms of communication besides language (gestures, facial expressions, augmentative communication devices), and symbolic play skills that are closely related to language development. Moreover, the clinician will check regularly that communication is used in an appropriate manner in the different environments of the child.

Case Study: Adam

> *Seven-year-old Adam was a quiet ASD boy with moderate learning difficulties. He found it extremely difficult to initiate speech and would often ignore adults or children who attempted to play with him. It appeared that Adam was not interested in interacting with others. It was clear from the LPAD report that he had a hard time working through the visual modality. Up until now, much of his speech therapy experiences involved pictures and pretend play activities. During initial therapy sessions, the Feuerstein clinician used auditory play activities, slowly drawing Adam in. For example, the speech therapist would play an instrument and encourage Adam to imitate her by playing the same instrument (e.g., tambourine, drum, triangle or castanets). This ensured that he understood the concept of imitation. Building up slowly, the clinician played a sequence of two or three instruments and allowed Adam to copy this musical sequence. Next, she used an echo-mic and enunciated a single phoneme, handing the mic to Adam as a cue so that he knew it was his turn to make the sound. Over the following months, Adam became more confident in his ability to make sounds and was willing to imitate short words. His parents and teachers were also instructed to act as good speech models, talking slowly and clearly and allowing him time to imitate words and phrases but never demanding that he do so (never tell a child to say or repeat something, as they may consider it futile: if you just said it, why should they bother repeating it! And often, if the child was able to say it, he would have!). At the age of eight, Adam's parents reported that he had begun using*

a few of the words that he had practiced in therapy sessions in a relevant context, at home. As Adam found the auditory modality easier to work through, therapy centered around auditory activities. Recent research has reported that high-functioning ASD adults can recognize emotional cues through an auditory modality (Lin, Tobe, and Kuriki, 2016).

Speech therapists tend to talk a lot. This can overwhelm some children, who may respond by speaking even less than they normally do. After all, why would they talk if the clinician is jabbering away! Paradoxically, silence is a powerful cue for speech and can provoke joint attention. If one makes a statement and then remains silent for a moment, it is a clear message to the listener that it is his turn to talk. Up to a point, the longer one remains silent the more powerful the cue becomes. As most people find silence quite uncomfortable, these gaps are quickly filled. Yet, precisely such pauses might cue a child to start talking. The child may also use the silent time to process what has been said and plan his own utterance.

In the Feuerstein Method, the clinician is responsible for *finding an entry* to the child. If he does not respond to the initial overtures of the therapist, rather than concluding that the child is "not responding," the mediator asks, "How can I change myself in order to elicit a response?" Some children prefer a quiet environment and a soft-spoken therapist. Other children may respond only after the clinician has provided a great deal of animated input. Hence, the clinician may need to alter the volume, tone and intonation of her voice in order to engage a child, using suitable gestures when necessary, and so generate intentionality within the clinical relationship. Positioning also matters when helping the child to gain eye contact. In this vein, consultations with occupational therapists are helpful. They can advise on how to seat children so that they are most comfortable and where clinicians should position themselves so that the child can best focus on them.

With respect to verbal communication, the length, complexity, and tone of an utterance when addressing a child are all crucial and adjustable factors in treatment. The same information can be conveyed in one complex sentence, in several phrases that are part of a single sentence or by using several short sentences. It is our job as mediators to adapt ourselves and the stimuli we are using so that it is a best-fit for each individual. This assists the child to engage so that we can achieve joint attention and an intentional and reciprocal relationship during therapy.

As noted, children can be wary of a test environment—and rightfully so! They may opt to ignore what is going on around them and even withdraw into themselves or cling to their parent. There are many ways to manage this impasse. One involves the presentation of a game without seeking the child's active participation. The speech therapist makes it clear to the child that she (the clinician) is going to engage in an activity. The parent may be invited to join in, but the child should receive no pressure whatsoever to do so. A child who has had a chance to observe an activity and has seen someone he trusts playing with the clinician may be more willing to attend to the activity and then participate himself. It ought to be noted that many repetitions may be required before this outcome is achieved.

At times, a clinician may be so focused on her therapy goals that she forgets to ensure that the child is enjoying the process of reaching these goals. Speech therapy does not have to be a taxing or tedious experience. In fact, the clinician must be on the look- out for any behaviors that indicate that the child (or clinician) is not enjoying the therapy process. If such behaviors are noted, it is time to take a step back. Reassess your short-term goals, analyze what you have learned about the child and redesign the therapy sessions to include activities that the child is more likely to enjoy. As children develop cognitively and learn to express themselves even at a very basic level, we have observed that they often become less anxious and more able to appreciate and enjoy the activities that are part of their daily life.

Case Study: Barry

> *Barry, a five-year-old boy, was frustrated when his clinician did not understand his attempts to communicate. Moreover, he had difficulty remaining focused on the play activities presented and would often choose not to participate in them. The speech therapist was aware that she needed to fundamentally change how the sessions were structured so that Barry could choose the activities that he wanted, and that the tasks were designed in such a way that they involved many small stages. In this manner, he could participate and remain focused on a single activity but move to a different stage of the activity when he wanted to do so (e.g., constructing a play village). Sometimes, Barry would move to a different stage and then return to something he was doing earlier in the same game. Barry was also given more specific verbal choices so that the clinician found it easier to understand him. In this way, Barry was happier to participate in the games that he had chosen and was able to attend to each task together with the speech therapist for a limited time. Moreover, this restructuring enabled us to work on his speech clarity without him becoming overly frustrated.*

The Feuerstein Method is investigative and flexible. What medium does the child prefer? Activities that take a longer or shorter time? Does the child learn better as a very active participant, or does he need to "act less" in order to focus on processing the information presented? Identify how the child prefers to learn and use it as a basis for treatment. After all, the materials do not make the treatment—the therapist and the child together use the materials to reach the planned goals. Stimuli are then mediated to the child in an intentional manner so as to modify the quality and structure of the interaction. Consult the child; how many more times does he wish to repeat the activity; or move on to something more challenging? Often as the treatment process progresses the child is more willing to participate in more challenging tasks. He has learned to trust the speech therapist, knowing that she will provide him with the tools that are necessary to perform the task, and his communication and cognitive repertoire has expanded so that he is often prepared to attempt tasks that he may have rejected earlier on.

The Concept of Language as a Means to Communicate

For some ASD children, speaking may be fraught with anxiety. The clinician should anticipate and appreciate such anxiety. As mentioned, a critical step in Feuerstein treatment is to clarify with the child what is expected of him, mediating for goal setting, planning and achieving. Specifically, he must understand the concept of language. Spoken language requires that a child knows that he needs to string together specific sounds to create a word, and that this word is meaningful to his listener. This understanding allows a child to develop a well-defined goal when he attempts to verbalize. Such strategizing is very different from using the random sounds that make up the jargon he may have relied on until this point.

Case Study: Nicky

> *Nicky was a happy and playful four-year-old who did not seek social interaction with her peers and used jargon-like utterances. When she had a particular need for something, she would either snatch the item or raise her voice, becoming frustrated when others did not understand her. During the first step of therapy, our goal was to enable Nicky to become aware that her jargon was not an effective form of communication—all the while ensuring that she did not feel criticized as this would reduce her motivation to learn to talk accurately and clearly. Nicky needed to think reflectively and understand that her jargon was not comprehensible to others, and that she needed to learn specific language skills if she wanted others to understand her. This relates to Feuerstein theory which explains how it is critical to both love and understand your child and at the same time believe in his potential to change and so help him modify his skill-set (Feuerstein, Feuerstein, and Falik, 2006).*
>
> *Initially, the speech therapist repeated Nicky's jargon phrase so that she could hear and reflect on it. At the same time, the clinician presented a puzzled expression to her, conveying that she had not really understood her communicative attempt. The clinician was always on the look-out for opportunities to clearly and slowly offer a short phrase that Nicky could use instead of her jargon phrase. The clinician demonstrated how these phrases were easy to understand, making it possible for her listener to act on her requests. After a few months, Nicky began*

to use less jargon, but it took nearly a year until she was articulating short phrases that were comprehensible to others. During this time, her parents and nursery caregivers were guided as how to offer her clear models to form phrases. It was also critical to reduce the anxiety of Nicky's parents when she began to talk less whilst she was shifting her communication mode from jargon to comprehensible speech. This is a common and natural occurrence: as Nicky began to grasp that her jargon was ineffective, she reduced this type of communication. Consequently, she spoke less while she was developing the language skills to form words and combine them to form comprehensible phrases.

In order for children to follow instructions, they need to understand the words we are using and to be aware that these words are a means for them to receive information. Thus, the clinician should be aware of the child's receptive language level and tailor her speech to this level. A careful assessment of receptive language skills is critical. We often assume that a child understands much more language than they actually do; the child is gathering a great deal from non-verbal forms of communication (paralinguistics; facial expressions, gestures, intonation, volume, pitch), as well as from context. A receptive language assessment can filter out these other forms of communication and so assist the clinician in gaining an accurate picture of the child's receptive language level. It is important to note that teachers and parents use multiple question words throughout the day, and a child may not yet have learned to distinguish between the terms "what," "when," "how," "where" and "why". One may think the child did not understand what has been said when, in fact, he has not understood the specific question word that was used.

In order to regulate his own behavior, a child needs basic tools of expression (e.g., being able to indicate "stop," "no," "more," etc.). Clinicians and caregivers must be sensitive to the cues of non-verbal children that indicate that the child is about to lose patience or *act out.* Once these cues have been identified, the child can be helped to express himself in a calmer, more effective, and consistent manner. Every child has a different set of cues. At such times, one little boy would move his hands about behind his head; a young girl, for her part, would make a quiet, sniffing-like sound. Such signs could easily have been overlooked as indicators of a child's volatility. Instead, they served as helpful hints of the child's threshold of tolerance. Full-blown outbursts can be the outcome of dismissing such signs. After such an outburst, part of mediating for regulation of behavior may involve waiting a few minutes and then gently trying to help the child return to the activities planned for the session. The child often needs longer than several minutes to regain his composure. Once the clinician has identified these subtle signs (which may not have been identified by the child's parents) or caregivers, she can assist the child to become aware of them himself and then support him to both take time to regulate himself and to communicate his discomfort in a way that others can understand. The clinician may reflect the child's behavior to him so he can experience how his behaviors are ineffective, then modelling possible options that that he can adopt. This should not be done at the time when the child is stressed, but rather at another time when the childis more open to mediation and in a calm manner so that the child can observe and choose which technique of communication is most effective for him. Initially this may ivolve just teaching the child to say or signal "no".

Despite its questionable reputation, "no" is not a bad word for a child to say. In fact, it is a critically important part of our vocabulary, and it is essential to teach children different ways to say "no." The ability to reject objects and actions can help to prevent aversive behaviors such as screaming, crying, throwing, hitting, and so on.

When developing a basic, cross-environment core vocabulary from which children can learn to articulate and use specific key words, we ask parents and nursery or school staff which words will be most motivating and useful for the child to learn. Following this, the clinician will start to work on increasing a child's MLU (mean length of utterance) without compromising on speech clarity. At the same time, she will work on grammar, syntax and language concepts. A speech therapist working with ASD children will also prioritize the development of pragmatic skills. These young clients may never become extroverts, but they can develop the social language skills we use in our daily communications. These include what we say, how we say it, awareness of body language and knowledge of context-appropriateness (as discussed later in this chapter). It should be noted that many people see their autism as part of their identity and it is critical that a speech therapist clarifies that she is not trying to "normalize" them, but rather aid their communication skills so that they can be effective communicators, whilst at the same time respecting their neurodiverse differences.

The Need to Communicate

A basic responsibility of the speech therapist is to ensure that the child understands the concept of communicative intent. Is he aware that speech is a medium to communicate his thoughts, requests, and ideas to a listener, and, by doing so, have an effect on the other? Signifying communicative intent is often challenging for children with ASD. This was the basis of the early therapy sessions with Nicky (introduced above). As mentioned, when she used jargon, the speech therapist would present a puzzled facial expression and check that she had observed and understood the meaning of this expression. Repeating a jargon utterance to her also enabled Nicky to appreciate that this utterance was not comprehensible to others. This helped her to begin to develop an appreciation for the need of a language system that can be understood by all those who are involved in the communication process. Modeling appropriate phrases using real words— *"Oh, you want more Lego blocks— more Lego please..."*

also demonstrated the idea of communicative intent by allowing Nicky to observe how using words that were understood by her listener could enable her to get what she wanted.

Case Study: Yasmine

Four-and-a-half-year-old Yasmine had not developed any way to communicate her preference when presented with a choice of two objects or activities. After carefully analyzing a chosen task, the clinician presented each activity on its own and played with each toy separately. Then, while playing with each one, she presented a picture of the play object, so that Yasmine could learn that the pictorial image represented the toy with which they were currently playing. Following this, every time Yasmine played with the toy, she was offered the pictorial image to pull off from a small Velcro board. Once the clinician was confident that Yasmine understood that the picture was a representation of the play object/activity, she began to work with Yasmine on scanning between two objects. Initially, the therapist helped her to scan between the objects by taking her hand and gently moving it between the objects and touching each one. (She had fair eye hand coordination before therapy began.) When the therapist was sure that Yasmine was aware of both play objects and was able to scan between the pictures with the knowledge that they represented the play activity, she mediated for planning behaviors and began to help Yasmine learn that, by scanning and choosing one of the pictures, she could determine what the next play activity would be. The speech therapist demonstrated repeatedly the scanning- choosing-playing sequence to mediate for systematic data gathering and to reduce impulsivity and regulate behaviors at the input phase. Initially, the clinician held Yasmine's hands gently on the table to ensure that she was first scanning and choosing rather than impulsively reaching for one of the pictures. The speech therapist mediated for transcendence so that Yasmine learned that making choices was a skill she could use both with concrete objects (the toys) and with pictures that represented the toys. The complexity of this task can be reduced by replacing one of the pictures with a blank card or something that the clinician knows is of little interest to the child. Adding more pictures broadens the child's choice and so increases the task's complexity, requiring more attention from the child. The clinician mediates to them to attend to more than one piece of information so as to allow more complex comparisons. Once Yasmine realized she could determine the activities that take place in the session, she became more attentive and alert. Yasmine's feeling of ability increased her intrinsic motivation; she had gained some autonomy and could use her newly learned communication skill to shape the therapy environment.

The Means to Communicate

According to Feuerstein, Cohen and Mintzker (1993), the mediation of words is central to the child: it is in this way that he can make sense of his world. Vygotsky wrote *"Real concepts are impossible without words, and thinking in concepts does not exist beyond verbal thinking"* Vygotsky (1962). It is frequently noted that an extended vocabulary is positively related to basic abilities such as intelligence, reading, comprehension and school success. Words can enable our cognitive processes and assist us to understand our environment. Vygotsky understood that children could learn new skills by communicating and then learning from others. He considered words and concepts to be a basis for thought. Children learn that a word can represent a concept and then the word can be used in their thought processes to operate that concept.

A child can learn that every person, object and action, has its own label. Learning labels for objects frees the child from dependence on concrete forms and allows him to refer to objects that are not in his immediate experience. It permits children to go beyond their sensory, concrete world so that they can develop a system of conceptual relationships, (How is my cup of milk related to the pool I swim in? They seem to be unrelated, but the concept of *receptacle* enables a connection.) Language as an abstract representational system is a characteristic of higher- order thinking that allows connections to be made between objects, actions or concepts that may otherwise appear unrelated. This stage of representational thought leads to the processing of language and is the "cognitive" aspect of the Feuerstein social/ cognitive approach. As we describe further this approach through the modality of speech and language, we will note other strategies that involve thinking, understanding, and communicational expression which bring the cognitive element into therapy. Having the ability to hear what has been said is critical at the input phase, and so it is worth repeating that a Speech and Language therapist must identify any child that may have a hearing impairment so that he can be appropriately aided by the relevant professionals.

Communication involves the child learning basic planning and processing behaviors, most often through the linguistic modality. This requires taking time to choose and retrieve the word/s that one wishes to use to express oneself. Planning verbal output can be similar to other planning behaviors. Frequently, the children we work with are impulsive. As such, it can be difficult for them to take the time to find the specific words they need and then to combine them in an appropriate manner to form a phrase or sentence. Some children may initially need a clear visual cue to remind them not to answer immediately so that they have a silent period in which to process their thoughts in order to plan their verbal output. Other children may need to be verbally guided, step by step, until they can learn to guide themselves in how to construct their desired utterance. In order to develop language processing skills, the speech therapist can introduce games that involve various sequential stages, such as construction, art or cooking projects. The child learns how the sequence of the task is critical to a successful outcome, as the therapist talks through each stage of the activity. These sequential activities aim to help a child realize how the complex skill of forming an utterance can take time, and there may be several stages that will need to be processed in order for them to be able to express themselves effectively. It is necessary to work together with the child to teach him how to process an utterance or/and how to form a response. The child may find it necessary to repeat a request in order to internalize it and then break it down so that he can ensure that he has understood all the words together with their grammatical and syntactic markers (e.g., what tense, number and gender markers are attached to the verb in the utterance they have just heard?).

Furthermore, there are many pragmatic language indicators that a child needs to understand. These may pose a particular challenge for the ASD child, since they may be both verbal and non-verbal and are frequently used to infer an implicit message, as well as to indicate situational clues that would then influence the response of a listener. For instance, the speaker is in a hurry, and this can be identified by observing that he is beginning to look away and leaning forward slightly in order to start leaving and talking a little fast; thus, a concise response is necessary in this case. (Further discussion on pragmatic skills is found later in this chapter.)

The output phase of articulating a word may be challenging if a child experiences oral motor coordination, phonological, muscle tone, voice, stammering or other neurological or biological issues. These can cause various difficulties in sequential phoneme production for speech. So, even when a child has managed to retrieve a relevant word, articulating it may prove difficult. Before we can expect a child to talk, we need to ascertain that he is equipped with all the necessary tools to carry out the task.

Another vital part of developing effective speech output most relevant to the needs of ASD children is helping them appreciate the needs of others and so reducing egocentric thinking. Thus, they will learn that in order for their speech attempt to be successful, it must be understood not only by themselves but also by others, both at a phoneme level and a word/phrase level.

Case Study: Helen

> *Nine-year-old Helen was a shy ASD child with a severe verbal dyspraxia. She was learning in a special needs class of eight children, many of whom had physical difficulties and were non- verbal. Most of the communication in Helen's class was carried out using augmentative communication devices. Helen lived with her parents and siblings who tried to understand Helen as best they could whilst she used gestures and facial expressions to express herself. Since she rarely used her augmentative communication*

device at home, her expressive communication was very limited. She had given up on becoming a verbal communicator and was very reluctant to carry out any exercises that required making sounds. The speech therapist noted that although Helen's present situation made minimal demands for her to be a verbal communicator, she still conveyed a desire to communicate, and the speech therapist harnessed this in order to allow Helen to realize her learning potential. The first year of therapy involved helping Helen to gain basic oral motor control using common oral motor exercises and pictures to represent sounds while mediating for feelings of confidence and ability —a slow but extremely productive process. This was a critical stage in the therapy process, since for many years Helen had felt that she was not able to speak and up to now was highly resistant to any attempts from various clinicians to help her talk. Now, she was beginning to recognize her own potential to change. Once she began to understand that she had some control of her oral musculature, Helen was more willing to attempt to make sounds. Next, we started to help Helen articulate some basic sounds in an intentional manner. Helen was given a lot of autonomy at this point, and she herself would choose which sounds to work on and which games to use in order to help her learn to articulate these sounds. At the same time, Helen was learning to read with another teacher at the Feuerstein Institute. Thus, the speech therapist was able to replace pictures with letters as visual cues to sound out particular sounds so that Helen could begin to understand how speech was made up of specific sounds represented by letters. This gave both the speech and reading lessons more meaning. Over the course of several years, the speech therapist worked together with Helen's reading teacher so that she could use the letters as visual crutches for speech. Moreover, the reading teacher was aware of which sounds Helen had learnt to articulate. Once Helen had acquired oral motor coordination, she realized that verbal communication was an accessible and efficient means through which she could communicate.

Repetition and Imitation as a Tool to Assist Speech

Repetition and imitation do not seem like sophisticated techniques to develop communication. Yet, at the right time and with the right tone, they can be critical tools in facilitating a child's speech development. Repeating a child's verbalizations can boost his confidence as repetition demonstrates that you have heard and accepted his communication attempt. If appropriate, sounds can be interpreted; for instance, if the child says "beb", the clinician may choose to respond "beb", Oh, you want to touch the baby." Children often express great relief when the clinician imitates their verbalizations. It is not unusual for repetition to spark the first *circle of communication* the ASD child has ever experienced. Child and therapist take turns verbalizing. Up to then, the child may have experienced people correcting him or telling him what to say or how to say it. By repeating the child's utterance, we give him some *control of the conversation*. The child can then begin to enjoy this verbal play and start to learn to control his sound output. Thus, the tool of repetition is a critical one. After initially repeating the child's utterance, we then also add or modify the child's output so that he can learn from the mediator. This is done slowly and with careful observation of the child's response to our slight changes to their utterance. Many children will spontaneously repeat from a model without being specifically told to do so; thus, the choice is theirs. In other words, the child has the autonomy to decide whether he feels able to repeat the modified form of his utterance. By imitating the model he has heard, the child is reinforcing that language structure within his language lexicon. This will make it easier to retrieve the structure in the future (Forestier & Oudeyer, 2017).

Skills for Using Language in Different Situations and Settings

For children with ASD, learning to talk involves a profound emotional aspect: the child needs to have confidence in his own ability to communicate. So many questions may go through the child's mind: "Do I want to communicate? Is it in my own interest? I want to, but I'm not sure how, or I lack confidence in my ability to communicate." The speech therapist conveys to the child (and parents) the idea that communication is both desirable and possible. ASD children may have a long history of failure in their attempts to talk, perhaps finally deciding to be more of an observer than an active participant in their environment. Thus, this calls for mediating for feelings of competence and the ability to achieve a specific goal. Another tool that an ASD child may adopt in order to avoid discourse is to employ scripted or stereotyped phrases potentially applicable in many different situations. The clinician can work with the child to help him to understand that these phrases may not always be relevant and that he has the ability to construct other more varied phrases (however simple they may be) in order to express himself in a more precise and relevant manner. Once again the clinician should ensure that their client is aware that we are not disrespecting their personal choices, but rather assisting them to communicate so that they can be an active participant in all their environments.

It is advised to start working on tiny steps towards a larger communication goal. If one can break up a task into phases and equip a child with the tools that he will require to complete each phase, then he can experience success in completing each part of the task. This success, in turn, will bolster his confidence in his ability to communicate.

It can be challenging for a clinician to help a child learn how to use language in a social setting within the confines of the clinical therapy setting. This is why a therapy group is often indicated when working on pragmatic language skills. If a therapy group is not available, then the child may have a joint session with a sibling or school/nursery friend. Skills such as learning to omit irrelevant details, refraining from inappropriate topic changes, and not perseverating on a particular theme are common goals with ASD children (Paul et al., 2009). These goals will often be met with an appropriate natural response from peers in the group. The group mediator may need to mediate these responses to an ASD child so that he can learn to identify them and understand why his utterances may have been unsuitable. The child will also need to learn to be an active listener within the group setting even if he is not being directly addressed. He can learn to respond to a group member's comments either verbally or using non-verbal cues, and he can request clarifications as well as learn to read cues from group members about when he must clarify his own comments. With younger children, learning to listen to their peers can be challenging. Hence, we practice this in a group setting by questioning each child about another group member's answer. Once children are aware that they will be questioned about another child's response, they become more cognizant of the need to listen to each other. For example, we might ask each child about his favorite foods, after which the children will be asked to plan a gift basket for each group member while taking into account his likes and dislikes. This sort of activity covers multiple areas: listening skills, reducing egocentric behaviors, turn-taking and building an awareness of the preferences of others and how they may differ from one's own preferences.

Becoming an Autonomous Communicator

After a child has learned to communicate, we ensure that he can actually use his speech. In other words, we ensure that he is able to initiate communication independently and sustain the interaction for as long as may be required in the circumstances. This does not necessarily mean a completely fluent interaction, but rather that the child can start and sustain a communicative interaction with someone outside of the therapy room. We note if the child has learned to recognize his need to communicate and can do so in such a way that his listener can understand his message. For some children, this may be a basic interaction such as indicating they want more of something either verbally or using a gesture or an AAC ((Augmentative and Alternative Communication) tool. It is important to remember that, up to now, the child may have had little confidence in his ability to express himself that he may have waited to do so until he was extremely frustrated—thus leading to other negative consequences.

A child's level of anxiety and other sensory stimuli in the environment must be taken into account when we develop activities designed to assist them to be an independent communicator. Initially we may set up specific and simple communicative tasks within the clinic so that the child can practice initiating an interaction (e.g., asking the secretary for paper for the printer). Parents can be advised how to create similar communication tasks.

Case Study: Elizabeth

Elizabeth had been in therapy for more than two years when we started to work on tasks that involved her initiating communication with people outside of her immediate family and her educational staff. After having practiced some tasks within the therapy center, we went to a nearby playground where we had arranged to meet another mother and child. Elizabeth had been prepared for this situation, and we had decided on a few verbal interactions that she could initiate with the other child (suggesting sharing a snack and/or playing with a ball together.) After several trips to the park, we decided to attempt a more challenging communicative task at a small local supermarket. Elizabeth was prepared for the trip, and we had a list of two items to buy. On the first two occasions at the supermarket, Elizabeth was not able to talk to anyone and could not find the items we had planned to buy. In fact, during the first visit Elizabeth sat down on the floor in the middle of an aisle and refused to budge! The clinician then understood that many other sensory stimuli were bothering Elizabeth in that situation, and we spent several sessions working with Elizabeth on remaining calm and focused when making a verbal request in a loud and busy environment. On our third attempt, Elizabeth managed to make a one-word request ("juice") to a supermarket employee. In our continued work with Elizabeth and her parents, she became more confident of her ability to express herself in such situations.

When working with ASD children on sustaining a conversation, we are acutely aware of the difficulties that they experience when talking to others. For example, they may be distracted by others' appearance or other background sounds in the environment. If so, the children need to learn to assist themselves in a relevant manner, which may involve asking the person they are with to move somewhere quieter, use fewer gestures while speaking, and so on. Other language issues which could be stumbling blocks include understanding the use of figurative language, including metaphors, idioms and irony, which can also be difficult for more fluent communicators. Some phrases may be so common that speakers may not notice that they are speaking in a nonliteral manner. Understanding the main message can be challenging and the ASD child may become confused by details, losing track of the main idea of what is being said to him. Alternatively, the child may pick up on some key words but miss the grammatical structures of the conversation.

Case Study: James

James, a friendly six-year-old child, was progressing well in many areas. It came as something of a surprise, that he would often do precisely the opposite of what we would request. When we discussed this with his parents, his father pointed out that when he was told "don't tear the paper" he would hear the key words "tear" and "paper." We worked with James on how words are embedded in a context and how this context of other words was crucial for understanding the meaning of a message.

It is also critical to consider that ASD children may deal with information in a piecemeal fashion and can experience difficulty in dealing with multiple pieces of information or connecting ideas. Specific therapy would involve mediating to the child how to consider and process two or more pieces of information. The child may make associations that may not be relevant to his listener and then lose the thread of the discussion. Additionally, a child's ability to sustain dialogue might be influenced by a reluctance to participate in a conversation (he may, thus, not give his listener time to respond). He may even non-verbally "engineer" ending an interaction by becoming offensive. Finally, the child must learn how the context of a conversation (time, place) can influence its duration and content (e.g., the difference between giving someone concise directions to a classroom when they are late for a lesson and discussing with friends in recess a favorite holiday destination).

Working with Families and Caregivers

Working *together* with the child and his caregivers is a necessary pre-requisite for successful therapy outcomes. Ensuring that there is reciprocity during therapy is an intrinsic part of the therapy process. The clinician must learn what the child needs in order to activate himself. There is no "quick fix" in speech therapy, and so in order for the therapy process to be effective and for long-term changes to occur, we endeavor to work together with the child, his educators, and his family. One cannot *"therapy the child"* and resolve his difficulties, but rather we attempt to develop a strategy that promotes reciprocity in order to create lasting changes. Our treatment of the child hinges on working with families and other caregivers. If a child has not been an active communicator, those around him may have developed habits of attempting to decipher what he wants without the child having to resort to clear communication. Parents may offer various objects, point to items or pictures, and use gestures, after which they will observe the child's response. These efforts can be a real relief to a child and serve to reduce his frustration; they can "work" within the family system. Thus, if the child's listener talks *for* him, offering suggestions of what he may want, or confines communication to his idiosyncratic language, the child will have no need to invest the enormous effort necessary to learn to communicate in ways that can be understood outside the home. In therapy sessions, the clinician demonstrates to parents and caregivers how to create a need system to motivate conventional, non-egocentric speech. For example, if the lid of the container of bubbles has been sealed tightly, the child will need to request assistance in opening it; if a key piece of a game or puzzle is missing, the child will need to utter a request for assistance: these requests become a therapeutic objective.

The parents/caregivers of a child with ASD have a tough job. Even though many embrace the challenge, they still encounter multiple complications and hurdles on the practical, educational and emotional levels. In an effort to help their child act and look as "normal" as possible, they may focus on critical activities for daily living (ADL) involving personal hygiene, bathing and grooming skills and so may not be available to address issues of cognitive development. While valuing the vital importance of ADL skills, a Feuerstein clinician will also recognize a child's learning propensity. She will assist the child to develop higher level cognitive skills that will enable him to better integrate into his environment and carry out ADL's in the long term.

Parents may experience an emotional block at various times during their child's development or feel tremendously overwhelmed, to the point of being temporarily unable to work on therapy goals with their child. Taking a break is an accepted and important option for parents. One father felt so distressed and needed such a break so he did not feel able to do homework with his child. He asked permission to video parts of the speech therapy session and allow his son to watch it every day. The speech therapist was careful to plan the part of the session that was being recorded in such a way that it would benefit the child while he was watching it at home. This plan turned out to be very successful: the child was able to practice the skills he had learned in therapy and would return the following week having done homework every day!

Part of the speech therapist's job is to empower parents and caregivers to assist the child in a way that is manageable for them.

Case Study: Mario

> *Mario was an energetic five-year-old ASD child who had not yet acquired speech and was having a difficult time relating to the other children in his nursery. On the recommendation of the nursery staff, he only attended the nursery three times a week. Mario's mother was attentive to her son, facilitating his development in whatever way she could. She was a good mediator and spent several hours a day working with her son. When Mario became frustrated, he would throw objects or hit his mother—who was afraid of these angry outbursts. At such times, she tended to give him whatever he wanted. Mario had learnt that he could use aversive behaviors in order to manipulate his mother. We worked together with Mario's mother to empower her so that she could continue to assist him without being afraid of him. Initially, it was critical for her to recognize and anticipate when Mario was upset or frustrated in order to reduce his initial anxiety. Many non-verbal children need adults to clearly demonstrate that*

they have understood the children's objection as quickly as possible, but for Mario this was not enough. His mother learned to introduce tasks slowly and clearly so that Mario would know ahead of time what was expected of him and so have time to prepare himself. When applicable she would ensure that he had understood the task by allowing him to imitate her while she carried out the task herself. In this way, he became familiar with the activity. Next, he could focus on the skills necessary to carry out the task without experiencing the anxiety that he would generally feel when faced with something novel. She would increase the length and complexity of a task very slowly, but not get stuck repeating an activity because that is what Mario likes and "it keeps him calm." Like many ASD children, Mario did not like surprises. Thus, his daily timetable was always carefully explained to him and visually presented. Mario's mother learned that she did not have to agree to all her son's demands. We mediated to her for feelings of ability so that she felt capable of following through on the assignments discussed in therapy; e.g. instead of moving seats on the bus at every stop, as Mario requested, she would allow him to choose the seats when they got on the bus and then explain to him at each stop that it was tiring and inconvenient for her to keep moving—but that she still loved him very much and the next day he could choose new seats. The first few days of practicing this new exercise were indeed challenging for Mario and his mother, but after five days he was able to remain in the same seat. This achievement was empowering for Mario's mother, who began to approach other situations in a similar way.

It is helpful to introduce an idea, concept or new activity in collaboration with other teachers and clinicians. In this way, the learning becomes less context-sensitive. This relates to the *Mediation of Transcendence*—the aspect of an experience that goes beyond an immediate goal or skill but can be projected to another time or place (see Introduction to the Theory). This quality of "going beyond" is an important part of MLE. For example, if a child has learned lip-rounding in a therapy session, the clinician might assign him a goal of applying the skill at home by drinking from a straw or apply it when learning to say an [oo] sound as part of a word or word approximation. Taking a different example, if a child is learning to use words to represent positions in space (on, under, next to, behind etc.), the more frequently one can demonstrate for the child how the words can be used in many different contexts the easier it will be for him to grasp how to use these word. In this way, we can ensure that transcendence of the new skill or concept learned will occur. It is for this reason that constant collaboration with others who interact with the child is an essential part of the therapy process.

In this vein, we turn to sibling collaboration. We have had many therapy sessions together with siblings so that they can better understand their brother or sister and learn how to respond to him or her in different situations. Feuerstein and colleagues (1991) discuss the process of individuation and how it is meaningfully enriched by a feeling of belonging and acceptance. This sense of belonging can be generated by joint sibling therapy sessions that often lead to an experience of synthesis between the ASD child and other family members. Bass and Mulick (2007) examined peer- mediated approaches to assist social play skill enhancement of children with autism. They found strong empirical evidence that siblings can help improve the social play skills of ASD children by helping them to initiate social interactions and respond to such initiation from peers.

Often parents, motivated by politeness, will agree with the speech therapist and her recommendations but will not be able to implement them and feel uncomfortable questioning the recommendations. It is the clinician's responsibility to understand the parents and set realistic homework assignments. We will often work together with parents when designing home activities so that the tasks can be accomplished easily within the home environment. We also encourage parents to inform us if a task needs to be adapted such that they feel confident to present it to their child. Feuerstein and Beker (1989) introduced the idea of "Shaping Modifying Environments," which proposes that fundamental change can be stimulated by planned active intervention that systematically makes demands on those within it for cognitive, emotional, and social modification in the context of their existing levels of development, skill, etc. It does not "accept the student where he (or she) is," but it does "start where the student is," building on existing competencies while providing for needed feelings of security. As competency and performance improve, demands rise accordingly, thus establishing ever higher levels of functioning. Whatever the specific setting, the task is to establish and maintain a modifying environment appropriate to the needs of the particular clientele being served. (Beker & Feuerstein, 1989b)

The goal is that students should not just learn to do specific tasks better, but rather carry them out in ways that will allow them to master similar tasks in the future. The child learns to adapt by developing cognitive and emotional flexibility and the capacity to modify his own thinking and behaviors. The basic components of the modifying environment include (1) the expectation of those in the setting that the child can succeed in achieving the desired growth, and that these components are critical for the child's learning; (2) the use and adaptation of resources, and (3); the flexibility of the mediator.

Let's take an example of flexibility in action. One mother told us in no uncertain terms that, as she was the only adult present in the home with four young children, she was not in a position to do homework with her son Neil. Neil had a significant motor coordination disorder that meant frequent oral motor exercises formed a critical part of the therapy process. Before we began working with him, we contacted his nursery staff and made arrangements for someone on that team to carry out homework activities with him. The speech therapist would send the nursery worker video clips of the therapy session with clear instructions, and this worked extremely well. In other cases, we have created online groups so that all the staff and family members working with a child can be aware of what they are currently learning in therapy.

As we have noted, the Feuerstein Method encourages parents and care-givers to attend therapy sessions so that they can learn to become effective mediators at home or in the child's educational setting. This home-med-iation promotes repetition and practice so as to promote the *transcendence* of new skills. Research by Pickles et al. (2016) and Green et al. (2017) found positive, long-term effects of early parent-mediated interventions for autism. In fact, the PACT (Pre-school Autism Communication Therapy) program and the parent-mediated social communication intervention described in these studies aim at refining parent skills so that they can mediate to their children after being guided by professional clinicians. This research resonates well with the decades-long Feuerstein Method of using the family setting as a natural environment for mediation.

Feuerstein in Action: Yana's Story

The Beginning

Yana came to the Feuerstein Institute for an assessment at age three and a half. She was an enthralling child who was quite wary of her new environment. Yana communicated using jargon with a rich intonation together with a basic com-municative intent, pointing to the objects she wanted. She moved quickly between activities, made sounds to express her needs, and made fleeting eye contact. She understood basic requests within context, such as "get in the bath" or "take off your coat." Yana had low muscle tone, an immature chew, and used her fingers to manipulate the food in her mouth. She could not straw drink or blow out candles, and, following her initial assessment, it was clear that she had an oral motor coordination difficulty—dyspraxia. Verbal dyspraxia denotes a difficulty in forming and coordinating the precise articulatory movements required for the production of speech. Oral dyspraxia refers to difficulties in making and coordinating movements of the vocal tract (larynx, lips, tongue, palate) in the absence of speech. Yana's parents reported that they rarely took her to public places because of her screaming and throwing behaviors.

As Yana found it difficult to relate to unfamiliar people, the dynamic assessment process was carried out over three visits. This gave her time to adjust to the assessment setting, and the clinician could learn which forms of mediation were most helpful to Yana. By the third session, Yana had become more confident in her abilities to communicate at a basic level and was able to gain eye contact with the speech therapist. At this point, she began to make more intentional communication efforts.

The initial aims of therapy were to enable Yana to accept mediation for communication and cognitive skills. Although there were many specific speech and language goals, the initial concern was enabling Yana to develop the perquisite skills for therapy. Thus, preliminary sessions involved mediation for regulation and control of behaviors, feelings of competence, basic planning behaviors, and acceptance of novel tasks.

The Initial Therapy Process-Understanding Communication

At the Input Phase

Initially, Yana needed to understand the concept of spoken language. She had to learn that in order to be understood she had to string together sounds that would form a word with meaning to her listener rather than rely on the random sounds upon which her current jargon was based. She also needed to understand the basic requests we were making during therapy sessions to which she was expected to respond. Thus, it was essential for the therapist to ensure that there was clear intentionality and reciprocity for every presented task. Additionally, Yana had to grasp the notion of communicative intent; that, when she used speech, she was able to communicate her thought/idea to her listener and, by doing so, have an effect on them.

At the Elaboration and Output Phases

At this point, Yana needed to acquire simple planning behaviors. For example, she had to learn that she could take time to choose and retrieve the sounds/words that she required to express herself. Her dyspraxia made the output stage particularly difficult, as it called for sequential phoneme production for speech. Even when she had retrieved a word and was physically capable of articulating each sound in the word, it was hard for her to articulate a string of sounds at will (at other times, some words would "slip out" spontaneously, as if bypassing the motor-coordination difficulty, a phenomenon sometimes observed win children with dyspraxia).

When analyzing the operations required by Yana to learn to articulate even short, basic words, it emerged that we needed to help her gain some basic oral motor control that would support articulation, as well as eating and drinking skills, and reduce dribbling. As Yana was not familiar with activities relating to oral motor exercises, it was several weeks before she was comfortable enough to engage in oral motor *games* during sessions. In order to deal with the novelty of the activity the clinician offered multiple examples and many repetitions. Oral motor activities for speech were always related to speech sounds; for example, round mouth for an "oo" sound or monkey noise and spread mouth for a mouse-like "ee" sound (an elaboration of these activities is provided below).

Developing Purposeful Communication

Teaching Yana functional words to replace noises and acting out behaviors was a primary goal. Initially, the clinician worked on the use of single useful words, such as *no* and *more,* as they could be quite meaningful for Yana and had a low level of complexity (i.e., words containing just two basic sounds: CV consonant vowel and VC vowel consonant words). Yana's first attempt at planned speech came several weeks into the treatment: she said the Hebrew word "od," a vowel consonant utterance meaning "more." The clinicians kept in mind that, because Yana was not familiar with the use of intentional meaningful verbal communication as a modality, the treatment would need to progress in a manner that took every small step of learning to communicate into account (from noises and gesticulating to articulation of meaningful words and intentional gestures). Her parents and personal aide were advised to respond promptly to all of her intentional communicative attempts. While she could not always have what she wanted, they were requested to demonstrate consistently that they appreciated her communicative attempt: "We heard that you said "no" and you don't want to get in the car now; we appreciate that you would rather stay at home, but we all need to leave for nursery now as we need to go to work…" After roughly two months of therapy, Yana was using the word "no" spontaneously to reject objects and actions. She still shouted and threw things at times, but she had become calmer and more willing to attempt play activities at home and in nursery. Her parents were advised to offer her a greater range of verbal choices, granting her more autonomy over activities occurring in the home.

After three months of weekly therapy sessions with parent collaboration, the clinician began working on using a string of two words and integrating a familiar word plus a new word to create meaningful phrases, such as *more water* and *no book.* This helped Yana to develop an awareness of how she might manipulate her environment via language. Yana's parents were asked to supply a list of words that would be useful for her so that the clinician could practice using these core vocabulary words in various contexts.

The goal was to reduce her frustration while refraining from pressuring her to speak—to help Yana experience the need to use her newly learned communication skills. At this stage, the clinician introduced oral motor exercises, demonstrating to Yana's aide how she could carry out these exercises at home in a stress-free, fun way. Next, the complexity of verbal output tasks was increased, so that Yana could start to use phrases of 2–4 syllables without compromising the clarity of her utterance (e.g., "more papers"). It should be noted that Yana's personal aide was present during most therapy sessions, and she was encouraged to ask questions and try out the homework exercises during the sessions so that the speech therapist could forestall any difficulties that might come up at home.

The therapy room can be a fairly sterile setting. Nonetheless, we introduced words to Yana in their natural context. When she would point at an object, a verbal model of the word was presented so that the function of the word was salient. Emotion words were introduced in a similar way. Whenever Yana became anxious, the clinician offered her verbal models to explain her anxiety; "I am tired and don't want to play anymore, I only want to play with the bubbles and not with any of the other toys." In doing so, the therapist mediated language as a means to regulate behaviors.

Organizing, Processing and Planning

This aspect introduces and expands cognitive elements. After a few months, the clinicians decided to work on joint focus of attention with Yana since this skill will often precede and predict language development (Markram, Rinaldi & Markram, 2007), and families can be taught to facilitate joint intention and other reciprocal social interactions during everyday activities. The course of treatment went as follows. The clinician would show an interest in Yana's play, as she played alongside her. She had to modify her behavior so that Yana would be interested in what she was doing, after which she started to comment on Yana's actions. Next, the therapist created a need system: she presented toys that she knew Yana enjoyed and waited for her to focus on the toy and initiate some kind of request (verbal or non-verbal). At that point, they would begin to participate in the play activity together. The clinician also modeled for Yana how to initiate a request to play. Gradually, Yana began to spontaneously attend to joint activities and request objects and actions. The clinician was careful to share her intention with Yana; in this way, there were no surprises and Yana was always aware of what was expected of her. As the tasks became more complex, the clinician would point out details, assisting Yana as to what they could focus on together. Next, the therapist began to engage Yana in activities that she (the clinician) chose, such as reading a book or a construction activity. In the beginning, these objects were placed in Yana's direct line of vision. Gradually, they were moved so the therapist and Yana could play/read together. As Yana became more familiar with these activities, she focused on them independently and took more of an interest in the activities the clinician presented.

The work on general planning skills was also continued, with activities that gradually increased in complexity. These included basic, non-connecting inset puzzles (introducing analyzing and scanning rather than trial and error placement), simple sequential stories and a model-building game that requires one to lay out a simple scene (using 3–6 objects) presented in a picture (e.g., a father sitting on a chair and a child sitting on a swing). Yana enjoyed learning to play using these objects, especially when the objects chosen were familiar and meaningful to her. If too many objects were introduced at once, she became anxious and threw the pieces around or slid under the table. For that reason, the therapist was careful to increase the number of items slowly and provide multiple demonstrations before encouraging her to attempt a task. At times, it was necessary to offer the closest form of hand-on- hand mediation in order to mediate for feelings of competence and ability.

Gradually, Yana was able to participate in play activities throughout a therapy session. The next step was to help her reduce her impulsivity and learn to participate in more complex organizational and processing skills, including scanning and planning behaviors. Initially, this was done in a non-verbal modality, which was easier for Yana to grasp. She was presented with a basic lotto game, was asked to match a picture to another identical picture.

This activity called for enormous effort from Yana at the input phase. She had to learn how to scan and identify the pictures on the lotto board. To reduce the complexity of the task, the board was partly covered. In that way, Yana would only have to scan three pictures in a single row; later, six pictures were presented in two rows. The chosen pictures were at a low level of abstraction—photographs of familiar, concrete objects which took minimal effort to interpret.

At the elaboration phase, the therapist checked that Yana understood the concept of "same" and "different," which was a prerequisite for this task. Yana and the clinician practiced matching objects and pictures. She was soon able to focus on this task and to choose two identical objects from a basket containing five objects. Personally meaningful objects, such as a brush, dog, and doll, increased Yana's willingness to participate in the task.

With respect to the output phase, the therapist mediated for the need of precision and accuracy. The goal here was for Yana to place the pictures in precisely the right places. Strips of Velcro were put on the pictures and the lotto board, which allowed her to see that they would need to attach and stick together. This activity also promoted the adoption of goal-seeking behaviors.

This task offered Yana the opportunity to learn many new concepts, such as "same-different, top-bottom, first, middle and last." After about two months, she was able to picture-match all six pictures on the lotto board.

The Role of Play in the Treatment Plan

Simultaneously, the therapist began to work on systematic play skills and engaged in activities that required sorting and categorization. These activities were used to assist Yana in organizing and processing the world around her and to reduce her impulsive and unplanned behaviors. This processing of the immediate environment helped Yana to slow down. A child's understanding of his environment can be expanded by helping him to describe/classify the things he sees. One might say, for example, "my doll is small but yours is big," "my doll has blue eyes and short hair," and so forth. Such practical terminology, drawn from real-life scenarios, is a good way to introduce crucial linguistic concepts.

Receptive Language Skills

Initially, it was necessary to offer Yana many contextual clues, both visual and gestural, to understand an instruction. It appeared that she did not have a speech listening habit, and thus had not yet adopted an auditory modality to process language. The therapist worked with her toward understanding the importance of listening to spoken language. Musical sounds were identified and matched to an instrument; next, the clinician requested that she give her one object from a choice of two, following a verbal request with no other contextual cues. It took several weeks for Yana to acquire the reciprocity required for this task. After about four months of therapy, she was able to consistently give the therapist an object from a choice of three items.

Oral Motor Skills

Yana's oral and speech dyspraxia compromised both her speech and her eating skills. Thus, oral motor exercises were practiced extensively for the first six months of treatment. Initially, she was quite resistant to these exercises. Time and again, the clinician demonstrated the tasks, making it clear to Yana what was expected of her. At the same time, it was critical to mediate for feelings of ability: Yana was well aware that these types of motor coordination tasks were challenging. After about ten weeks, Yana gained lip rounding with the aid of a straw and produced a centralized air flow to blow out a candle. She also learned to blow a whistle. These are no small accomplishments for a child with severe oral dyspraxia. Following these successes, we started working on oral motor coordination to produce specific sounds, starting with the [u] sound that requires a clear lip round position. We played fun sound-making games in front of a mirror in which the clinician would imitate Yana and she could observe herself. In this way, she could see how she was producing each sound and so become more aware of her verbal output. Gradually, the props (straw, whistle) that assisted Yana to produce a central air stream were removed, so that she could develop the oral motor coordination to obtain a central airflow without a prop. Yana slowly learned to blow independently.

Moreover, Yana learned to take bites of her food, chew the food using a mature lateral chew, and not to stuff too much food into her mouth at once (in the past, such behavior had resulted in her spitting out much of her food). She also adopted neater eating habits, and between bites she began to lay her food down in a specific place rather than throw her food after each bite. The clinician used close, hand-on- hand mediation to help Yana adopt these new eating habits. Over time and with the help of her personal aide, who observed the sessions and then practiced with Yana at every meal, she became an independent, relatively tidy eater.

Social Communication Skills

After a few months, Yana began to make improved eye contact with the therapist and to transition calmly between tasks. As she learnt to accept the mediation offered, the clinician presented her with increasingly structured play activities and introduced the concept of turn-taking. At this time, Yana also adopted some goal-seeking behaviors. For instance, she began to analyze tasks in order to understand what was required of her to complete them. Initially, modelling was used, tasks were repeated and simplified, and physical and emotional support was provided. Each incremental achievement was clearly acknowledged, affording Yana many chances to appreciate her own changing capacities. At first, it was hard for her to grasp that the clinician also wanted a turn. Thus, mediation for sharing behaviors was provided, helping her understand that others have needs and desires. Other social speech skills, such as greeting people verbally and requesting clarification, were also introduced. Since Yana had already learned some basic language skills, she now appreciated how to greet people and the positive feedback she naturally received from this. Requesting clarification and being able to communicate that she had not understood something was more challenging, and for many weeks the clinician modelled phrases such as "I don't know," "Tell me," and "Help me," with an exaggerated affect. Yana considered requesting help an inadequacy and did not want to appear "weak," preferring instead to play independently. As such, requesting assistance was not a skill she experienced as necessary. The clinician mediated strongly for meaning, demonstrating to Yana how asking for help was a positive action, a means to an end that could enrich her play experience and allow her to enjoy more varied play activities.

Twice-weekly treatment over a ten month period saw Yana able to engage throughout the forty-five-minute therapy session. She had developed some oral motor coordination and chewed her food in a mature and organized manner. Moreover, she attempted to use two-word phrases (not always articulating all the syllables in both words) to express herself and displayed an understanding of several language concepts (big and small, take and give, body parts, etc.). Yana's nursery teacher met with her clinicians at the Feuerstein Institute so that they could share information and learn which new skills should be prioritized.

Consolidating Progress and Moving On

Language: Over the next six months, the clinician aimed to help Yana adopt a consistent "yes/no" response. She also assessed that an awareness of speech clarity was the next target goal, since as the length of Yana's utterances increased, her clarity was compromised. Analysis of her speech revealed that she was omitting most word and syllable final consonants, which was impacting her speech clarity. The clinician did not want to continue correcting Yana and demonstrating how to say these final sounds. Instead, the idea was to shift responsibility for speech clarity over to Yana herself, so that she could understand that if she did not speak clearly, her communication attempts would not be effective. In addition, the clinician used *minimal pairs* exercises to demonstrate how the final sounds of words were critical to comprehension, and that if she omitted a final sound the meaning of her utterance would be changed (e.g., "bow/boat, car/card, toe/toad"). Further language concepts were introduced following the consultation with Yana's nursery school teacher, and the clinician continued to work on more advanced oral motor coordination activities. Yana's aide and parents were also introduced to the Feuerstein tool of Mediated Self Talk (MST; as described at the end of this chapter), so as to broaden Yana's vocabulary and assist her to achieve better speech clarity.

Pragmatic and Play Skills

As noted, people often told Yana to "slow down," "wait," "don't hit," and so on in order to help her regulate her behaviors. We aimed to introduce the use of verbal tools to help Yana learn to regulate her *own* behaviors so as to facilitate the development of inhibitory control, better planning, organization skills and more cognitive flexibility. Initially the clinician would describe Yana's behaviors to her so that she could learn to begin to recognize her own frustrations and become more aware of her abilities so that she could be more independent (e.g. "Yana you are waving and hitting the table with the puzzle piece, is it hard to find where it should be placed, you can tell me, it's difficult, I don't know where to put it"). We also mediated to Yana how she could start to consider alternatives and then make her own choice, such as: "We can continue playing this game, we can add more characters to the game or stop and choose another activity". She was encouraged to reflect on past experiences, using them as a guide for future choices: "Last week you found it difficult to construct this model and then threw it on the floor; would you like me to show you how the pieces fit together?" As Yana became more aware of her feelings, she began to make intentional choices and to enjoy play activities. At this point, the clinician introduced mediation for independent problem- solving. Games were chosen that helped Yana to regulate her speech volume and physical movements. Concepts such as "loud and quiet," "fast and slow," and "hard and soft" were introduced. We practiced shouting and whispering and discussed in which situations we may use different voice volumes. Sessions became very active as the therapist and Yana stamped feet, clapped hands and banged drums using different intensities. All this was aimed at encouraging Yana to become aware of her voice and her physical movements. While working on these skills, the speech therapist coordinated self-regulation skills with Yana's yoga and cognitive- movement teacher at the Feuerstein Institute.

As Yana developed self-awareness, the next goal was to encourage sharing and other social behaviors. Until this point, Yana would simply grab the objects she wished to play with, as she lacked the language to form requests. The therapist role-played asking for objects, and slowly Yana began to request objects that she wanted while she and the therapist played together. This activity was good preparation for the group therapy that was being considered for Yana.

As Yana's receptive language skills improved, the clinician introduced more complex symbolic play sequences which included some abstract concepts. The theoretical links between symbolic play and language and literacy are explicit in the theories of Vygotsky (1967, 1978) and Piaget (1962, 1970), who examined the role of symbolic play in preschool children's cognitive and linguistic development. More recently, Smith and Jones (2011) investigated the developmental pathway connecting visual object recognition, object name learning, and symbolic play, and proposed that they were not simply causally related to language delay, but that their absence is an indication of a problem in language acquisition. Symbolic play supports the development of representational thought, which with practice becomes more abstract. The representational competency that Yana gained through these play activities generalized to other language skills, and she began to understand longer utterances containing more information. Consequently, her speech expanded. At first Yana was able to pretend to feed herself using an empty cup and pretend food. Next, she involved a doll and a teddy bear in pretend play, and she could follow an instruction such as "give the doll a drink." The concrete objects like the cup and spoon were then replaced with hand gestures. It should be noted that Yana tended to be more verbal when she was leading the play activities. Now that she was using her verbal choice-making skills both in therapy sessions and at home, it took another few months for these skills to transfer to her nursery setting. Yana's parents also noted that she was starting to need less adult direction at home, a development that they experienced with much relief.

The Power of the Group

After a year of individual therapy, Yana had made tremendous progress in her oral motor and expressive and receptive language skills. However, speaking in her nursery school context was still difficult for her. Thus, the next task was to help her understand the social dynamics of a group setting so that she could develop the confidence to express herself with her peers. Social and pragmatic skills are infamously challenging for children with ASD, so it was critical to address these issues as soon as

Yana was able to express herself. The clinician did not wait until Yana was talking to her peers or was considered "ready" to be part of a group. Rather, group therapy is initiated precisely in order to teach children how to interact. While ASD children are often deemed "unready" for group therapy, they tend to adapt well beyond these expectations. For the first few weeks, Yana remained quiet in the group. The speech therapist appreciated that she was fully occupied observing and trying to understand the group dynamics and familiarizing herself with the other group members. The clinician that ran the group was concerned about her level of participation but resisted the urge to push her to start talking before she was ready. After several weeks, Yana began to interact with the other group members. These children were good models for Yana; observing their behaviors during a play task fortified her confidence to attempt the task. The initial goals of the group therapy were for Yana to:

- Interact directly with other children
- Attend to another child in a small group setting
- Become more aware of her speech clarity, as she could note whether the other children had understood and responded to her
- Participate in activities that required sharing and turn-taking

After several months of both group and individual therapy, Yana's teacher reported that she was now interacting with her classmates, at times even initiating communication with her peers. At this point, the group therapy goals were expanded to include:

- Ensuring that Yana was listening to her peers and carrying out instructions given or commenting on another person's remarks
- Awareness of what may cause communication breakdown— i.e. not understanding requests, lack of speech clarity, not waiting for a response from her before continuing a conversation, shifting topic
- Practicing empathy and awareness of the needs of others; listening to the difficulties the other children may bring up and suggesting help, e.g., thinking what Mommy or Daddy may want as a birthday present (very often children will suggest gifts that they themselves would want to receive!)
- Practicing how to receive assistance from peers
- Working on narrative skills through stories and relating personal experiences, the children need to be aware of presupposition (i.e. what information they have and what their listener has and how much information they need to share: not too much and at the same time be aware that the others don't know the background to their story.)
- Learning strategies for dealing with communication breakdown. Specific repair strategies such as repeating, revising and expanding a message (Brady, Halle, and Reichle, 2002)

- Requesting clarifications. Observe your listener to ensure you have his attention, check that your listener has understood you and allow your listener time to respond and have an active part in the conversation. (Many children launch into a monologue and then another child will often just walk away.)
- Learning how to respond when someone else is talking to you—acknowledging them and responding appropriately
- Seeking assistance from an adult when necessary

Group therapy sessions featured games in which the children needed to explain things to one another. Construction activities were also used so that parts were distributed to all the children in the group, and they had to work together in order to build their model.

At the time of this writing, Yana is integrated in a first-grade class and is able to express herself to her teacher and peers. She will often talk using phrases and sentences of 6–9 words and her speech clarity is reasonable. We are starting to work on structuring a narrative, being aware of her listeners and whether they have understood everything she has said. Future therapy is set to include higher-level language processing skills since Yana is still very impulsive and her teacher reported that frequently she responds to questions in class without having processed or manipulated all the information necessary for her to construct an appropriate response.

Considering the Feuerstein Approach together with Recent Theories of Linguistics

For many years, the field of language acquisition was dominated by Chomsky's theories of universal grammar that specify that young children come equipped with the capability to form sentences using abstract grammatical rules. More recently, many linguists have rejected Chomsky's theories in favor of the view that children learn simple grammatical patterns and gradually discern their underlying rules. Other factors, including memory, attention and social capabilities, are now considered central to language acquisition—these are the cognitive elements that form the core of the Feuerstein approach. Many of the children whom we meet with ASD are impulsive or may not be able to fully attend to their immediate environment. This affects their ability to make spontaneous analogies, so they experience more difficulty in acquiring language.

Case Study: Carrie

> *Carrie fitted this description and had been seeing a speech therapist since she was diagnosed with ASD when she was three years old. She was blessed with parents who diligently carried out all the homework exercises set*

by the clinicians and created a rich language environment for their daughter. Consequently, Carrie was a fairly fluent speaker by the time she was seven years old, but still made various grammatical and syntactical errors. These errors included irregular plural and past tense forms. Carrie tended to be somewhat impulsive and even after having learnt the correct forms several times she still found it difficult to inhibit her first regular conjugation of the verb, i.e. she would say "I eated" rather than "I ate." Ibbotson and Kearvell-White (2015) noted that the development of non-linguistic faculties such as executive control can assist in the understanding of language acquisition. During our therapy sessions with Carrie, we did not just work on her language issues but mediated for reducing impulsivity and worked on many general self-regulation skills in order to promote her higher-level language skills.

Since Chomsky's theories have lost their prominence, a usage-based approach to learning language has arisen that proposes that children are equipped with tools such as categorization, understanding "communicative intention" and "analogy making" so that they can build grammatical rules from the language that they are exposed to. Feuerstein's technique of Mediated Self-Talk (MST; Feuerstein, Falik, Feuerstein, and Bohacs (2013).) seems to be a natural development in view of these findings.

Mediated Self-Talk

Mediated Self-Talk encourages parents and caregivers to create a rich language environment by verbally mediating a child's environment to him using repetitions, analogies and multiple examples. MST can be an extremely effective tool to aid a child's language acquisition. As speech therapists at the Feuerstein Institute, we also have access to Feuerstein's Instrumental Enrichment tools such as "Comparisons," "Categorization," "Temporal Relations" and "Analogies," which we use to assist children to develop skills that will in turn assist their language development. This represents a further infusion of cognitive development into our approach.

MST aims to help parents and caregivers encourage their children's communication so that a child can receive frequent mediation of language by exposure to language models. Using this method, a child is exposed to structured language sequences which are directly related to a specific activity/process/situation that he is experiencing or observing. This process helps the child to relate the specific language structure being focused on at that particular time to what he is observing or experiencing and so make the structures being taught more meaningful. Parents and caregivers are guided by the speech therapists to choose topics and language structures appropriate for their child's needs, such as appropriate sentence length, expanding vocabulary, specific grammatical structures such as question forms, specific sounds the child has difficulty articulating or use of idioms and colloquialisms. We also work together with parents and caregivers to guide them as to when to introduce new language skills into their MST and how to make it appropriate for their child's language development.

The rationale for MST is presented to parents and caregivers early on in treatment, so that they can appreciate why this is an effective tool for developing a child's language skills. Already at a very young age, children understand language even though they are not talking. It is at this point that adults in their environment must remember to talk to the children even though they may not yet be verbal communicators. Most children with ASD understand language long before they begin to express themselves. Understandably many parents experience difficulty talking to their child when they does not respond verbally. It is critical to encourage parents to talk to their children even when they are not responding since the children are often both able to understand them and can continue to learn language from listening to others.

MST can be a verbal translation of one's thoughts and movements that presents a language template to the child. As mentioned earlier, one should be a good speech model and speak slowly and clearly, using short, clear phrases that we think the child will understand. The language used should be at a higher level than the child's so that he learns from the adult's enriched model. Unlike a conversation, eye contact is not critical during MST. Nonetheless, we do want the child to listen to what we are saying. In order to get the child's attention, the adult may need to vary the volume of her voice and modify/exaggerate intonation. A child must also be motivated to listen to what is being said. Thus, one should choose a topic of interest to the child or discuss something he is currently experiencing or planning to do.

In the MST, we carefully choose which language skill or concepts we wish to mediate and then slowly increase the complexity of the language structures. The mediator offers many examples in different situations in order to ensure that bridging occurs. A wonderful aspect of MST is that it can be done almost any time: bath-time, in the supermarket, driving, walking to school/nursery, cooking, and so forth. Ideally, though, MST is done when both adult and child are relaxed and thus more open to mediation.

In conclusion, this chapter encapsulates a transformative approach that combines the Feuerstein Method with conventional speech therapy techniques. It emphasizes the necessity of a dynamic assessment process that is not merely evaluative but also contributes to a constructive intervention strategy. The child's inherent communication abilities are the focal point, with therapy tailored to harness these skills as a foundation for development. Parental and caregiver involvement is integral, fostering an environment that extends beyond clinical settings and into the child's daily life. The case studies presented not only illustrate the method's practicality but also demonstrate tangible progress, reflecting the profound impact of a personalized, cognitive-focused approach. The method aligns with contemporary linguistic theories that advocate for cognitive and social factors in language acquisition and reinforce the Feuerstein Method's relevance. This chapter aims to provides both a theoretical framework and a practical demonstration that can guide professionals and families towards realizing the communicative potential of children with ASD.

References

Bass, J. D., and J. A. Mulick. "Social Play Skill Enhancement of Children with Autism using Peers and Siblings as Therapists." In *Psychology in the Schools* 44, 7 (2007): 727–735.

Feuerstein, R., Falik, L. H., Feuerstein, R. S., and K. Bohacs. *A Think-Aloud and Talk-Aloud Approach to Building Language: Overcoming Disability, Delay, and Deficiency*. New York: Teachers College Press, 2013.

Green, J., et al. "Randomized Trial of a Parent-Mediated Intervention for Infants at High Risk for Autism: Longitudinal Outcomes to Age 3 Years. *Journal of Child Psychology and Psychiatry* 58 (2017): 1330–1340.

Ibbotson, Paul, and J. Kearvell-White. "Inhibitory Control Predicts Grammatical Ability." *PloS One* 10, 12 (2015), e0145030.ICDL http://www. icdl.com/home.

Pickles, Andrew, et al. "Parent-Mediated Social Communication Therapy for Young Children with Autism (PACT): Long-Term Follow-Up of a Randomized Controlled Trial." *The Lancet* 338 (2016): 2501–2509.

Smith, L. B., and S. S. Jones. "Symbolic Play Connects to Language through Visual Object Recognition." *Developmental Science* 14, 5 (2011): 1142–1149.

Vygotsky, L. S. *Thought and Language*. Cambridge, MA: MIT Press, 1962.

Vygotsky, L. S. "Play and its Role in the Mental Development of the Child." *Soviet Psychology 5*, 3 (1967): 6–18.

Vygotsky, L. S. (1978). "Interaction between learning and development." In M. Cole, V. John-Steiner, S. Scribner, & E. Souberman (eds.), *Mind and Society: The Development of Higher Psychological Processes*, pp. 79–91. Cambridge, MA: Harvard University Press.

Chapter 7

Mediating Thinking Skills through the Feuerstein Instrumental Enrichment Program for ASD Individuals

Julie Jamet and Refael S. Feuerstein

The Feuerstein Instrumental Enrichment Basic Instruments: "Identifying Emotions" and "From Empathy to Action"

Feuerstein's Basic Instrumental Enrichment (FIE- B) program consists of a battery of modules or instruments designed to enhance cognitive development in young children and those with a younger mental age. The Mediated Learning Experience (MLE) method describes the effective and necessary interaction in order to develop learning and thinking skills. The interaction of the mediated learning experience shapes each event, stimulus, and occurrence in a way that allows the recipient of the mediation to derive cognitive benefit from it. There is no event, or occurrence of any kind that has no cognitive component. Serve lunch to a child. It is a completely physical event. But did anyone prepare the food? There is a process here that caused the creation of food. Does the food have a specific purpose? Was it served at a certain time? in a certain place? All of these cognitive considerations seem to be 'hidden' within the concrete situation. The purpose of the mediator is to reveal these considerations and enable the recipient of the mediation to understand them so that they will be able to use them independently in the future. He can then learn to take into account the appropriate timing and location and other important factors that are necessary when planning events such as a meal.

The FIE program is a kind of concentrated 'antibiotic' of the MLE. It focuses on specific cognitive goals and allows for intensive MLE intervention around specific goals. For example, there is a module that deals with data collection and there is a module that deals with understanding relationships between events and objects, other modules work on comparisons, understanding instructions, organising information, and drawing conclusions. Thus, we see that the FIE program allows the professional to give MLE in a focused manner. The program is made up of sophisticated exercises that are based on critical skills that are necessary to create a scaffold to support the cognitive operations required for learning.

DOI: 10.4324/9781003451136-8

When working to together with ASD persons, we emphasize the cognitive operations most relevant for their individual needs. These often include the need to develop interpersonal communication, understanding relationships in their environments and understanding instructions.

Three of the FIE instruments focus specifically on the development of emotional intelligence through cognitive mediation. The first instrument is called "Identifying Emotions," the second "From Empathy to Action," and the third deals with conflict prevention, "Think Learn and Prevent Violence." This chapter will discuss the first two instruments.

The "Identifying Emotions" instrument aims to address the client's ability to recognize the seven basic emotions: surprise, joy, anger, disgust, pain, sorrow, and fear. Research has demonstrated the universality of these emotions; they are independent of cultural context (Ekman, Friesen, O'Sullivan, and Chan, 1987). The instrument focuses on two main areas. The first is body language—specifically, facial expressions (and how they express a certain emotion). The second area asks the child to match an emotion expressed in a portrait to one of a number of situations presented pictorially (see Introduction to the Theory). The situation should match both the content and the intensity of the emotion presented in the portrait. Situations are constructed in such a way that they do not provide a clear answer, but rather allow for a discussion of the emotion and its implications.

In our clinical experience, we have found that a significant percentage of ASD children have a great deal of difficulty identifying emotions. They may not notice a change in someone's expression or even understand that it is possible to "read" someone's facial expression. This is because they cannot easily recognize these emotions in themselves, something which is necessary before they can recognize these feelings in others. Some children with ASD may be able to identify whether an emotion is positive or negative but label all negative emotions as "anger," even if a picture expresses disgust, or all positive emotions as "he feels good," without being precise as to the specific positive emotion. When treating children with ASD, emphasis is placed on mediation for deciphering and defining the feelings that they themselves experience. Before beginning the mediation process, it is important to ensure that the child can see the difference between eyes that are wide open or squinting, or a mouth that is wide open and tight shut. They may notice the difference, but not know how to associate them with the different emotions.

It is important to emphasize, however, the wide range of abilities and difficulties that exist for children on the spectrum. This is also the case for children not on the spectrum but with other intellectual/developmental disabilities. Some of these children are more likely to notice that a facial expression has changed or may understand that one can "read" someone's face. One child may be able to identify the specific emotion while another will find it difficult to *name* what he sees in someone's body language or facial expression.

Case study: John

> *Thirteen-year-old John did not understand social situations and was unable to decipher facial expressions. For example, when someone laughed at him, he did not interpret it as something negative directed at him. In extreme situations, he noticed if an emotion being directed at him was positive or negative, but he did not understand its meaning. Oftentimes, he imitated the unpleasant facial expressions/words directed at him and directed them towards other people, to the extent that he could meet a stranger on the street and repeat back an unpleasant sentence he had been told at school. Seeing two people in conversation, he would interrupt with no understanding that he was disturbing them. John was not able to notice the expression of the other person who was unavailable at that particular moment. He would tell someone "You are ugly" and not notice by the listener's expression that he felt insulted. If John saw the person whom he insulted crying, he understood that something was wrong, and may also have understood that something on his part was not right, but he would not make the connection between his behavior and the crying.*

Some children with ASD may sense that the atmosphere in a room is uncomfortable, for example, without grasping that they did something to cause this atmosphere. In response, they may begin displaying repetitive, stereotypical behaviors.

Case Study: Anna

> *Eighteen-year-old Anna did not receive sufficient mediation until she reached the Feuerstein Institute. She had an urge to peel off any label she saw. One day she peeled a sticker off a game which we had taken a long time to carefully prepare. Of course, we were not angry with her, but she realized that something disagreeable had happened. In response to the negative atmosphere she felt, she began to bite her shirt. She needed a great deal of mediation to understand that it was indeed annoying that she peeled off the sticker, but it was not terrible either. In short, the intensity of her emotion was not in line with the situation.*

Case Study: Sam

> *Fifteen-year-old Sam could not rely on facial expressions in order to understand whether what he did was right or wrong. He had to be told explicitly whether he had succeeded or failed. Even after the therapist gave him a verbal response, he was not always sure that he understood and could respond with loud singing and inappropriate shrieks. It seemed that Sam was aware (at least at a certain level) that he was expected to understand the situation,*

but it bothered him that he did not comprehend everything going on. The gap between what he felt was expected of him and his ability to fulfil this expectation produced a strong sense of tension in him. This affected his functioning at home, at school, and elsewhere. Complicating matters was that the people around Sam did not mediate or verbally explain the situation to him. First and foremost, his treatment plan focused on identifying emotions. Working with him required a great deal of flexibility. The mediator had to be active and theatrical, using a variety of stimuli including his/her voice to express feelings, perhaps even exaggerating the stimulus.

Step one in mediating the meaning of different facial expressions involves teaching the different facial features: eyebrows, eyes, cheeks, lips, teeth (revealed or exposed), and so forth. Sometimes we ask the child to put stickers on the therapist's face to show he understands each feature, e.g., a sticker next to the eyebrows, next to the lips, etcetera. This is done in order to help focus the child's gaze. If the child agrees, we may place stickers on his face too. We often work in front of a mirror to mediate the different facial expressions that appear in various emotional situations.

The next step after identification of the emotion is imitation of facial expressions representing different emotions. We usually use images from the child's life—pictures of the child's birthday, for example, when discussing happiness. Only once this stage is completed do we move on to connecting the situations to specific emotions. It is important to emphasize here the degree to which ASD children interpret situations in ways that might differ from our expectations. The instrument creates a variety of interpretive situations that the mediator explains to the child. For example, most children who see the image of a girl receiving a letter will not interpret it as a surprise; however, the child with ASD might interpret it as a surprise because he has never received a letter. Many children do not understand what a surprise party is because they have not been invited to many parties. Furthermore, a party is often not a source of joy for them, but rather a source of distress since it involves a sensory flooding. Sometimes, what surprises us does not surprise them and vice versa, so the therapist must explain to the ASD child the reason why she might feel surprised in a given situation.

These children seem to suffer from mediation deprivation. They do not have the same understanding of everyday phenomena that children without communication difficulties automatically absorb from the environment and accordingly build up an understanding of reality. This absorption allows them to put together the pieces of the puzzle to understand their environments. ASD children do not spontaneously absorb the same daily stimulation from their environment because of their communication and learning difficulties. Often their family and educational environments don't know how to mediate to them those same "puzzle pieces" that surround them. They live in a sort of glass bell where they can see what is going on but the information is not absorbed—leaving them unable to attribute meaning to those events. The therapist's role is to break open this transparent bell and instill in these children these experiences and their meaning.

The second instrument is called **"From Empathy to Action."**

In the "From Empathy to Action" instrument (see above), a crisis situation appears at the top of every page. For example, we see a sad child sitting on the sidewalk with his broken bicycle in front of him. Below this picture, we encounter four other images. In each of them, another figure appears, in different response states. Each of the four images express a different response. Thus, in one picture we will see the figure appearing to ignore the suffering child. In another picture we will see the same figure kneeling, crying and trying to comfort the child. In another picture, he is seen trying to tie the fallen wheel with a rope, a clearly improbable solution. In the last picture we see the figure putting the child on his own bicycle, leaving the broken bicycle behind.

This instrument (from empathy to action) is a more advanced tool than the "Emotion Identification" instrument: it not only requires that a situation be matched to a particular emotion, it also asks the learner to match a behavioral response to a particular emotion. The child must follow a chain of events and examine the nature of the relationship between them. It turns out that what initially seems more complex is actually simpler. This is because all the pictures are about the same story—with a specific focused change. The continuity reduces the stimulus load imposed on the child at the input phase. This reduction allows the therapist and the child to focus more on processing the situation than on gaining control over the data load.

Case Study: Maria

> *Maria is a charming four-year-old girl. No one had worked with her on her feelings, so she did not understand what was happening for her in the emotional realm. When she was hungry, stressed, or sad, she would say that she was nervous. If the game that the therapist was playing with her was difficult, she would say, "I'm nervous" and not "This game is too hard for me." The moment she said she was nervous; she would put her head down between her hands. We worked with Maria a great deal on emotional tools, emphasizing the naming of emotional states. As a result of this intervention, a real change took place. She became able to describe her feelings quite well. Her ability to define her emotions led to an ability to ask for something specific. She thus learned to say "I'm hungry" instead of "I'm nervous." If this was said in the middle of a lesson, it was possible to find a solution and continue with the lesson. Her parents' increased ability to understand what their child was going through and respond accordingly caused a significant reduction in tension at home. She also learned to ask for help, which was a significant achievement, since it means she learned that her emotions are not closed off in her inner world but rather they allow focused communication with the people in her environment.*

FIE-BASIC **FROM EMPATHY TO ACTION**

Describe the problem(on the right)

What does this picture show?

Describe the solutions(below)

1.What did he / she do?

2.Why did he / she do it?

(Write answer below each picture)

1.
2.

1.
2.

1.
2.

1.
2.

Feuerstein Instrumental Enrichment - BASIC

KEY 1.Appropriate emotion & appropriate action   3.Appropriate emotion but inappropriate action
2.Appropriate emotion & appropriate action but not effective   4.Inappropriate emotion & inappropriate action

Figure 7.1 Empathy to Action Instrument from FIE-Basic.

The "From Empathy to Action" instrument enables ASD children to better understand themselves and their environment, which in turn reduces their level of anxiety. Additionally, this instrument contains another important principle that is often new to the ASD individual—the understanding that you can change a situation in order to solve a problem. The child on the spectrum will often be helpless in the face of a situation that he not only does not understand, but also does not know how to manipulate or change. The instrument counters the child's passivity in the face of reality and builds in him the awareness that he can manipulate situations in order to change them.

The image of the child sitting helplessly in front of his friend with the broken bicycle represents the ASD child's psychological stance in the face of crisis situations. He will cry and feel sad alongside the suffering person, but he will also feel helpless to do anything to make a difference. With this instrument, we mediate to the child that there are ways to act in order to change reality. This is a transition from a passive attitude to an active approach.

The Feuerstein Instrumental Enrichment Basic Instruments: "Learning to Ask Questions for Reading Comprehension"

The "Learning to Ask Questions for Reading Comprehension" instrument is one of a battery of instruments that make up the Basic "Feuerstein Instrumental Enrichment" (FIE-B) program. This instrument aims to teach individuals easy-to-use processes in order to develop reading comprehension skills. In the instrument, each sentence is mediated as an answer to questions. Thus, the idea is that the questions can serve as a methodical tool for deciphering the meaning of the sentence. The instrument consists of short stories built from sequences of short sentences, with pictures appearing next to each sentence depicting what is written. Some of the follow-up sentences are in the third person; for example, "Danny is climbing a tree" may be followed by "He is holding on to a branch with his hand." The instrument is divided into three parts, differentiated by the complexity of the sentences the individual learns to decipher. In the first part, one learns to apply the following three questions to each sentence: 1) who is this about? 2) what was his/her action? and 3) on what object was the action carried out?

Analyzing the first sentence in Figure 2 using these three questions yields the following answers: a) Danny, b) climbing, and c) a tree.

1   He is holding onto a branch with his hand.
2   He sees a birds' nest.
3   He sees baby birds.
4   He gives them seeds.
5   They eat the food out of his hands.

A common problem encountered in clinical work with some children on the autistic spectrum occurs during reading aloud. Reading comprehension might be challenging for some people with ASD. In some cases, if the individual encounters a word that he does not recognize, he might feel frustration, and, without having learned skills to figure out the meaning of the sentence, break eye contact with the mediator, stop reading, and throw down the book. Feuerstein argued that this kind of behavior is caused by a deficient cognitive function at the output phase, known as "Blocking." This phenomenon stems from inflexibility due to an excessive need to be exact that cannot be realized because of an unfamiliar word. And, it would seem that the verbal passivity many of these individuals display does not contribute to their ability to overcome this obstacle. This phenomenon might not appear in the same way when they are asked to read silently and do not feel the mediator's expectation that they read with comprehension. In reading aloud with ASD individuals, an unfamiliar word turns the reading into a technical process, lacking comprehension.

The "Learning to Ask Questions for Reading Comprehension" instrument provides several tools to deal with this problem. First, many words are repeated in the stories, making it easier to read and understand. Recalling the first story in the instrument, the words "tree," "branch" and "he" appear frequently in the sentences (see picture above). Repetition reduces stress because it increases familiarity and lowers anxiety about unfamiliar words (the stories do not require a broad vocabulary). Repetition is crucial because it allows the individual to connect with the text and feel more comfortable, which increases cooperation with the mediator. Any other simple story could be organized this way. As we see in Figure 3, the sentences in the story are separated from each other, thus avoiding the pressure of a dense paragraph. In the "Learning to Ask Questions for Reading Comprehension" instrument, each sentence stands alone. Furthermore, each sentence is accompanied by an illustrative picture. The pictures help the individual fully understand each sentence before moving on to the next. Moreover, they promote a calming effect, since comprehension is not only dependent on the verbal modality, but also the visual modality. This alleviates the pressure an ASD individual can feel when faced with a written text.

Additionally, the questions stimulate an analytical process. Thus, the sentence is broken down into its main elements, which facilitates an understanding of these parts, and is then reconstructed in order to grasp the sentence as a whole. This process ensures good sentence comprehension, which creates a solid foundation for deciphering and understanding the next sentence. The cumulative effect of reading in this way is linked to the *Mediation for Transcendence* that is, mediation that seeks to change

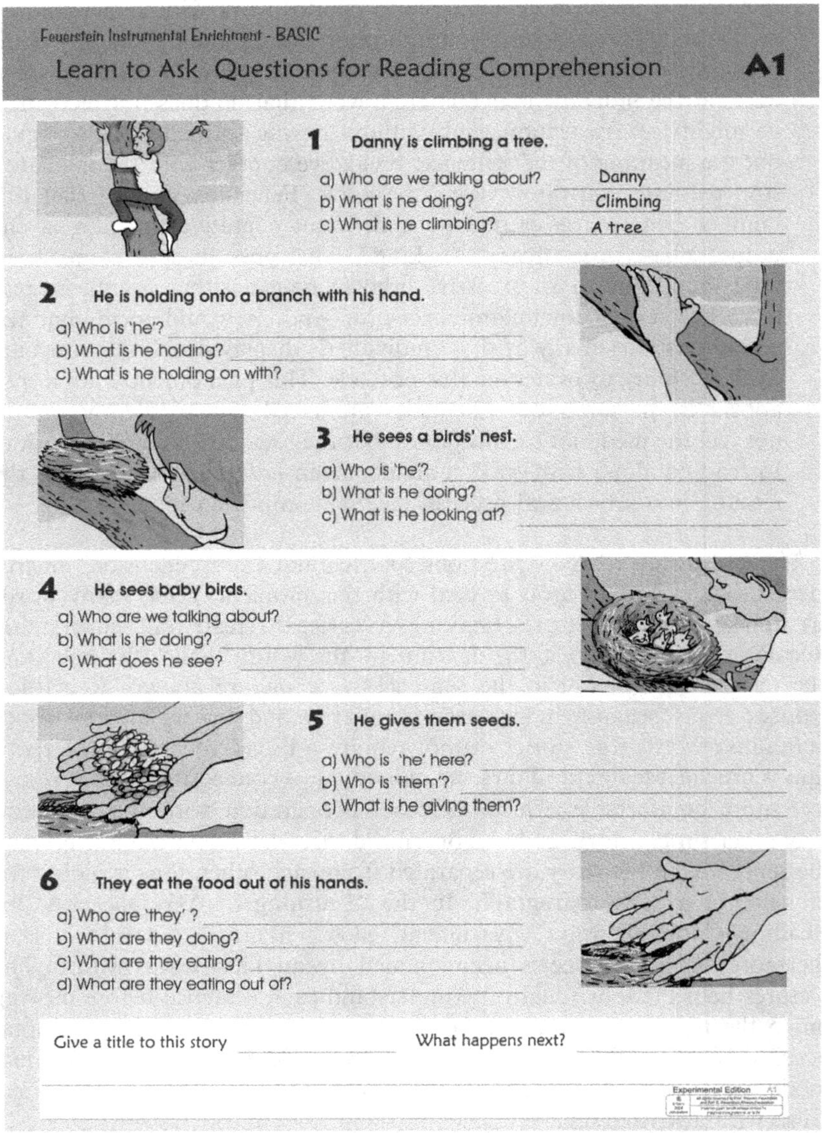

Feuerstein Instrumental Enrichment - BASIC

Learn to Ask Questions for Reading Comprehension   A1

1   Danny is climbing a tree.

a) Who are we talking about?   Danny
b) What is he doing?   Climbing
c) What is he climbing?   A tree

2   He is holding onto a branch with his hand.

a) Who is 'he'?
b) What is he holding?
c) What is he holding on with?

3   He sees a birds' nest.

a) Who is 'he'?
b) What is he doing?
c) What is he looking at?

4   He sees baby birds.

a) Who are we talking about?
b) What is he doing?
c) What does he see?

5   He gives them seeds.

a) Who is 'he' here?
b) Who is 'them'?
c) What is he giving them?

6   They eat the food out of his hands.

a) Who are 'they' ?
b) What are they doing?
c) What are they eating?
d) What are they eating out of?

Give a title to this story _____   What happens next? _____

Experimental Edition   A1

Figure 7.2 Learning to Ask Questions for Reading Comprehension from FIE-Basic.
FAMILY RELATIONS All Rights Reserved ©

the autistic individual's approach to all written texts and which should become a cognitive structural change. Mediation aims to produce in those on the spectrum the perception that they *can* understand and find meaning in a written text. Moreover, mediation attempts to teach them about internal logic, in which each sentence supports the next: each sentence creates the knowledge base upon which the next sentence rests (this may be called "necessary continuity" in a text).

Alongside this, in the "Learning to Ask Questions for Reading Comprehension" instrument, the individual is challenged by the text. For example, the sentence "He is holding onto the branch" does not mention the name of the person pictured, and the accompanying image does not show his whole body but rather his hand holding the branch. Here, the deficient cognitive function "episodic grasp of reality" (see Introduction to the Theory, and Feuerstein, Feuerstein, Falik, & Rand, 2006) plays a significant role at the elaboration phase. This relates to the difficulty many ASD individuals have in connecting the parts to its whole; the tendency to see parts of the whole as stand-alone items, without making connections between them. Someone with ASD may view each sentence as a stand-alone statement; thus, the word "he" will not be understood if it is not associated with the previous sentence that mentioned the name "Danny."

Some ASD individuals will say that the hand holding the branch in the picture refers to another person. Here, the mediator will step in, and build connections between the sentences for him. Moreover, the mediator will aim to create the tendency in the individual to seek out and create connections between items with the goal of connecting them together to make a "whole." This is vital preparation for the world of more complex texts, in which a deliberate effort is required to create connections between

paragraphs and sentences. Sometimes the mediator will read the sentences out loud and skip the questions, all the while explaining what he is doing. Gradually, the mediator transfers responsibility for reading to the student. It should also be noted that the instrument's simplicity enables parents and teachers to repeat it, thus creating a cumulative effect.

In summary, the task is built in a way that it remains familiar to the individual, fostering trust and reducing anxiety. Nevertheless, it also presents a challenge, as the tasks are diverse. This is also true of the writing required in this task. Many ASD individuals are apprehensive about writing, and so emphasis is placed on reducing the anxiety or fear of failure that often blocks them from writing (see also Chapter 10). The mediator may write the word first to create a model, or initiate a role-play game: "I will write first and you will write after me." Later in the task, the child is required to give a title to the story he has read. Many ASD individuals find this difficult and thus tend toward the concrete (e.g., "Danny and the Bird"). Here, mediation is required for the deficient cognitive function at the elaboration phase described as an *"inability to select relevant, as opposed to irrelevant, cues in defining a problem"* (see Introduction to the Theory, and Feuerstein, Feuerstein, Falik, and Rand, 2006). Entitling things requires abstraction, and an understanding of a higher order of meaning. Here the individual needs to understand that there is no explicit answer in the story.

The next step requires the individual to invent a continuation of the story he has just read with the mediator. In our example story, Danny remained on the tree. Many ASD individuals find it hard to imagine a situation different to the one presented, such as Danny descending from the tree. Their rigidity and tendency to be concrete limits their imagination and creativity. Interestingly, by the fifth and sixth stories, some ASD individuals will already begin to think of ideas for the story's continuation even before they are even asked (while they are reading the story for the first time). Humor is one of the most effective ways to mediate the ability to invent a continuation to a story. When the mediator offers his own idea for a funny ending, individuals are more likely to open up and offer their own suggestions.

Case study: Bruce

> *Bruce was diagnosed with ASD when he was a little boy. He was integrated into the regular education system, but the integration did not work out. He switched to home schooling but participated in many activities such as sports, and art, in normative groups. When Bruce came to us at the age of nine, he spoke a great deal and could recognize letters but could not yet read. We started working with him using the "Learning to Ask Questions for Reading Comprehension" instrument. The initial goal was for him not to panic when confronted with a written text, and to be able to sit down in front of a reading task. When we started working together, he could only sit and work for a maximum of ten minutes. Each short story took 2–3 sessions, and I would read and write for him. Towards the end of the period (after about a month), we could sit reading together for 45 minutes straight, and he would point to the correct word in the text that answered the question I had asked. It should be noted that Bruce's mother invested a lot of effort in working with him. After a year, Bruce could read by himself. When he returned to the Feuerstein Institute at the age of 11, he was reading and writing independently, and only asked for assistance when something was difficult. His answers to my questions reflected an understanding of the texts, and there were no robotic answers.*

In an analysis of our work with Bruce, we found that he knew much more than he let on. We noticed that he would look at a certain word and focus his gaze on it without responding, or in response to a question, he would scan the text with his eyes. We also saw that although he did not read and did not respond, he was nonetheless interested in the text. In our view, Bruce was a child who had learned from direct exposure (without mediation), which enabled him to absorb a great deal—although not enough to assist his initial reading skills.

Bruce's mother, who was present in the room during the treatment, was concerned that he would become unruly during the lesson as he was afraid of failure and reacted to it badly. However, this instrument enabled him to experience success, and to reduce his anxiety about reading and writing. The combination of the repetition inherent in the instrument and the strategies that we mediated to him created his first experience of academic success. This tool allows one to focus effort on a small amount of cohesive information, in this case, a sentence (i.e., field reduction). Furthermore, since the answers to the questions we asked were to be found in the text itself, Bruce did not have to produce answers out of thin air, reducing his stress level. The instrument makes it simple for the mediator to create a positive learning experience, since the person receiving mediation has few options to fail.

Over time, Bruce answered our questions more quickly and with greater accuracy. He did not achieve complete independence in his ability to answer the questions, but his way of dealing with the questions improved markedly. His case demonstrated how the use of cognitive intervention can reduce anxiety, remove obstacles to success, and reveal hidden abilities (capacities that had been more or less present but were concealed due to emotional barriers).

Imparting World Knowledge through the Feuerstein Instrumental Enrichment Standard "Family Relations"

Many children with ASD face a lack of general knowledge. This, of course, makes it difficult for these children to integrate into normative society, which is the ultimate goal of our efforts. Their communication and learning difficulties act as a kind of barrier to the world, to the extent that one 13-year-old boy who we were seeing did not even know the terms "male and female." He understood that there were boys and girls, but he did not know the different terms or how to distinguish between them. No one ever mediated this basic concept to him. Many families never think to explain such things to their ASD child because those are things that a neurotypical child would perceive as self-evident. This is especially the case when the child with ASD has highly developed knowledge in other subjects that interest him.

The *Feuerstein Instrumental Enrichment Basic* (FIE-B) instruments, particularly "Learning to Ask Questions for Reading Comprehension" (discussed at length just above), enable therapists to mediate basic common knowledge to children with ASD. For example, the "Learning to Ask Questions for Reading Comprehension" instrument contains a picture of animals in a cage in the zoo. Security rules might be unclear to some children with ASD. For example, ASD individuals might not understand why it is forbidden to climb on a cage, or to put one's hand near a lion's mouth. They may not know that touching broken glass can injure their hand, or how one can use special cream to prevent mosquito bites. This is due to the fact that their communication difficulties impair their ability to learn spontaneously, so information that they are exposed to every day is not processed and fully understood. Some parents are unaware of this deficit in their child, some do not have the tools to correct it, and some do not believe that they can correct it.

Transmission of knowledge is not complete without mediation, especially *Mediation for Transcendence,* that is, the transference of the skill/knowledge learned to other areas (see introduction to the theory). For example, one may mediate to an ASD student that he should say hello to his teacher and friends when they enter the classroom, and he may internalize this. Nonetheless, he may not apply this principle in other contexts; for example, by saying hello to someone he knows at the grocery store or bus stop. In other words, the mediated skill (to greet people) will not necessarily become a general principle—or, in the terms of Feuerstein Theory, a "cognitive structure." Therefore, it is important that the mediator actively transfers the skill to other situations. Without mediation for transcendence, the skill may remain concrete and focused rather than used to change the child's functioning.

Of course, the imparting of basic world knowledge is not unique to "Feuerstein Instrumental Enrichment." Thus, one might ask, how does it contribute to this area in a unique way? The answer lies in the structure of the instruments. The instruments are built so that each image or task is directly related to or built upon the preceding image or task. This repetition enables the consolidation of information while also introducing new information and enabling transference to other contexts. This gradual structure can reduce the ASD individual's fear of the unknown and provides a kind of "cognitive crutch."

The "Family Relations" instrument (Feuerstein 1965) also helps the ASD individual acquire basic knowledge. The child is part of a nuclear family, a larger extended family, and the social community of his parents and family. Lack of adequate understanding of these relationships makes it difficult for the child to integrate into his natural surroundings.

The family structure is unique in that it both maintains stability and is dynamic. For example, one of our client's sisters got married and moved in with her husband. This made a significant difference in her way of life and family status, but she still remained the child's sister; the family relationship did not change. Our client responded with great confusion. This is where the cognitive function in the input phase *"Lack of or impaired conservation of constancies across variations"* is expressed. The aim is to be able to isolate and differentiate components that are not related to the essence of the object. For example, changing the color or size of a table does not change its function as a table. The fact that one's sister is married and has a spouse does not change her status as a sister. The child with ASD may have trouble understanding the relationship between the constant factor and the variable one. Accordingly, we often see that a family wedding, especially of a brother or sister, causes confusion and stress among children with ASD. A situation of divorce in the family, beyond the inherent difficulty, may also undermine the child's understanding of the family institution. My father continues to be my father, and my mother continues to be my mother, even though my father married another woman, or vice versa. It is easy to imagine the intensity of the anxiety that a simple misunderstanding of this state of affairs could generate in an ASD child.

A related difficulty concerns the nuances of different relationships. For example, we expect children to understand that their relationship to their brother should be different from their relationship toward a classmate. The child with ASD needs to learn not just the relationship between himself and other people, but the quality, the nature, and the strength of each relationship; what is forbidden and what is permissible. It is here that the cognitive function "episodic grasp of reality" (in the elaboration phase) is expressed. This involves difficulty in producing a complete picture of the relationship, function, and behavioral rules that derive from that same relationship. The ASD child has trouble making connections between different behaviors and the family relationship. Here, intervention must mediate integration.

Often, it seems that a deductive approach is more effective than an inductive one. In other words, it is easier for the child with ASD to understand the abstract idea of the "family" than to understand the connections between the individuals that make up the family. The details are more understandable to them when they are embedded in a general way that is, one might say, mathematically logical. Therefore, the most effective intervention in this situation will be "top-down" and not "bottom-up." There is something in abstract thinking that enables the children to have a clear understanding without the emotional burden of dealing with concrete reality. Indeed, the Feuerstein Method, as conveyed in FIE, enables the abstract refinement of relationships and their subsequent implications for reality, with all of its complexity.

This inflexibility, where the child finds it difficult to accept changes, is expressed in other contexts, such as in the following anecdote: "I met one of my clients, aged 12, while on a day out with my family on the beach. He said to me 'I don't want to be here; I am supposed to be at my computer right now.'" Many ASD children exhibit this rigidity and are unable to adapt their behavior according to the situation they are currently in, such as in the classroom or at home with their family. This inflexibility stems from the ASD child's difficulty in making connections between appropriate rules of behavior and different social environments.

The causes of an "episodic grasp of reality" are often emotional— every change creates a certain tension in all of us. There is probably an evolutionary explanation that change may involve situations of uncertainty and danger, and therefore alertness in these situations can almost be described as a condition for survival. The sensitivity and alertness of a child with ASD may create emotional flooding that can make it particularly hard for him to cope. The boy with ASD wants the situation to remain the same; that it will remain as it always was. I'll be in my room with my sister when she's thirty- five, and Mom and Dad will be here forever. It reassures him when everything is normal and everything is going on as usual and this way, he is not overwhelmed emotionally. When things change within the family, the influence on the child can be immense. Every shift in routine is like a stone thrown into the sea, resulting in ripples.

We have a 15-year-old boy whose parents are in the process of divorce. He does not want to talk about it because emotionally it is difficult for him, but we are working on the "Family Relations" instrument. He understood that in a diagram depicting a family, the line between parents and children never changes.

He kept the line connecting him and his mother, and him and his father, but he erased the line between his father and mother. Understanding these "rules" helped him deal emotionally with the complicated situation he was experiencing.

The use of the Feuerstein Instrumental Enrichment Standard "Instructions" in working with ASD individuals

This instrument is oriented to deciphering and processing written instructions, "translating" these instructions into pictorial form and back again into written instructions. It aims to improve the ability to understand and follow various kinds of instructions and to break down complicated instructions into a series of simpler instructions. Particularly important for our purposes, the instrument teaches the student to overcome ambiguity and thus express himself in a clear way, and to follow instructions accurately. These goals are a strong advantage when working with ASD individuals, as their achievement provides such individuals with communication skills and a better understanding of themselves and their surroundings.

The instrument deals mainly with geometric shapes. The first part of the instrument presents simple geometric shapes and the relationships between them. The learner must identify and interpret the instructions' keywords and draw conclusions, with an emphasis on the order of implementation of the different instructions. The next section of the instrument presents different types of instructions; for example, instructions which prescribe a certain order of implementation, or instructions that can be translated into several parallel action plans, requiring the use of divergent thinking. Other instructions require arrangement according to a given criterion. The second part of the instrument presents instructions on complex geometric concepts.

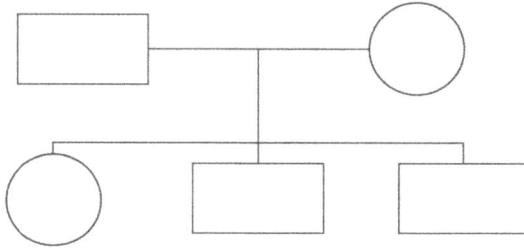

Above you see a diagram of a family.

Such a diagram is called a genealogical map. The map is blank (empty).

Place the names in the blank genealogical map, as indicated by the following sentences:

    a) Arthur is Rita's father.

    b) Simon and Jerry are brothers.

    c) Jerry is Laura's son.

Answer the following questions with the help of the map.

    a) Who is older, Rita or Laura? _____

    b) Who has two brothers? _____

    c) Who has a brother named Simon and one sister? _____

Complete:

    a) Arthur and Laura are the _____ of _____ .

    b) Arthur and Laura are _____ .

    c) There are more _____ than _____ in the family.

    d) There are more _____ than _____ in the family.

FAMILY RELATIONS   All Rights Reserved ©

Feuerstein Publishing House LTD
Realizing Human Potential
© All Rights Reserved
Jerusalem 2014

Developed by: Prof. Reuven Feuerstein

Figure 7.3 The Feuerstein Instrumental Enrichment Standard "Family Relations". © Feuerstein™ Publishing House Ltd.

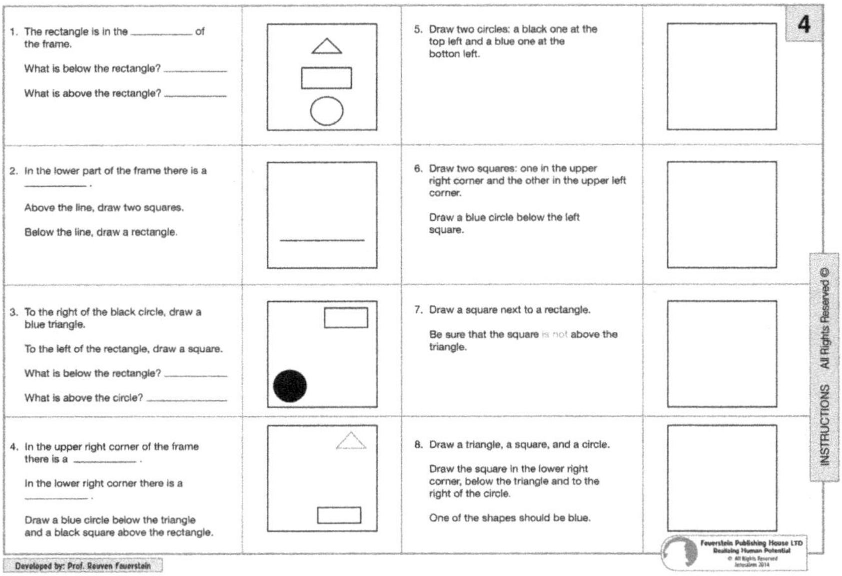

1. The rectangle is in the _____ of the frame.

   What is below the rectangle? _____

   What is above the rectangle? _____

5. Draw two circles: a black one at the top left and a blue one at the botton left.

2. In the lower part of the frame there is a _____ .

   Above the line, draw two squares.

   Below the line, draw a rectangle.

6. Draw two squares: one in the upper right corner and the other in the upper left corner.

   Draw a blue circle below the left square.

3. To the right of the black circle, draw a blue triangle.

   To the left of the rectangle, draw a square.

   What is below the rectangle? _____

   What is above the circle? _____

7. Draw a square next to a rectangle.

   Be sure that the square is not above the triangle.

4. In the upper right corner of the frame there is a _____ .

   In the lower right corner there is a _____ .

   Draw a blue circle below the triangle and a black square above the rectangle.

8. Draw a triangle, a square, and a circle.

   Draw the square in the lower right corner, below the triangle and to the right of the circle.

   One of the shapes should be blue.

Developed by: Prof. Reuven Feuerstein

4

INSTRUCTIONS   All Rights Reserved ©

Figure 7.4 Instructions.

Family Relations

Therapeutic aims

The primary goal of this instrument in working with ASD individuals is to improve verbal communication ability, especially vocabulary. A second goal is to create a need for precise and detailed verbal descriptions so as to be clearly understood by others.

One of the main advantages of this instrument is that it is concrete. Instead of being asked to describe emotions, learners are asked to describe objects (geometrical shapes, e.g., circle, triangle, square); each with its own rules. On the one hand, the shapes are simple and concrete, so they do not "threaten" the inner world of the person with ASD. On the other hand, the shapes require detailed and precise descriptions, a task that pushes the learner out of his comfort zone.

It is important to clarify that the purpose of the instrument is not to study geometry, but to understand the importance of words in interpersonal communication (see Chapter 6). Often, when a learner is asked to describe a square, he will simply say: "square"; when the therapist asks him again, he is likely to become impatient. The therapist is seeking for him to describe the square's four right angles and the four sides of equal length that are parallel to each other. The learner usually recognizes the features of the square, as well as other shapes: he just has to give these features expression. It is easier for him to describe a square than to describe anger, as it is difficult for him to distinguish between - or even name - different emotions. He may have difficulty identifying emotions, let alone one particular feeling. Furthermore, understanding emotion requires higher abstraction than understanding geometric shapes.

Case Studies: Carlos and Joseph

> *Eleven-year-old Carlos functioned at a high level and was integrated in regular school, but he had many difficulties. Every lesson began with my question, "What did you do yesterday?" And he always would answer "I went for a walk." My request for a more detailed description was not met with information. While working on the "Instructions" instrument, Carlos came to me and said, "On Saturday I went for a walk on the beach with my father." He said this as soon as he entered the classroom, so it seemed to me that he had thought about what to say during the week and planned to tell me.*
>
> *Fourteen-year-old Joseph is an immigrant to Israel. He spoke his native language fairly well, so his speech therapist worked with him on the relatively new Hebrew language. Nonetheless, he did not really progress. Following my work with him on the "Instructions" instrument, I suggested that she avoid asking him questions that do not lead to specific answers and avoid the use of vague pointers that he does not fully understand. Instead, I advised that she provide him with short, focused instructions that allow for brief and focused answers. As a result, the speech therapist moved to the "Reading Comprehension" instrument (described earlier). The breaking down of sentences into small parts and the focused questions worked well for Joseph, and he showed sudden improvement. The "Instructions" instrument also uses precise targeting and breaking down of instructions, which helps many children to make progress. There is always reference to the "whole"; for example, rather than asking, "what objects are there"? the therapist will say, "We are in the kitchen; there are a lot of utensils here, which utensils are there in the kitchen?" The focus on utensils will be with reference to the "whole," in this case, the kitchen.*

This instrument emphasizes precision. The therapist will often make a "mistake," and then ask the person receiving mediation to correct it. Additionally, the instrument stresses distinguishing between relevant and irrelevant components. Some ASD individuals focus on irrelevant forms or colors in the background that are not related to the task at hand. This instrument places a strong emphasis on the output phase, which is responsible for transferring the product of the processing stage to the environment. Individuals diagnosed with ASD will often understand a question, but their output will be egocentric and therefore not understood by others. In order for those around the ASD individual to understand his response, output precision is required. *Mediation for Meaning* (see Introduction to the Theory) in this tool focuses on the ability of others to understand the learner's message. Lack of precision in the output phase will make this difficult.

References

Ekman, P., W. V. Friesen, M. O'Sullivan, A. Chan, et al. "Universals and Cultural Differences in the Judgments of Facial Expressions of Emotion." *Journal of Personality and Social Psychology* 53 4 (1987): 712–717.

Feuerstein, R., R. S. Feuerstein, L. H. Falik, & Y. Rand, *Creating and Enhancing Cognitive Modifiability: The Feuerstein Instrumental Enrichment Program.* Jerusalem: ICELP Press, 2006.

Feuerstein, R.S., Feuerstein, R., & Falik, L. (2005). "The Feuerstein programs for early assessment and intervention: The LPAD-Basic and the IE-Basic." In Oon-Seng Tan and A. Seok-Hoon Seng (Eds.), *Enhancing cognitive functions.* Singapore: McGraw Hill Asia.

Feuerstein, R. S., Feuerstein, R., & Falik, L. (2009). *The Feuerstein Instrumental Enrichment-Basic Program: User's Guide* (2nd revised edition) Jerusalem: ICELP.

Ben Hur, M. & Feuerstein, R., S (2011). "Feuerstein's new program for the facilitation of cognitive development in young children." *Journal of Cognitive Education and Psychology,* 10(3), 224–237.

Chapter 8

Imparting Writing Skills to Children with ASD

Bruria Avichay, Gili Amorai and Refael S. Feuerstein

Introduction

In this chapter, we will address the importance of imparting writing skills to ASD children. Writing is a critical facet of communication; it functions as both a means and a goal. In this respect, writing is a kind of outward departure from the child's inner world to the external social world. It must be noted that reading and speech accompanies the acquisition of writing, so these skills are also strengthened in the process of that acquisition. Here, however, we place the emphasis on writing as it is more directly associated with interpersonal communication, which is a central goal for the child on the spectrum.

Moreover, writing is crucial to integrating the child with ASD into regular educational and employment frameworks. In order to ensure that the integration is genuine and not purely "geographical," that is, a physical placement that does not involve emotional/intellectual connection, we must see to it that the child's writing skills are effective and accessible.

In this field, we generally see two types of individuals: low and high functioning. The higher-functioning children acquire reading and writing very efficiently; some have even taught themselves to read and write. Intervention with these children focuses on reading and writing comprehension, and we may take advantage of their proficiency by teaching them its full significance. Those with lower functioning have difficulty with the mechanics of writing, as well as understanding the technical process of writing.

In addition to serving as a means of communicating ideas to others, writing facilitates the organization of information so that it can be verbalized. Thus, the speech therapist will often work in conjunction with the occupational therapist, the former dealing with conversation and the latter with the organization and the imparting of communication through writing. It is precisely writing that makes it possible to teach vital rules that are hard to learn otherwise, such as how to compose an e-mail to a family member versus one to a friend or teacher, or how one organizes an idea to craft a coherent sentence and paragraph. Children whose thoughts flow

DOI: 10.4324/9781003451136-9

too fast find it difficult to express this fluency. Writing slows down the pace and allows for clear organization and expression.

Case Study: Simon

> *When I asked 15-year-old Simon what he did yesterday, he tended to focus on one specific event that he particularly enjoys, for example, "the swimming pool." When I asked him how it was, he would say "fun." However, when I asked him to write down his answer, I receive a much more comprehensive description: "I went to the swimming pool on Monday with my mother, I like to go to the pool, I like quiet in the water, then I ate potato chips, then we had guests round - Sally and Matt. I played piano with Jack."*

Simon's response seems like a sort of "grocery list" of activities, but after working with the Feuerstein Instrumental Enrichment (FIE; see Introduction to the Theory and Chapter 9) tools on emotion identification, and work on text construction, his answers became more detailed and structured: "I did not go to school during the holiday. I lit candles with my father and mother and then I ate donuts. Then I went to the beach with Jack and Liz and it was fun because I love the water." When I asked Simon to describe in words what he had done, he recounted it in a fairly elaborate way, without reading the text. In other words, the writing process helped him to organize his experiences such that he could convey them well in conversation.

In Simon's case, the separation between the elaboration phase and the output phase permitted proper output in the form of writing. Owing to its more complex technical aspects, writing leads to slowing down, allowing the elaboration phase to operate well because the pressure to provide immediate output is reduced.

Furthermore, the writing process reduces the intensity of the stimulation in the input phase. In a conversation, the speaker needs to observe the face of the person with whom he is talking and take into account the overall situation of the room and the people around him. Thus, input processes allow more background noise to penetrate and disrupt Simon during a conversation. When writing, by contrast, Simon only needs to concentrate on the page in front of him. He is not exposed to an interpersonal interaction that requires him to activate the input phase, with emphasis on the emotional and social aspects of the conversation. The elaboration phase is also freed up to organize the ideas and express them in the output phase (written) in a more optimal manner. Once the elaboration phase is completed, the verbal output phase becomes more efficient and communication-oriented. Hence, when I asked Simon to tell me verbally what happened yesterday, he was able to do significantly better after he had processed and written down his ideas. In other words, the Feuerstein Method allows us to analyze thinking processes and causes for certain behaviors, and, if necessary, to isolate different phases of thinking to improve functioning.

Case Study: Isaac

> *Isaac is a 17-year-old, high-functioning boy who attended a special education school. It was very difficult to hold a conversation with him or to get an answer in response to a question: "Who are your friends at school? How was school today?" The only method that was found to be even slightly effective was to present him with two choices from which he had to choose one. This communication option had its drawbacks, however, as he had a tendency to choose the second answer that was presented to him. Then we turned to writing -I would write the beginning and he would continue. His favorite subject was baseball, in very broad contexts. He told me that he goes to a baseball game every Saturday, which seemed unlikely to me. Around the same time, I taught him how to navigate the internet, and we learned about the role of the various icons. He kept searching for baseball videos and wrote how he goes to a baseball game every week. When I told his parents, it turned out that Isaac's father was a baseball coach and that he indeed took his son every Saturday to watch the games. He was sure that Isaac did not understand anything about the game and its rules. He did not even know he was interested in baseball at all. Yet it turned out that Isaac was very interested and even understood the game well. Writing seemed to release many barriers for this young man, allowing him to express himself more freely and at a high level of detail and content. This enabled us to identify his learning ability. As previously mentioned, the Feuerstein Method emphasizes the ability to learn as a key to the process of human rehabilitation. It turned out that Isaac had a high self-learning ability, and the therapeutic rehabilitation process had something to base itself upon. This knowledge also opened a window for renewed communication between Isaac and his father. His father created a video presentation for Isaac which included all the information about baseball his son was interested in.*

It is important to emphasize that, from a therapeutic point of view, there is no difference between writing by means of an electronic device and writing with pen and paper. The main aim is that the client is able to express himself through writing, which often releases many barriers. Sometimes we skip writing with pen and paper and move straight to the tablet or vice versa. Nonetheless, digital communication devices are less favored by us as they lose a lot of the richness inherent in writing. Sometimes we use these devices to construct an idea but quickly move on from there towards writing with pen and paper as a means of communication.

Teamwork plays a pivotal role in our therapeutic work (see Chapter 5). The synergy that develops among team members can be leveraged to increase the effectiveness of each person. After successfully working with Simon on writing texts, I suggested to my colleague, who deals with imparting thinking strategies through Feuerstein's Instrumental Enrichment program (see Chapter 7), to use writing as a means of communication with this young man. When I found it difficult to work with another client who had trouble calming down, I consulted with the team therapists who work through movement (see Chapter 9). They advised me to sing a particular song with the client that produces a particular breathing pattern, and this suggestion proved highly successful for the treatment.

The therapy dealing with writing is composed of a number of important "building blocks" that are worked on simultaneously. The work is done in an integrated way, working in parallel on several building blocks. When progress is made in an area that is more advanced, it builds on more "basic" building blocks that were previously treated. These interactions are not random but are a direct result of the mediation process, which is concerned not only with imparting the specific building block but with linking it to the previous blocks.

Building Block #1: Acquiring a Spatial Frame of Reference

Building Block #1 deals with the creation of a spatial relationship system (see Introduction to Theory). In the first stage, we mediate for the child the concepts of the body, including spatial references to the different body parts. In the second stage, we mediate with regard to the space in the room so that he can apply these spatial concepts to writing.

In this building block, we also mediate for the graphic aspect. Importantly, however, we do not begin with the letters which are complicated and abstract. We do not draw a letter and ask the child to identify and copy it. Instead, we are engaged in creating a cognitive-conceptual system of the basic lines and shapes from which the letters are composed. We focus on an orderly comparison process between the different shapes, and naming the forms, lines, and positions in which the lines and shapes are located in the letters.

At this stage, we are not satisfied with the verbal channel itself, but actually draw the different basic shapes. At the next stage, we develop the ability to take apart and reassemble these shapes, so that the child will be able to build letters and words from them. This is where Feuerstein's cognitive approach, which tries to bring the person receiving mediation to control the perceptual side of actions through thinking, clearly emerges. One might say that we teach the child "to think the letter" rather than simply to see it.

The third element of this building block is developing the ability to continuously and systematically scan, distinguishing between the images and the background and identifying differences. In the input phase, this process is a precondition for the ability to control letter continuity and, subsequently, word and sentence continuity. In this context, the *mediation for regulating behavior,* which will make it possible for the child to avoid focusing on a more familiar or more prominent letter or shape at the expense of the continuous scan. Naturally, faulty scanning habits tend to result in distorted or omitted letters. Feuerstein calls this deficient cognitive function in the input phase "blurred and sweeping perception."

Case Study: Lucy

> *Lucy is a nine-year-old girl who arrived at the Feuerstein Institute with a long history of frustration from failed treatment attempts. She had been treated with the ABA method (see Chapter 3), which succeeded in motivating her to perform some actions, but no learning or understanding underpinned that behavior. Because the actions that she had learned were external to her, she had no experience of her capability, even when she succeeded. It was as if the success was not hers.*
>
> *From a grapho-motor point of view, Lucy struggled to identify the four sides of a square. She even struggled to distinguish that the square comprises four sides, not to mention their directions (vertical, horizontal, left, right) or even where a particular line begins and ends. It took about a year for Lucy to understand these concepts. As she suffered from dyspraxia (difficulty in planning movement), it was hard for her to plan the continuous movement needed to reach a target. In practice, the continuous motion suffered from complications and performance failure. For example, a child might know that he should climb onto a chair, but, in practice, when he tries to sit, things go very wrong.*
>
> *One day, Lucy arrived at treatment distraught. She had trouble focusing on tasks and fiddled with her clothes constantly; everything was very complicated. Lucy had brought to the office a bag full of dolls. She occupied herself with taking out these dolls, returning them to the bag, and repeating this process. When we asked Lucy to sit on a chair - something that would have taken a normative child perhaps two seconds to do - she experienced this as a complex process. She had to plan how to sit next to the table, from which side she would sit, and where to put her bag. At one point, she placed her bag on the chair and then saw that she had nowhere to sit—then, she tried to understand where to sit. It took Lucy five full minutes to deal with this problem. She ultimately sat down, but with her feet pointed in the wrong direction. In order to fix things, she tried to turn the chair instead of turning around herself. When she saw that that would not work, she got up from the chair and started from the beginning. She tried to move the chair and the table, which she naturally could not do. After all that, verbal mediation began. "Where will you hang your bag? There is a hook in the room, or maybe hang the bag on the chair? Now, stand with your back to the chair and bend your knees. How should the feet be placed on the chair?" She could not answer me. Thus, I told her, "forward." But Lucy still did know how to accomplish the goal. I*

explained to her that the feet should touch the floor so that they wouldn't tire. She tried and still could not place her feet the way they should be. After several sessions during which she practiced these steps, Lucy arrived one day and simply sat down, with her feet forward. Throughout this process, she strongly resisted the mediation.

Let us return for a moment to the scenario described above, in which Lucy arrived with her bag and dolls. She very politely showed me them one by one, and then began to arrange them in a particular order. Next, she put them back into the bag and took them out. At some point, I had to separate her from the dolls so that we could begin working. Yet, as I sensed that Lucy was in a power struggle with me, I tried to give her some control. Thus, I asked her where she wanted to put the dolls - on the windowsill or the table? She cooperated and put them on the windowsill. But shortly afterwards, she wanted to put the dolls back into her bag. I wanted to teach her the sides of a square, but she wanted to play with the dolls. I did not tell her what to do, but I instead informed her that we were beginning to draw a dollhouse that would not get wet in the rain. While she was playing with the dolls, she would steal glances at what I was doing. Slowly, she helped me close the house by drawing lines to protect the dolls.

Over time, Lucy was able to plan her sitting more efficiently. She built a kind a scenario of what she should pay attention to, and, after several months, she organized herself in the room unaided. Once, when she reverted to bringing in the bag with the dolls and playing with them, I asked her, where should the dolls be? I could now talk with her about this—we had established trust, which allowed me to tell her things that were unpleasant for her without her becoming destructive.

If we analyze Lucy's case (which we will continue below), we see two interconnected lines of intervention. One of these lines concerns building the ability to engage in mediated interaction - what the theory refers to as *Mediation for Intentionality.* Lucy's anxiety, which led to her need to control events, prevented the application of mediation for change. In Feuerstein's language, the cognitive structures are wrapped in a near-impenetrable protective layer. The mediator had to work hard to find an opening in this shield to mediate with Lucy (on mediation, see Introduction to Theory). She cooperated with the mediator in her games with the dolls, showing them to the mediator. But the cooperation was bounded by the rules that Lucy set. It was challenging to change these rules. The mediator used strong mediation to "direct her"; that is, to create the trust essential to change the structures of thinking and functioning. This was undertaken by creating a demand for change, while empowering her sense of control rather than harming it. Thus, the mediator asked Lucy to decide where she wanted to put the dolls—given particular choices. She would decide, but she would make the decision within the activity space that the mediator determined. "Will you put the dolls on the windowsill or on the table?" the mediator asked. Gradually and firmly, the mediator broke through the wall to the cooperation necessary for fruitful mediation processes.

The mediator's second line of intervention turned on the need to deal with Lucy's notable difficulty in planning motor actions (the dyspraxia described above). This is where a further prominent aspect of the Feuerstein Method was expressed. For example, the mediator did not ask Lucy to kiss her mother because that would have been impossible; the child was liable to encounter great difficulty if the mediator were to ask her to make the lip movement of a kiss. This example reflects the limitation of the purely functional approach, even when it is accompanied by appropriate reinforcements. The Feuerstein Method, by contrast, focuses on the cognitive element of functioning. Hence, the mediator built cognitive scenarios of the required action with Lucy. In effect, the mediator teaches the client "to think of the action" rather than simply how to act. For this purpose, the mediator undertook two critical processes. The first was to break down the action into its primary elements. In the example above, we saw the breakdown of the steps required to sit: where to put the chair, its location vis-a-vis the table, where to put one's bag, where to stand before sitting, how to bend one's knees, put one's feet on the floor, and so forth.

The second process undertaken by the mediator was to create cognitive awareness of the actions required, and to understand the meaning of those actions. Thus, we aim to move beyond the instructions, "Stand, bend, move," to an understanding of why these actions are important.

Nonetheless, the mediator does strive to make broad cognitive change. In the case at hand, she was not interested merely in teaching Lucy how to sit efficiently, how to reduce the process of sitting on a chair from ten minutes to perhaps one second. Rather, she sought to change Lucy's pattern of actions: she tried to mediate the cognitive function of planning, which is part of the elaboration phase, as Feuerstein defined it. As we saw above, in Lucy's case, the mediator mediates the planning process, which is comprised of two basic elements: breaking down the complex process into sub-actions, and mediating the understanding of the purpose of the different actions, including understanding their place on the continuum of actions; how they are based on the previous step and lead to the next one.

Lucy, like many other ASD individuals, had difficulty creating a system of spatial relations. The ability to organize a space requires understanding the space and the application of an appropriate system of concepts. It should be noted that Lucy knew these concepts as words, but she understood the words passively rather than as tools that would enable her to organize reality. To turn these concepts into active ones, or "psychological tools" in Vygotsky's (1962) terminology, the therapist must use concepts in as many situations and ways as possible (Feuerstein refers to this as a cognitive function in all three phases, namely, "using concepts").

Let us take, as an example, spatial concepts for which the therapist applies movement in a maze. Thus, the therapist moves a magnet in a maze following the instructions of the client, who must use the concepts of left and right, forward and backward. If the client makes a mistake and "hits" a maze wall, the client must repeat the instruction. The concepts are also written on a paper and on a map in terms of space. It ought to be emphasized that these processes take a great deal of time and require great patience until they are expressed spontaneously.

Another difficulty that might be expressed by the creation of a spatial frame is the deficient cognitive function in the input phase of the simultaneous reference of several sources of information (see Introduction to the Theory). This function refers to difficulty with dividing one's attention among multiple factors simultaneously. The significance of this function is that its absence hinders the ability to compare and create links between different objects or events. If one can only think about one thing at a time, he will find it difficult to see the whole picture and navigate between the different items of information. When the issue is the creation of a spatial relationship, many ASD individuals will struggle to express or even identify "the upper right-hand corner" because of the difficulty in relating to "right" and "upper" at the same time. This requires mediation by analysis and synthesis, such as, "Where is the right side?" "Where is the upper side?" "Now let's connect them..."

Consider orientation within a written text, where the line begins and where it ends, where one line is located and where the line beneath it is. Without a spatial relationship, reading and writing cannot make any real progress.

Case Study: Daniel

> *Daniel came to us when he was seven years old. His basic level of functioning was very low, and he strongly resisted treatment. Daniel had a hard time leaving his parents, but it was also difficult for him to function when they were in the room. He did not make eye contact or speak; dinosaurs were his sole interest—and he preferred to be alone on this subject as well. It took a long time to get Daniel into the room, and seating him next to the table was also difficult. He had very little experience in writing, and he lacked basic writing concepts. It was necessary to start at the very beginning. I began with a computer game to teach him basic spatial concepts. We leveraged the computer game to the world of writing concepts.*

As noted above concerning this building block, we focus on two core objectives: instilling a spatial relationship system and instilling geometric concepts. The two objectives frequently cohere and support each other. When I teach clients to draw a particular geometric form, I often use spatial concepts to control the geometric shape, such as the concepts of the descending vertical line or a right-to-left horizontal line. It is important to note that I do not wait for the child to acquire the world of spatial concepts before I teach the world of geometric concepts. We teach the two subjects together, and when a client is stuck on a particular stage, we can focus on it and return to the integrative work later.

At the end of the system of Instrumental Enrichment tools, there is a module that engages the spatial relationship system with an affiliation to geometric shapes and the actual writing ("From Lines to Shapes" and "From Lines to Letters").

From Lines to Shapes

The chapter on implementation of the Feuerstein Instrumental Enrichment tools in working with ASD (see Chapter 9) sets out the advantages of using structured tools (pencil and paper) of the Feuerstein Program (Feuerstein Instrumental Enrichment), but there are ASD clients who resist using structured instruments and even feel threatened by them in the first stage. Thus, we often undertake preparatory intervention before the structured work on the program's pages. To narrow the range of uncertainty, we present a problem and show the client two answers, one correct and the other incorrect, and ask him to choose the correct answer. This method may serve to reduce anxiety and increase cooperation.

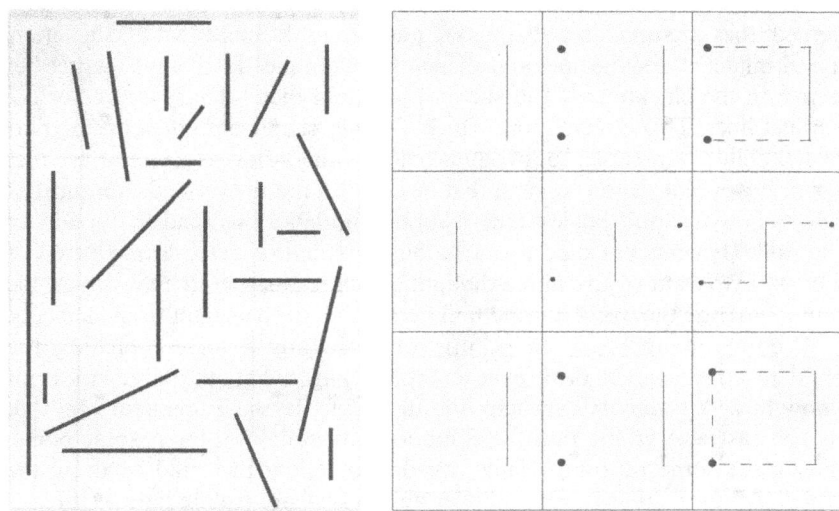

Figure 8.1a and 8.1b Lines to Shapes.
Source: © R. S. Feuerstein™ Publishing House Ltd

Building Block #2: Mediating Grapho-Motor Skills

In the first stage, we teach the basic shapes that form the letters: the horizontal line, vertical line, diagonal line, and circle. In the second stage, we use these basic shapes to assemble letters. In the third stage, we reduce the analytical element of the intervention and switch to writing and reading as semi-automatic processes. We de-emphasize the geometric elements from which each letter is built, and rather stress the letters as a whole.

In the first building block (mentioned above), we do not refer to the letter as a drawing, but disassemble it from top to bottom, using spatial concepts for this purpose.

It is at this point in treatment that we use images from the client's world and connect them to the relevant shapes. For example, we will draw a square and then turn it into a window or a gift in order to impart meaning to what we are doing. ASD individuals often have trouble connecting different shapes in their imagination to any particular shape; for example, what would happen when we place a triangle on top of a square—what do they create together? There is a strong expression here of a deficient cognitive function in the elaboration phase, which Feuerstein called an, expressed as difficulty in see the part-whole relationship (see Introduction to the Theory). Those with ASD will therefore struggle to say that a triangle placed on a square forms a house. This lack of connection between items may be expressed in not applying today a rule taught yesterday, as if there is no connection between yesterday and today.

The child may therefore encounter the letter "p" and not see the similarity between its shape and those of the letters, "d" and "b." As far as he is concerned, they are unrelated shapes. We mediate to the child that all the letters are ultimately the same lines and shapes. For example, the therapist writes her name on the blackboard, and she and the child then identify and color the vertical lines. This intervention, which involves significant effort on the part of the child, is intended to give him reading and writing tools in a broader form. It would be easier to insist that he copy his name over and over until he knows how to do it, but we take the long and laborious road that mediates the skill. (Feuerstein called this a "thought structure"—see Introduction to Theory.) We want to give him a thought structure; a structure that will enable him to analyze the world around him, to see the world as built from elements.

A common approach in occupational therapy involves teaching the child to copy a great deal, even complete pages. Yet, the child does not know how this activity can help him in his life. In the Feuerstein Method, by contrast, everything that the child does, including on the graphic plane, must have some meaning. Thus, we do not allow the child to draw the letter "A" or a square over and over again. Instead, we mediate writing as a means of communication and as a medium for creating something abstract; a concept, thought, or word.

Case Study: Lara

> *It took Lara a year to learn to write her name. She was highly resistant to these attempts. Hence, we began to teach her to draw the elements of the letters (lines, circles, etc.) before moving on to drawing a house. The moment that Lara felt that she had control over this drawing and the relevant geometric concepts, she opened to further mediation. In Lara's case, the first stage was mainly to bring her to the point that she was willing to work with us. As her confidence in her ability to represent things in graphic form grew, she opened up to the possibility of learning to write letters.*

The basic principle is to take an abstract concept and connect it to a concrete action that is relevant to the child. For instance, a child interested in numbers (see Steve's case, below) selects a number, which then we use to teach him the principle of vertical and horizontal lines.

Building Block #3: Mediating Symbolization

The letter system that we mediate for the child is a system of symbols that constitutes an alternative reality. Rather than listening to a particular sound, we indicate it with a graphic symbol. Instead of pointing to a "water bottle," we write the graphic symbols that mean "water bottle." The arbitrary nature of letter symbols is quite challenging: there is no connection between the shape that we draw for the letter "D" and the sound that we produce when reading it. Many children diagnosed as ASD struggle to understand language because they do not know how to deal with its abstract and arbitrary nature. In effect, when we teach reading, we essentially teach two languages: the concrete language—English, Hebrew, or Arabic, say—and the underlying language, which is the "language of the language," or, put differently, the language of symbols.

Our world is saturated with symbols. Thus, the language of symbols has broad consequences that go beyond a specific language. Look at the packaging on the simplest snack food and notice how many symbols are present. When driving, note the many symbols that shape your conduct: traffic signs, various lane markings, traffic lights, and so on.

Some children learn easily enough to copy letters (although we have described contrary cases), but do not learn to use them. Writing is a highly technical act when it is devoid of meaning and context. Below we meet Nate, whose treatment illustrates some of these issues.

Nate, who came to the Feuerstein Institute at the age of five, was diagnosed with ASD. In sessions he rapidly learned to write his name, and he even understood that the continuum of letters expressed his name. Shortly thereafter, however, Nate began to scribble letters with no meaning or context. The therapist explained, unsuccessfully, that the "words" he was writing were meaningless. At some point, she began to read his "words" aloud; he, realizing their absurdity, began to laugh. The therapist then wrote a meaningful word and read it aloud, which led Nate to understand that the continuum of letters could and should have meaning. Initially, she produced meaningful words at random. The next stage was to mediate for him that direction and effort were required to form meaningful words. Hence, the therapist asked Nate, "What word shall I write? Perhaps I'll write something that I like to eat? Perhaps I'll write a word about something I like to play?" She then showed him how she selected letters to form a meaningful word. Next, Nate imitated the process that the therapist demonstrated until he succeeded in forming single words. By the end of the year, she was able to write sentences.

Occupational therapy with the Feuerstein Method is highly oriented toward the semantics of writing. This approach diverges strongly from perspectives that focus the occupational therapy on the technical side of writing. In the Feuerstein Method, however, we believe that there is no point, and it may also be very difficult, to teach a particular technical skill, such as writing, without the child understanding its meaning. Moreover, if the child does not understand the meaning of the acquired skill, he cannot make use of it.

We frequently use the Feuerstein Instrumental Enrichment tools, "A World of Symbols" and "From Object and Event to Symbol and Sign (R. S Fuerstein 2009)."

Figure 8.2 Visual Thinking: From Object and Event to Symbol and Sign.
Source: © Feuerstein™ Publishing House Ltd, R. S Fuerstein 2009

We use these tools to reveal to the child the world of symbols that surround him. For example, we take the image of an elephant and tell the child that this is not the image of an actual elephant, but nevertheless represents one. The mediation method to establish this understanding is done by understanding the *reduction of the symbol*. Thus, the pictured elephant is not grey, he is very small, and he makes no sound at all. So how can this image represent an elephant? Because it has several essential characteristics: size, four feet, a trunk, and big ears. Such systematic mediation instills symbolic thinking in the child.

An important feature of working with ASD children, as compared to children with Down Syndrome, for example, is that the latter have a rich world in internal meaning which can be used to impart language. Children with ASD seem to have a kind of "meaning vacuum": many subjects simply do not interest them, and to create a world of meaning for them is a major challenge. This challenge is related to the child's difficulty in communicating, which stems from the lack of a real need for communication - and the basic significance of language as a means of communication does not exist for him. One of the main advantages in teamwork (see Chapter 6) is that it facilitates our ability to find points of meaning for the child. If one therapist sees that reading a story appeals to the child, and another sees that a particular motor activity appeals to him, the other therapists can adopt these meaningful anchors to create change in their fields of therapy.

Building Block #4: Mediating Analysis and Synthesis

Analysis and synthesis are preconditions for reading and writing. We have to deconstruct the letters into the lines that form them, and then connect them to the whole. Distinguishing the same letter is also accomplished through the processes of taking apart and reassembly. A complete word is often comprised of several letters. We have to take apart the word into the letters that comprise it and then connect them to the whole that constitutes the complete word. When we come to the sentence, we have to take it apart into words and then reconnect them to the whole sentence, the sentences in the paragraph, and the paragraphs in the complete story or article.

We mediate this skill of analysis and synthesis to the child. The transcendence principle in mediation requires it to "go beyond" the concrete task to other tasks in order to create a principle or cognitive structure (see Introduction to the Theory). For example, I might wish to teach a child to jump. The jumping process will be broken down into its components (analysis). We first stand with our feet together, then bend the knees, lift our heels off the ground, and, boom... we have jumped. In the case of writing, the mediator moves the process to the cognitive level of "understanding" the letter through deconstruction and reassembly, as we have described these actions.

It is important to note that the mediator is not satisfied with imparting writing skills. Rather, she seeks to give the recipient of the mediation a thought structure with extensive effects. In this sense, writing and its importance are a means for the crucial skill of analysis-synthesis. We teach the child the principle that everything in our world is comprised of sub-systems/elements with part-whole relations between them. The client, whose behavior is frequently characterized by Feuerstein's deficient cognitive function of the *episodic grasp of reality,* struggles precisely at the interface between the part and the whole. He struggles to connect experiences, to link one behavioral stage with the next. His life is made up of isolated fragments.

Our work breaks down this block of analysis and synthesis into three treatment stages:

1   The first part treats analysis and synthesis through lines and shapes.
2   The second part goes from the shape mode to the verbal mode. It deals with the relationship between the part and the whole in the world of words.
3   The third part refers to the part-whole relationship in the world of the word, sentence, paragraph, and concept.

Let us consider the first stage, that of lines, shapes, and letters. Many ASD individuals have good visual perception but are missing the cognitive operation that verbalizes the parts and the whole. As a result, they are unable to rely on their perception, no matter how good it is.

Steve is a fourteen-year-old autistic boy who has been treated with the Feuerstein Method at the Feuerstein Institute since he was four years old. He began working with me on the "Organization of Dots" instrument.

The client uses the "Organization of Dots" instrument to deal with a random cloud of dense points to find a pattern given to him in advance as a kind of model. As can be seen on the page shown here, the models are made from a square and triangle.

The desired shapes "catch ones eye", but when I asked Steve to describe how a square is built (e.g., "From how many lines?" "What is their length—equal or unequal?" "How many angles does the square have?" "What is an angle?"), he could not respond. Additionally, he did not know the relationship between the different shapes comprising the square or triangle. We saw that Steve's problem was not just his inability to apply the different shapes and connect them; he would also not use the strategies that we tried to teach him.

Understanding the part-whole relationship of shapes, is a precondition for writing. We first deal with the shapes' characteristics, which are not necessarily graphic. Moreover, we try to start this preparation at a very young age. We talk about writing with the child, but we don't really start there. I shall elaborate on this now.

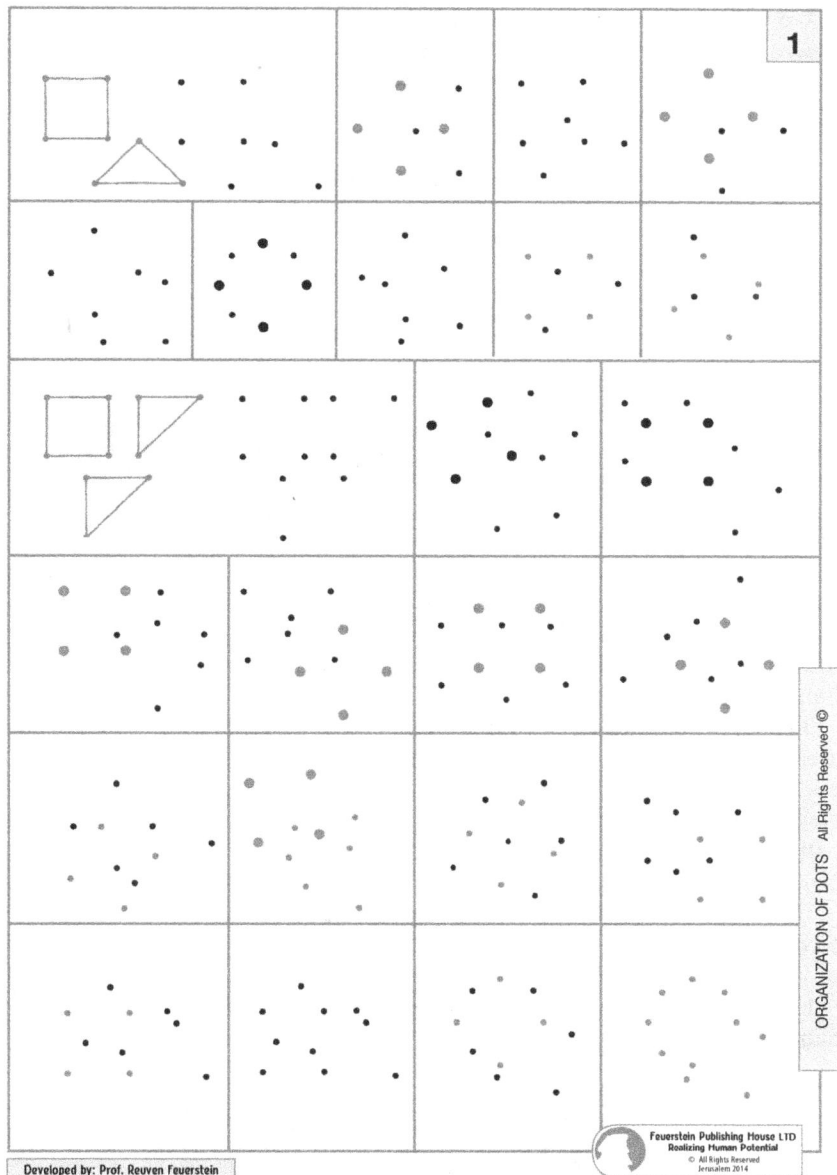

Figure 8.3 Organization of Dots.
Source: © Feuerstein™ Publishing House Ltd, R. Feuerstein (1960)

We will be dealing here with two types of mediation: *preparatory mediation*, and mediation that concerns actual writing. We begin the *preparatory mediation* at the age of two or three, at which point we already apply tangible means to mediate the part-whole relationship. For example, we might take a fruit, cut it in two, and then put it back together. All along, we show the child how we take it apart and put it back together into a whole. Additionally, beginning when the child reaches the age of two, we try to teach him to say words in their correct context of "part whole" relationships.

We use puzzles that are built on the part-whole principle, or dolls that can be taken apart and reassembled. The emphasis is on the use of objects known to the child from daily life, from which the understanding of the part-whole relationship emerges.

We gradually move from the tangible to the more complex, such as picture cards followed by more figurative and less realistic picture cards and puzzles of animals. These are followed by puzzles in which each part has no meaning unless assembled, such as a puzzle of the human body comprising hands, feet, head, and so on. The next stage deals with spatial relationships such as "left-right" and "up-down." We accompany each demonstration with verbalization in order to create internal representations that are the basis for comprehension. The objective is to develop in the child an internal language that he can later use to explain the world to himself without external mediation.

The mediator tries to expand the part-whole perception to other content areas; this is the goal of mediating structural change (*Mediation for Transcendence*). We want the child to be able to handle a social problem in the classroom; thus, we want him to know how to ask himself: "What do I do with this friend? I see from his face that he is angry or happy. I angered him, or alternatively, I said something nice to him. How shall I go on from here?"

In the third stage, we move on to apply the same mediation at the level of the word, sentence and paragraph. This time, the analysis is at the level of the word, which has to be broken down into letters.

Hebrew, for example, has two kinds of letters: print/machine letters and handwriting. (See Figure 8.4)

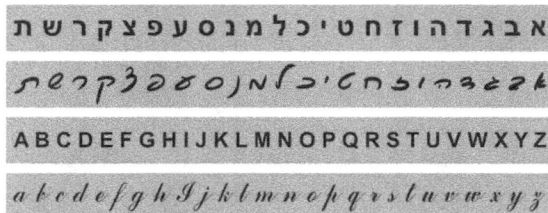

Figure 8.4 Hebrew and English Alphabets.

These letters somewhat parallel writing in European languages. Schools tend to begin handwriting with rounded script, which allows for a full flowing movement. There is no need (and it is also difficult) to use such script for analysis and synthesis. The letters are written by a full hand movement, so there is no need to refer to the parts of the letter. That is why many schools print letters (comparable to using capital letters). Conversely, we recommend starting with printed letters, because that makes it possible for us to break down the operation into its parts, and to mediate with the child how to interpret visual stimuli as well as letters and words that he encounters. Furthermore, as we have emphasized, it is necessary to mediate to the child how to organize the world around him even without external mediation.

It takes a long time for some clients to learn to read and write. They may acquire reading *through* writing because we prefer to combine the activities rather than isolate them—the latter is liable to severely burden their input processes. Additionally, we integrate the two processes because we want the writing process to be more than merely technical or functional; that is, we want it to have meaning. By using letters that I wrote for something, I can read them, I can write to someone. This is not a technical process. It is what Feuerstein called *Mediation for Meaning*; namely, the mediator creates with the recipient of the mediation an emotional urge to use information mediated for him. He is not just a mediator of skills or knowledge; he creates the internal urge to use them.

It is important to note that the aforementioned mediation process is not dichotomous. Thus, the stages have no sharp beginning and end points. We move back and forth between them, from the level of the letter and lines to the level of the word. When we have reached the level of the word with the child, we return to the part-whole level of the letter, lines, and shapes, in order to strengthen what has been taught but, even more, to create a coherent understanding of the part-whole. This, then, is not a separate topic, but a single principle applied across the different levels of function.

Lucy, whom we met above, was diagnosed with autism at an early age. When she came to us, she showed significant behavioral control difficulties and obsessive engagement with objects and their order. She also suffered from severe motor dyspraxia (difficulty in performing planned actions), expressed in simple motor activities. We observed the deficient cognitive function of *impulsive behavior* and, frequently, even aggression. Furthermore, it was extremely difficult to reach her for reciprocal communication. Even in the presence of adults who were very attached to her, Lucy was preoccupied with an imaginary world which (as we saw) included arranging all her dolls and objects. She resisted cooperating in both structured tasks and freer ones, such as tasks of enjoyment. In one class, the treatment task was writing, which was undertaken simultaneously with the reading acquisition process. These efforts followed numerous attempts in other places and by other methods.

Case Study: Lucy (continued)

> *Lucy arrived at the Feuerstein Institute with an experience of previous unsuccessful attempts to bring her to acquire these skills. The treatment goal was to help her integrate into a school structure. She learned how to write her name after a year of intervention. Lucy exhibited a significant blocking response to the very engagement in graphic activities, even when they were wholly spontaneous, because of a fear of failure. Even after she succeeded in achieving some kind of output after investing a great effort, and the output was comprehensible and good, she tore up the pages and scribbled on them. Despite the motor graphic difficulty, she grasped the substance of writing. She understood that writing is a means of communication and the development of ideas. She understood exactly the uses that she could make of writing. "I can write a letter." "I can make a shopping list for mommy." Nonetheless, she struggled to muster the strength for the task of writing. Her difficulty was centered on analysis and synthesis; thus, it was hard for her to distinguish between the different parts that comprise each letter. Later, we also observed that she struggled to establish the relationship between letters and words. It was difficult for her to read a whole word as she tended to drop and transpose letters. This difficulty also appeared in copying shapes. Thus, when she had to copy a square, for which purpose she was asked to say how many lines it had, she would say as many as seven or eight, or three; in other words, even when she did not need to create a graphic form or draw what she saw, it was difficult for her to distinguish the shape. She simply did not see the starting point and terminal point of the line.*
>
> *To introduce Lucy to the world of writing in a way that would be less threatening to her, it was clear to us that it was necessary to delay her writing skills until she achieved success in the* Mediation for a Feeling of Competence. *We began with an intervention in drawing, a favorite activity for her. Through drawing, it became possible to mediate for analysis and synthesis.*
>
> *At this point, Lucy's drawings became rather repetitive. They were usually images of a boy, girl, and dog, and later, a house. She represented them with circles and lines. It was very important to Lucy to combine the known with the familiar, which was a new phenomenon for her. Retaining what was taught gave her the sense of experiment and capability about this skill, which initially was exceedingly difficult for her.*

Conversely, through the mediation, it was possible to add things that were new to her, based on what she already knew. In this way, on the basis of the shape that had been learned, it was possible to add new items. If Lucy had learned how to draw a square, it was possible to mediate her to draw a triangle, and subsequently to use the square and triangle for the dog of the family house into which she inserted the different figures. We tried to instill in her some kind of symbolic meaning to emphasize that the drawing was not merely of people, but of her family or her beloved cousins. The mediation process was based on a process of building and dismantling drawings. We then moved on to tactile shapes, using different colors for lines in different positions. We sought lines of different directions and lengths in a room. After we felt that she really controlled the part-whole relationship in the different concepts, we switched to the graphic modality that was so strongly blocked. It is important to mention that this entire process was accompanied by highly intensive *Mediation for a Feeling of Competence.* The advantage of using the tactile shapes was that even if she made a mistake, it could be corrected. We also worked on the graphic modality such that the client drew line after line until the square was complete. Feuerstein called this process *Distance Mediation.* Thus, we did Mediation at Zero Distance, in which the mediator actually holds the hand of the recipient of the mediation; as success and capability are achieved, she distances himself from the recipient. This model, in which the mediator and Lucy simultaneously drew lines, helped Lucy to restrain her impulsiveness.

Ultimately, Lucy succeeded in performing the task herself. She did not even need to copy the shape because she had internalized the shapes through the conceptualization and verbalization built into the mediation process. This process of analysis and synthesis helped Lucy far beyond forming the simple structure of a letter; it helped her to grasp her need for *planning and precision.* We might say that it built her need to construct internal schematics and precision of concepts, a need that had not appeared spontaneously.

One might ask: why did we persist for so long in our mediation attempt? The answer is that we were essentially teaching Lucy a new language. We observed how she grasped the principle and learned to apply it in diverse disciplines. Lucy is now freely writing full pages.

The third stage in this process is understanding the relationship between the part and the whole in a sentence, paragraph and idea. This concerns less the technical aspect of how I shape a letter or assemble a word and more the aspect of content. It is important to realize that, in order to attend to content, a certain degree of fluency in the technical skill of writing (or reading) must be present. For the child to be able to produce letters and words automatically, he must understand how to break them down and reassemble them. At that point, he can pay more attention to the concept, and the analysis and synthesis become far more abstract.

There is a major shift from the second to the third stage, when we reach the section and paragraph stage. The analysis in this stage not only includes reference to words, but also how we break down the concept that we want to write about.

Let us return to Steve, whom we met above. Steve has very strong abilities in some fields; he can even be called an autodidact. He taught himself to read and write at a very young age—but only technically, without any functional use in either reading or writing. In contrast to Lucy, who saw letters and words as a way to communicate and as a means to express ideas, Steve did not understand the communicative aspect of words. But he did grasp the technical aspect with ease—again, unlike Lucy. Treatment aimed to help Steve make functional use of reading and writing as a means of communication. We began with writing email to family and friends. In each session, Steve would choose someone he wanted to write a letter to, and that is how we practiced writing.

The analysis and synthesis mediation process began in emails sent to him, to which he sent an email in response. The analysis process included reference to the context of the text sent him, the syntax of the text, and its language structure. We took letters and analyzed their structure. Thus, he came to understand that, "first of all, there is a request with my name, followed by a question, 'How am I?' I am then asked a question. I am included in some kind of experience, with more and more information added."

The first step was to teach Steve to systematically analyze the text and mine it for retrievable principles which could be used to write letters of his own. The use of analysis and comprehension of how letters are built helped him to understand the nature of his communication through writing. Writing became another tool for describing his experiences in his internal world, experiences that he struggled to convey verbally. He also learned to tailor content to the different people he corresponded with; thus, one email to someone was based on the previous email to that person. In this way, his communications systems ceased to be *episodic*. The reader will note that the operation of analysis and synthesis is multifaceted and has many consequences. It can be seen how, in this case, the mediation, which emphasizes cognitive structures of analysis and synthesis, influences subjects that are not cognitive in themselves. The ability to communicate, to write—that is, social skills—were all harnessed from this cognitive operation. Steve developed an ability to use his friend's name, his cousin's name, and his brother's name as a result of these processes. In effect, the third part of this building block deals with context in its broad sense; the ability to see the parts in the context of a whole—the ability to see their relative relationship in the overall context. And the context, unlike previous stages, takes into account the child's inner world, as we saw in Steve's case study. This means that the "context"' includes at this stage also the inner world of the child. This naturally touches on the parameter of the learning, which mediates such *Mediation for Meaning* which is largely responsible for creating internal motivation (the interests) of the child. Because the challenges facing them on the technical level are liable to be very great, we insist that the effort that the child has to invest will be meaningful for him. For one child, it might be a beloved snack; for another, it could be dinosaurs or important people, such as his father and mother.

As Feuerstein Method therapists, we never leave the meaning to a later stage. The *mediation for meaning* accompanies the mediation throughout the different operations. Even when we do not find a topic that is significant for the child, we will mediate and build it for him.

It is important to remember that in the context of *mediation for meaning,* we also try to increase the *mediation distance* and gradually bring the child to independence in this area.

Case Study: Jason

> *Jason struggled to write, and when he successfully wrote letters and words, he struggled to connect them. We struggled to find something that would be a meaningful factor for him. It was suggested to us that we use the bathroom euphemisms "number one and number two", because that is something that every child knows. The breakthrough came through numbers. He enjoyed arranging numbers and his writing began with numbers, which are very significant for him. He gives them meaning. If, for example, we arrange numbers by order, "1" represents the first thing in the treatment, "2" represents the second thing, and "3" the third thing. The numbers 1,2, and 3 represent candies that the child wants to receive. The idea is to give meaning to a number for a continuum so that the numbers do not remain abstractions. Thus, writing numbers took on a communicative aspect—something with meaning that was not merely technical.*

One of the stages that we see with ASD clients in the area of writing is the point at which the child understands someone else can understand what he wrote, which means that it can serve as communication. It is a major breakthrough when a child realizes why he is writing.

Case Study: Steve (continued)

> *As Steve's mother was ill at the time of one appointment, he came with his father. It was hard for the child to cope with this change. It was a stormy day and also just before a long vacation. Numerous things were bothering him. He was my third client of the day; I was preceded by two therapists who tried to calm him down, with only limited success. He was still extremely excited when he entered my office. I tried to talk with him about what had happened and why he was so excited. Steve ultimately took a piece of paper and wrote, "I want to go to the bathroom." I told him that I now understood that something was bothering him, that he asked to go to the bathroom, and that I would wait for him. When he returned, he was still very excited. I told him, "Steve, you said that you needed to go to the bathroom, and you went. What do you want now? You're excited and it is hard for you to sit. You want to say something?"*

He wrote, "I'm excited that my father is here in Jerusalem."
This use of a piece of paper as a means of expressing emotion and needs
vis-a-vis another person was a breakthrough, following prolonged effort.

With young children who have not yet reached this stage, we take the sheet of paper on which they wrote outside the therapy room and show it someone, thus mediating for the child his use of the writing as a means of communication. At the end of class, we show the text to the parent, and we might buy something at the Institute cafe and show the note, or hang it on the notice board. Naturally, we mediate the step with the child so he will understand its significance.

It is important to note that, frequently, when one teaches writing, one does so in the context of a developmental continuum (e.g., the Hebrew alphabet, where it is much easier to write certain letters than others, which are built on the diagonal). We could deal with the diagonals at a later stage, because they require the use of the brain's two hemispheres and demand use of the diagonal line.

Yet, we do not do this. Rather, we begin with letters that are difficult to write but which have personal significance for the child (e.g., those that make up his name). This seems like an absurdity; it is precisely with the child who struggles to write and may even have dyspraxia that we start with the difficult letters. But because communication is intrinsic to writing, we favor it over the developmental continuum. This continuum would suggest beginning with the easier letters, whereas the Feuerstein Method holds that we should engage in meaningful writing by choosing letters that are significant to the child.

Case Study: Lucy (continued)

A therapist presented Lucy with an ornamented designer notebook of the kind that she liked. Initially, she wrote items related to the games that she played during the treatment. If a memory game was being played, for example, she wrote down the words on cards that she had found. It was clear to her that this writing helped her. Accordingly, she was prepared to make an effort to do something that she had been previously unwilling to do.

In this chapter, we have tried to show the real goal of mediation. Crucially, mediation does not consist of teaching skills—that, rather, is the goal of instruction. The goal of the Feuerstein Method, by contrast, is to change the way that one approaches the world. The specific skill—writing, in this case—is a means for instilling a proper perception of the relationship between the child and the world around him. It can be said that within the cognitive structure of communications and the correct relationship with one's surroundings, writing is an important element—but only one element among many that Piaget and Feuerstein called a cognitive structure.

Moreover, we have tried to illustrate the spiral-like nature of mediation; it entails an ever-expanding circling back, an encircling that nourishes the growing interior circles. Thus, the process is distinctly non-linear. We saw how the three stages in the process mediate the analysis-synthesis operation—developing, repeating, and strengthening the previous stages.

The third important principle is *Mediation for Meaning*. We saw how we choose to create meaning for the child even at the expense of the convenience of teaching particular content. This principle guides many of the Feuerstein Method interventions, because when the mediation recipient experiences meaning, it causes him to gather the resources needed to deal with the many challenges that he faces.

Finally, and no less importantly, meaning creates a tangible connection between the acquired skill and the world. It is meaning, first and foremost, that ensures that the child's new skill will become part of him and used by him to relate differently to his surroundings.

Reference

Vygotsky, L. S. *Thought and Language.* Cambridge, MA: MIT Press, 1962.

Chapter 9

Cognitive Therapy through the Motor Modality with ASD Individuals

Debbie Nadler and Ayelet-Hashahar Aithan

Introduction

The Feuerstein Method (FM), used in various fields and modalities with children diagnosed with ASD, is based on Feuerstein's Structural Cognitive Modifiability (SCM) theory and Mediated Learning Experience (MLE) theory. For the Feuerstein therapist, conclusions made by a static diagnosis/assessment (see Introduction to the Theory) do not constitute a final and absolute judgment. Instead, we set far-reaching goals based on the results of Feuerstein's cognitive-dynamic assessment (LPAD; see Chapter 4 and 5).

The main goal of this method for ASD individuals is to develop their learning modalities, emotion, communication, and operational thinking, and to provide them with tools for improved adaptation. We must believe in their ability to make a significant change in their functioning and to always assume that they understand more than we would think they do. Taking into account not only what we see at the present time with an ASD individual but also what we might see in the future will change the way we relate to them. The changes we seek to achieve are structural ones that impact the overall functioning and development of the individual.

Dynamic cognitive therapy through the motor modality is one of the therapies based on the FM for treating those on the autism spectrum. This form of therapy aims to draw ASD individuals out of their "bubble," to explore, discover, and experience the world as a safe place full of meaningful experiences which can be empowering and enjoyable. The therapy combines different types of movement (e.g. aerobics, yoga, therapeutic sports, etc.) depending on the client's age, level of functioning and treatment goals. The uniqueness of the treatment is that it uses MLE criteria (see Introduction to the Theory), and it aims to strengthen the deficient cognitive functions and operations that are necessary for acquiring basic life skills (as defined by Feuerstein).

There are intervention methods that emphasize the linear transition between development stages and argue that it is not possible to move to

DOI: 10.4324/9781003451136-10

the next stage if the previous step has not yet been achieved. Feuerstein, by contrast, argued that while the sequence of stages is important, the transition through them is not necessarily linear. Mediation has the power to precede the acquisition of one stage before the other, and vice versa.

In dynamic cognitive therapy through the motor modality, the ASD individual is exposed to a wide range of cognitive, motor, sensory, and emotional experiences and stimuli. We encourage the client to progress and provide him with mediation and complex tasks. The treatment follows the dynamic approach, which attempts to discover the child's abilities and make the mediator, parents and child aware of which mediation methods and thinking strategies were most effective for the child.

Therapy using the FM is interdisciplinary, as described at length in this book. Treatment through the motor modality has unique advantages:

1   Movement is a primary ability in the development of our early sensory systems. It affects motor-perceptual skills (e.g., auditory distinction, speech and language, visual discrimination and intentional activity), and other higher-level skills (e.g., complex motor skills, organized behavior and self-image; Kranowitz, 2005).
2   Physical activity promotes the creation of new nerve cells and increases oxygen supply to the brain. This, in turn, improves concentration and learning ability (Ratey & Hagerman, 2008).
3   Therapy using the motor and sensory modalities comes naturally to children; they enjoy the treatment and it helps their brains regulate sensory information that affects their functioning. Therapy through movement creates openness to mediation, improved listening, and implementation of instructions in a practical and effective way.
4   The movement modality is universal and does not depend on prior knowledge or a particular culture. This enables optimal adaptation to each child and collaborative work with children from completely different backgrounds and different levels.
5   This modality is particularly suitable for children diagnosed with ASD because it is concrete. Thus, non-verbal children can take an active part in the therapy, which does not require language for its implementation.

Case Study: Martin

Seven-year-old Martin, diagnosed with ASD, had no verbal ability. He received treatment at the Feuerstein Institute for a total of four weeks. During this period, a marked improvement was seen in his communication abilities and cognitive abilities. In one conversation with his parents, they expressed their disappointment that Martin was unable to communicate and play with his only brother, who is very close to him in age. We invited Peter, Martin's brother, to the Institute for a joint lesson to see how we could develop the communication between them. For this purpose, a lesson was chosen in the movement modality that enables children of different levels to work together. The treatment was exceptionally successful. At first, Peter sat in front of Martin. They were asked to perform quick tasks that did not require much planning, such as inserting blocks into a specially designed bar. Martin took out a cube, placed it close to him and called Peter to take the cube (as requested by the mediator). Martin looked at his brother, took the cube from his hands and placed it in the bar. Afterward, the roles were reversed, and Martin imitated the model his brother used in the previous task. The tasks presented to them were adapted for working together using different sensory stimuli. The activities were goal oriented and included turn-taking, consideration for the other, flexibility, accuracy in carrying out tasks, and more. After creating an atmosphere of movement and learning in the room, we were able to move on to tasks that required processing and storage of more complex information, such as arranging objects in sequence according to their size and other criteria. Martin showed great tolerance towards his brother and was very focused on the tasks. The treatment was exciting and aroused interest in both of them; in fact, Peter enjoyed the session as much as Martin. The results of the intervention changed their parents' emotional stance, since the treatment provided clear evidence that Martin and Peter were able to achieve a mutually enjoyable interaction.

Thanks to the motor aspect of this activity, in which the brothers shared interest and ability (movement), they engaged enjoyably with one another. In other modalities, this was not possible, owing to the large gap between them with respect to interests and motivation. Because the movement modality invites nonverbal communication such as eye contact, facial expressions, gestures, and joint action, it fosters connection.

This modality is suitable for intervention from an early age. Cognitive learning through movement is not based on prior formal knowledge. As such, it is also suitable for children without formal knowledge or with a history of failure in formal educational frameworks that created blocking responses, opposition and avoidance behavior.

Case Study: Bryan

Bryan is an eighteen-year-old boy diagnosed with ASD. He has no verbal ability and has dyspraxia (difficulty in conceptualization, motor planning and skilled performance of unfamiliar activities), which makes it hard for him to perform daily tasks. Bryan displays a pattern of passive behavior and lack of initiative. He tried multiple therapy methods over the years with some success but had a lot of bad experiences. Upon arrival at the Institute he demonstrated a great deal of anxious behavior and passivity. He received daily treatment at the Institute for a long period of time, accompanied by his mother. The multidisciplinary team worked intensively with Bryan and his mother to increase his independence and help him become more active. Bryan did not show any interest in cognitive therapies that aimed to develop his thinking skills and learning strategies. He would stare at the therapist, make noises, flap his hands, and take a long time to answer or follow instructions. In the movement therapies, on the other hand, Bryan would function in a completely different way. As soon as he grasped the rhythm and sequence of action (or counting), he was able to perform exercises involving movement imitation, to continue/repeat the exercise as many times as he was asked and even initiate some activities of his own. Following a process or sequence was generally very difficult for him, but here in the movement modality, Bryan was eventually able to completely internalize various complex movement sequences. Considerable improvement was seen, and progress was made in his ability to achieve fuller independence.

In this modality, one can study content that requires complex and abstract thinking such as the establishment of basic concepts, reading, and mathematical thinking. Many studies have found that the use of "space" is more efficient than formal learning (e.g., Prostig, 1994) emphasizes the connection between learning and movement). Mathematical reasoning, for example, can be learned through movement; ascending and descending steps invites counting and the conservation of quantity. The development of symbolization (necessary for language acquisition) can be carried out through the practice of body posture and naming exercises, where students learn to associate a pose and carry out a body posture according to its name. Symbolization is often challenging for ASD individuals. When children learn to associate a pose with its name or perform a body posture according to its name, they are learning symbolization. That is because learning the name of the posture depends on an associative relationship between it and the object it mentions. We may use a children's card game where each card has two tabs: one is a picture of a child doing a pose and the other is the object it is associated with. The child is asked to choose from a number of options in order to match the pose with the object or vice versa in a form of a matching pairs game. This game allows for nonverbal expression.

Furthermore, ASD children may feel a strong need for movement or sensation, and thus may struggle in formal learning settings which require sitting for extended periods of time on a chair.

The movement modality provides the ASD child with the opportunity to expand his repertoire of movements, social games, and pursuits. It helps him to use tools and objects in a functional way, such as correctly using forceps to grasp objects or a hammer. Stereotypical motions that seem pointless can be transformed into functional target movements. Thus, repetitive movements like tapping on the table can be encouraged at a certain rate, using counting and stopping, or obsessive movements such as the excessive rotation of objects can be used to spin a spinning top.

Certain targeted movements stimulate and activate brain areas that require development. For example, the crossing of the body's midline and cross and parallel movements create a balance between the brain lobes. This can promote thinking processes and functioning in ASD children.

The Building Blocks that Constitute Intervention Targets:

Therapy using the movement modality is composed of a number of important "building blocks" that are worked on simultaneously. The work is done in an integrated way, focusing in parallel on several building blocks. When progress is made in an area that is more advanced, it builds on more "basic" building blocks that were previously treated. These interactions are not random but are a direct result of the mediation process, which is concerned not only with imparting the specific building block but with linking it to the previous blocks. For example, treating Building Block #4 (developing the ability to imitate movement) rests on Building Block #1 (developing communication ability). Building Block #6 (developing spatial concepts) builds on Building Block #5 (creating the perception and understanding of the part-whole relationship and body schema).

Building Block #1: Communication Ability

ASD individuals tend to require a great deal of mediation for establishing contact. They are likely to exhibit the cognitive function in the output phase called *egocentric forms of communication*. This communication is not necessarily understood by others. Thus, the client will receive mediation in order to develop basic communication abilities such as recognition of the "other," eye contact, reciprocity, and sharing.

Communication begins with the parent-infant relationship. At its root rests physical contact, eye contact, fulfilment of the baby's needs, and maternal speech to the baby. Think, for a moment, of the parent's smile as they attribute meaning to their baby's involuntary lip twitching. Responding to the baby's needs is an important component of the parent-infant relationship. This is the first stage in the development of communication—in order to get his/her needs met, the baby learns to express them. When communication difficulties are apparent, we select activities and stimuli that will stimulate the client's need for and motivation to cooperate, respond, and communicate.

Many individuals diagnosed with ASD have sensory difficulties. Stimuli that provide a response to sensory needs create and strengthen internal motivation for collaboration, learning, mediation and communication. This treatment is accompanied by a *Mediation for Meaning*—needs are met in joint activities, and it becomes pleasant to be in contact with others.

In order to lead the client to change, the mediator will first try to connect with him where he is. From there, the mediator will slowly but surely lead him where they wants to take him. A famous story from the parables of Rabbi Nachman of Breslau[1] (Hazan, 1896) demonstrates this sort of treatment: It seems that the son of a king "went crazy" and thought he was a turkey. Sure enough, in good turkey fashion, he sat beneath the table naked, eating breadcrumbs. The doctors despaired of healing the prince until one sage arrived, undressed, and joined the young man under the table. He too, he explained to the prince, was a turkey. In this way, the sage slowly succeeded in bringing the king's son back to health.

In the current case of Building Block #1, mediation is provided on focusing on others, establishing emotional contact, eye contact, reciprocity, and sharing. Initially, the mediator follows the child's gaze in order to get him to lock eyes with him and tries to maintain it, taking advantage of the intervals to establish contact (bonding). Props such as rattles can attract the child's attention and cause him to focus his gaze on the therapist in order to strengthen eye contact, and accessories such as massage balls help address the client's sensory needs and boost his motivation to forge a relationship. Through eye contact, cooperation and recognition of the other, are built. Thus, a child who is more interested in objects than in people finds himself in contact and communication with others and enjoys the benefit of joint activity and mutual communication. The mediator reveals this to the child verbally, thereby deepening the experience.

Mediation for Sharing Behavior is done gradually in a relaxed, enabling and accepting environment, which respects the child and his need for space. A balance is maintained between actively trying to engage the child and giving the child space to approach the mediator when he wishes. During treatment, activities are chosen that encourage the development of eye contact and reciprocity with a partner, such as passing a ball from one to the other. Movement imitation exercises are chosen that encourage focused eye contact, and sometimes the mediator will even hold the child in front of him and focus him as part of the movement.

The mediator will provide *Mediation for Intentionality*. Thus, he will use different means in accordance with the needs of the child, such as varying speech tones and rhythms, facial expressions, proximity to the child, presentation and use of stimuli, and so on. The purpose of this mediation is to get the child to focus on the mediator. Later, mediation is reduced in accordance with the child's responses.

Case Studies: Jon and Liam

Jon, aged six, is a charming, gentle, and intelligent child diagnosed with ASD. Jon had sensory sensitivity to touch and sound (the auditory system) and needed sensory stimulation. He came to the Feuerstein Institute for 6 weeks of intensive therapy. At first Jon walked around the room, barely cooperating and made little eye contact. The mediator had to gently follow Jon in order to try and initiate interaction, eye contact, and connection. Whenever Jon responded to contact from the mediator, his need for sensory stimulation was provided for by means of accessories, touch, movement and the use of quiet, soft, slow speech. The mediator remained fully present with Jon the whole time, joining his activities and imitating his behavior. At first, Jon looked only at the objects but gradually, he started to look more and more at the mediator. She was able to slowly and gradually pull him in to a joint activity on the mattress. The mediator used positions and movement that enabled eye contact, focused gaze, and concentration on others. The activity was accompanied by emotional reflection and the mediation for the meaning of communication. 'When you express your needs, I can meet them and then you feel more comfortable.' 'Isn't it fun for us to play together.' 'I am so happy that you look into my eyes and hold my hand.' 'I am happy to see you happy and relaxed.' Eye contact, connection and attachment increased in quantity and quality. Slowly but surely, Jon responded to the mediator's attempts to connect with him and later even initiated contact with her. An increase was seen in reciprocity, cooperation and enjoyment and they built a close and warm relationship.

Five-year-old Liam was diagnosed with ASD and referred to the Feuerstein Institute after receiving treatment in several other settings but in which he had trouble participating. His parents reported that the initial stage of making contact with the therapist was a stumbling block for Liam that often kept the treatment short. When a therapist would approach him, talk to him, show him attractive stimuli or invite him to interact, Liam would feel threatened and shut himself off, fleeing to the other side of the room. When the therapist was stricter or forced him to sit or cooperate, Liam resisted and blocked any interaction. When Liam entered my room, I noticed that he briefly looked at me with a fearful look in his eyes. He ran to the corner of the room and sat down on the floor. From this, I understood that the first thing I should try to do was create a relaxed and non-threatening atmosphere for him. I stayed where I was and started talking to Liam's parents. I tried to speak in a calm, slow voice with pauses between sentences. I introduced myself to them and explained to them what I do in my treatment, when in fact my main intention was that my words should reach Liam. I respected Liam's personal space and did not try to invade it prematurely. From time to time, Liam would turn to look at the table where we were sitting and then hide his face between his legs. Over time, something in his expression seemed to soften. I played with his parents a game they said he liked, and then I clearly saw that he was watching and following the game. I felt that Liam was getting used to my room and my presence. When I took out a ball and approached slowly with a smile toward Liam, he made prolonged eye contact with me. Liam reached out his hands and together we began to roll the ball on his body, which answered his sensory need and enlisted his motivation to cooperate. It was then possible to roll the ball between us - an action chosen for the purpose of building a relationship and reciprocity. The treatment continued using the motor modality which met his sensory and motor needs and was done in a slow, relaxed manner that respected Liam's personal space. Mediation for Intentionality and Reciprocity through the motor modality built a connection and enabled the treatment to move forward and for Liam to achieve significant goals.

After actively trying to engage the child, we try to entice him to initiate contact with the mediator. At first, we may do something fun or something that meets his need in order to capture his attention and try to increase the number of times he responds as mediation is reduced. A balance must be struck between actively drawing him in and encouraging him to approach the mediator himself.

Throughout the treatment, the mediator supports the appearance of any communication from the client. Non-verbal individuals are required to communicate through learned gestures or an augmentative communication device (or a combination of them) and thus express their wishes and needs. The communication device may includes universal symbols of several words which the therapist will verbalize as he points to them (hello, goodbye, more, finished, happy, tired, frustrated, need for toilet, etc.) Each device is built specially by the department's speech and language therapists to match the client's needs. The communication device is used as an initial "cognitive crutch" for the client to acquire and use language. All the while, the mediator moves the client toward being able to initiate, be understood by others, and express himself, thus preventing frustration and eliminating egocentric communication. Later, we try to lead the client to use clear language.

Children often show increased motivation when using communicative language for sensory stimulation, such as the use of the word "more" while the therapist turns the child on a specially designed plate-like device, and the word "this" when selecting a preferred physical activity (from cards displaying pictures of various activities, such as trampoline, balance board, basketball, etc.). We have seen many children who, when in motion, produce spontaneous speech—words come out without them realizing it.

Case Study: Russell

> *Russell is a sweet and graceful six-year-old boy. He was diagnosed with nonverbal ASD and has been using assistive communication through his iPad. Russell has a sensory difficulty characterized by an intense need for sensory stimulation to feel satisfied. He constantly searches for sensory stimulation in the form of deep pressure touch, mainly by taking off his shoes at every opportunity and jumping on tiptoe. Russell also exhibits hypersensitivity to any sudden or strong noise, becoming tense and restless. He responds positively to* Mediation for Intentionality and Reciprocity *as well as to slow speech that is quiet and accentuated with exaggerated and clear facial expressions. Under these conditions, he can maintain eye contact with the mediator for a long time and express his enjoyment when engaging in joint activities with*

the mediator. A sensorimotor activity within the treatment framework provides Russell with alternative proprioceptive stimulation. This is provided in conjunction with mediation and communication with the mediator. For example, jumping on a trampoline with the mediator in front of him holding her hands and jumping at her counting pace creates a state of openness to mediation, where Russell trusts the mediator and allows her to lead him more easily to what she has to offer. He is willing to experiment with new and complex tasks he has not previously agreed to. After this sort of activity, sitting at a table and concentrating on lengthy cognitive tasks becomes much easier for Russell.

In the FM, treatment is frequently one-to-one, which permits focused work and the formulation of goals that match the needs of each child. However, dynamic cognitive therapy using the movement modality can also be provided in small groups (about five children) with several staff members. If the children in the group are low functioning, sometimes it is necessary to assign a mediator to each child to mediate when necessary. Group therapy allows for work on communication and social components that are expressed more naturally in a group setting. Emphasis is placed on the transfer of skills learned in the group to everyday life. The mediation given in the group is more distanced and requires the child to focus his attention on a mediator who adapts himself to the entire group. A prominent advantage of group therapy is the child's natural imitation of others in the peer group.

Case Study: Matthew

Matthew is a six-year-old boy diagnosed with ASD. He was non- verbal and physically disabled (mostly in his lower extremities). Matthew came to the Feuerstein Institute in Jerusalem for six weeks of intensive therapy to try and advance his skills and to provide his parents and teachers with recommendations for continuing treatment. In one-on-one treatments, Matthew showed little interest in interacting with the mediator and in the treatment itself. Despite the extensive use of mediation and efforts to find things of interest that might arouse his curiosity, he showed passive, unmotivated behavior and lack of interest. He bowed his head and looked at the shadow created by the movement of his hands and did not want to stop to look at the therapist or an object. After some time, partial success was seen in attaining eye contact and paying attention to stimuli, and he would sometimes express short-term pleasure from an activity. However, all the therapists had the same feeling that Matthew still had built a 'wall' that we had not yet been able to penetrate and discover his true abilities. After integrating Matthew into group therapy in the movement modality with three other children, he appeared to suddenly 'come alive.' Even in the first activity (passing the ball back and forth between the children and saying their names), Matthew raised his head and showed great interest in the group members. He approached the boy who was sitting next to him, looked at him and smiled at him. During the activity, Matthew seemed to want to get close to the group members, but he did not know how to approach them and make contact in a meaningful way. Most of the group activities encouraged all the children's cooperation, such as transferring elastic bands from one child to another in a circle, etc. Matthew got involved in most of the group activities and expressed great pleasure throughout the treatment. The motivation Matthew revealed from the group therapy was taken advantage of in order to teach him social communication norms, openness to mediation and interest in tasks, which influenced his subsequent his individual treatments sessions.

Building Block #2: Building an Understanding of the Therapeutic Framework

Children with ASD may have trouble feeling comfortable within a group or framework. Many ASD children prefer to spend their free time alone. A child with ASD does not necessarily understand (without mediation) what is expected of him and how he should adapt himself. For example, he may not know that in school he is expected to sit quietly on a chair like the rest of the students, and at a family meal he has to abide by appropriate table manners. He may not know what he needs to do and how he needs to behave at celebrations and social events. Understanding where one is and what one needs to do, develops a child's sense of belonging to a particular place, society and framework.

A child with ASD requires an optimal treatment environment that allows him to bring his abilities to the fore. The therapeutic framework aims to enable the child to bring his abilities into expression. In addition, meeting the requirements of the framework prepares the child for inclusion in school and in society in general. The therapeutic framework consists of two dimensions: treatment content, and the manner in which treatment is carried out. The framework describes what drives the selection of the activity that constitutes the treatment. The therapy uses three dimensions of mediation that transform the nature of learning into mediated learning: *Intentionality and Reciprocity, Transcendence* and *Mediation for Meaning* (see Introduction to the Theory).

Treatment is of a structured nature, with much repetition, in order to create a sense of order for the child. This feeling of order enables him to overcome an *episodic grasp of reality* and to build the ability to understand the sequence of the lesson itself (the order of the activities being done). Maintaining the sequence of the lesson is a means of mediating the continuity of time. This may prevent recurring questions like "what is happening next?" or anxiety as a result of uncertainty. The beginning and ending of each session, like some fixed activities during the lesson, remain constant (the order of activities may vary). Alongside repetition in different forms, new content helps develop flexible thinking that enables better internalization of the learned material. Plenty of time is given to the child for information-processing and responses, and a calm and relaxed atmosphere is created with clear boundaries. All these allow the child to bring his learning ability into expression.

Internal motivation is mobilized to encourage learning and avoid conflict and power struggles. The child will be given a choice between two activities and between ways to carry out what is required. The mediator uses positive phrasing—telling the child what is permitted instead of what is prohibited. Additionally, communication should be empathic with clear boundaries—the mediator will listen to the child while offering a limited number of fixed choices and a similarly limited number of flexible ones.

The child is given *Mediation for a Feeling of Competence*. This mediation is provided by recalling successful experiences, setting clear goals, planning, executing, and then interpreting the results. Positive feedback reflects where, precisely, the child succeeded and how, as well as what needs to be improved and how. The feedback enables learning and the ability to reconstruct successes and correct errors.

Case Study: Andy

> *Andy, a five-year-old child diagnosed as low-functioning ASD, was seen at the Feuerstein Institute on a weekly basis. Andy was not verbal and did not use assistive communication spontaneously and consistently. His dynamic cognitive therapy in the motor modality was structured and repetitive in order to help him internalize and assimilate the treatment goals. The therapy made use of Andy's interest in music; mainly playing and listening to songs alongside movement. The treatment began with a preparatory stage where Andy was seated on a mattress, he chose a musical instrument and the mediator sang with him a song he knew. Andy was then required to select a motor activity from two picture cards offered to him. The selected card was attached to the board, thus creating a sequence of activity cards. The treatment ended with Andy lying on the mattress unwinding while he named body parts and did controlled breathing exercises. The structure and sequence of the treatment was emphasized in each session verbally and by singing a short song. In my last treatment with Andy, he surprised me. Uncharacteristically, as he entered the room he sat down on the mattress and reached for an instrument. After the opening song, he went to the place where the picture cards are placed and at the end of the lesson he lay down on his own initiative. This proved to us for the first time that Andy had indeed internalized the treatment framework.*

Building Block #3: The Development of Sensory Movement

Many children on the autistic spectrum exhibit over-reactivity in certain sensory systems and under-reactivity to sensory input from other sensory systems. Sensory imbalance and difficulty in sensory integration make systematic, clear and precise input difficult, and produces an *episodic grasp of reality,* difficulty in combining *sources of information,* and difficulty searching for connections between units of information. All of this creates a screen that interferes with the child's ability to make contact with others—as expressed in the standard diagnosis as a lack of social interest. A child with difficulty in sensory regulation is not "available" to learn. He is busy trying to regulate himself through behaviors that are mostly non-normative.

Feuerstein's dynamic cognitive approach looks for *islets of normalcy* (see Chapter 2) in the child's behavior and ways to expand them. The idea is to use one area of strength to develop other areas of difficulty, in order to build a sense of competence. The movement modality can help children develop strong sensory-motor abilities, through which other areas of difficulty can be strengthened.

Case Study: Julian

> *Julian came to the Feuerstein Institute for a period of five weeks. He was seven years old and diagnosed with ASD. According to his parents, the acquisition of his motor developmental milestones was within the normal range, and some were even earlier than the norm (such as walking before one year of age). Julian's parents reported that he was having a hard time functioning at school and socializing with other children. His strengths lie in his motor skills. For Julian, the most enjoyable part of the entire day is his time spent in the playground. From the moment he reaches the playground, he becomes active and does not give up on any apparatus. He climbs the monkey bars with confidence, swings high and climbs the ladders quickly.*
>
> *Cognitive therapy in the motor modality made use of Julian's strength in this area, where he felt a sense of competence and worked with high motivation and interest to develop areas that were difficult for him. Julian was also required to perform tasks and movement exercises with emphasis on accuracy and quality that were a challenge for him. Examples of activities done with Julian include: an obstacle course involving jumping in hoops, slalom walking between cones, walking under a beam and aiming a ball into a basket. The next time Julian was required to do the obstacle course, the rules changed slightly, and he had to be flexible in how he planned his movements. He had to hop on one leg in the hoops, jump around the cones, go over the beam and then hit the ball with his right hand, and so on.*

When the sensory-motor needs of ASD individuals are met, they become more open to mediation and exploring the world. The mother of Ruth, a four-year-old girl diagnosed with ASD, describes this process in the following way:

> *When I returned home with Ruth after intensive movement therapy, I felt that she was suddenly free to look out into the world and discover it. On the way home, she noticed animals and vehicles that passed by, something that she did not naturally do before. There is no doubt that the sensory-motor treatment accompanied with mediation brought her back into the real world.*

Cognitive dynamic therapy through the motor modality aims not only to help the individual process sensory input in the primary processing system (located in the brain stem), but also to store the sensory information in a more efficient manner (in the cortex). The treatment seeks to create a structural change that can be expanded and transferred to additional fields—and whose influence will continue autonomously. Therefore, stimulation is not just done through the sensory-motor channel, but also involves cognitive components. The therapist provides *Mediation of Meaning* in which the client is helped to understand why he is doing a certain activity; for example: "We will do a weight-bearing exercise so that your hands become stronger and you can write more easily." Proper preparation and explanation for future sensory experience reduces the client's anxiety about the unknown. It also helps him to regulate his emotions and behaviors and ease the transition between different activities and different parts of the day.

A program is built for each client in collaboration with the Clinic's occupational therapy team, which specializes in sensory integration. The program is shared with the client in order to help him regulate himself during the day. The program can be incorporated within home and school activities; it can be done with friends or alone.

David's mother explains:

> *Until he was five years old, our son David, diagnosed with ASD, was in a constant state of frustration and tension; he would bang his chin on the table until he bled. We tried to calm David in every way we could, and worried about him a lot. We arrived at the Institute after much trial and error that did not yield fruit. After the diagnostic process, we received a detailed explanation from the Institute's professionals about David's sensory need, which is 'hunger' for him, owing to the flood of other stimuli around him. We began to understand the source of his difficulty and how much it affected his life. David began to receive intensive weekly therapy at the Institute which included cognitive therapy with Feuerstein Instrumental Enrichment tools (see chapter 7),*

speech therapy and motor modality therapy. Observing his treatments at the Feuerstein Institute modeled for us how to mediate the world to David at every opportunity that arises, and we received recommendations and guidance for implementation. We immediately saw significant improvement in David's behavior. His tantrums and outbursts then diminished over time, until they completely disappeared. When David began to verbalize his difficulties and search for solutions to feelings that caused him discomfort, there was no limit to our joy. We found that the Mediation for Meaning—*the explanations behind the work and preparation before difficult situations we used so frequently with David— had entered his consciousness. For example, instead of us reminding him before a big event to put on his headphones to help him filter the loud noises around, he asked to do so of his own initiative. Today, David is 14 years old, integrated in a regular school, and completely unlike the withdrawn and frustrated child he used to be. His academic achievements are better than average in some subjects, and he is considered a favorite among his classmates. He still has communication and sensory difficulties that can frustrate or overwhelm him from time to time, but in general he manages to regulate himself with a regular daily routine including a half hour of exercise in the morning before school where he does pullups, push-ups and other dynamic exercises. Furthermore, during school breaks, David often runs around the school building several times. One can clearly see the positive influence of movement on David. He continues to come to the Feuerstein Institute once a week, and we feel that the treatment he receives promotes him to higher levels of thinking that we never thought he would reach.*

Building Block #4: Development of the Ability to Imitate

Learning by imitation is a primary learning ability, and its development strengthens general learning ability. Learning to imitate requires acknowledgement of others, and thus also develops communication, reciprocity, and sharing. Learning by imitation begins with the normative development of movement imitation. For a baby, imitating movement is a kind of instinct. The ability to imitate a movement continues to develop in the first year of life.

Children with ASD have difficulty acknowledging others, and this leads to difficulty in imitating movement and learning from a model. In fact, these children have less of an ability to imitate than children with normal development and even children with developmental intellectual disabilities. For children with ASD, imitation is often not spontaneous. For example, they will have difficulty replicating actions in which the parent manipulates objects or imitating body movements, such as clapping or stomping with the feet.

Imitation behavior can be mediated and encouraged. ASD children may not be willing or motivated to imitate. In these cases, efforts must first be devoted to mediating the act of imitation itself. Thus, the mediator will mediate to the child what imitating behavior is and encourage him to want to imitate—that is, to be interested in the person who is demonstrating, to look, to listen, and to repeat (Feuerstein, Feuerstein, & Mintzker, 2006).

ASD children do not spontaneously scan relevant data; they may focus on irrelevant information about the person or object in front of them. A baby will naturally focus on the center of his mother's face when she sings a song, while a child with ASD may scan her ears, mouth, hair or chin. The development of the cognitive function *the ability to choose between relevant and irrelevant data* at the elaboration phase is based on the ability to scan and focus on information that is important to the nature of the task. *Mediation for Focusing* and *Mediation for Systematic Scanning* of the model will help those with ASD reach appropriate conclusions for the task at hand and will make imitation more effective and accurate.

Case Study: Lorenzo

> Lorenzo, a seven-year-old boy diagnosed with ASD, was required to throw a dart at a dartboard. Prior to doing so, Lorenzo was asked to observe his father doing the task and imitate his movement. While his father was showing Lorenzo his hand's position before throwing the dart, it seemed that Lorenzo was looking at his father intently. Upon closer observation, however, it was clear that Lorenzo was actually scanning his father's legs and looking at body parts that were irrelevant to the movement. The mediator who noticed this turned Lorenzo's focus of attention toward his father's hands and the dartboard so that he could later mimic the movement.

Mediation for Intentionality is provided to create connection, eye contact, reciprocity, and cooperation—all of which strengthen the ability to imitate. The mediator takes advantage of the intervals of eye contact to perform a pose or movement as a model, and mediates for the child to imitate. Sometimes the child needs assistance in order to perform the pose or movement; in such cases, the mediator will either hold his hands or sit with him so that his body learns the movement. Later, the pose can be done by the child himself. Repetition is vital here. Aids may be used to attract the child's attention and make him look at the mediator who is modeling the behavior for him to imitate. The mediator may imitate the child and then ask the child to imitate them. In this way, the mediator acts as a model for the child. She accompanies this request with mediation that explains what is required: "I made a movement like you, now do as I do." Parents also sometimes serve as models in the treatment session. In

Feuerstein terms, this is *Mediation for Reciprocity.* Importantly, the mediator will make her request along with statements like the one above, where she reflects what is required of the child. This transfers the instruction from the functional level to the child's metacognitive level, in that he now also understands the meaning of the instruction.

The child is asked to perform body postures or movements by imitation and listening to instructions. One mediates in accordance with the child's need. Some children show the ability to mimic immediately, and some need more assistance. Some will observe, listening to instructions, and after many repetitions by the mediator, they will be able to imitate the movement. In such cases, there is a need for more intense mediation to strengthen the ability to imitate movement and learn from a model. Mediation is provided in accordance with the difficulty observed in the child. When we see difficulty in planning movements, spatial awareness or clumsy motor skills, we emphasize *Mediation for Planning* movement, execution stages, sequence of movements in stages, analysis, and synthesis. Many repetitions are given, the pace is slowed down, and the stages are emphasized.

Examples of other activities that encourage imitation include finger songs (mimicking the movement of the fingers of the hands) and movement imitation through aerobic dance (opposite a mirror in order to receive feedback on the quality of imitation). The development of imitation can be consciously activated, and it can also encourage the child to spontaneously imitate normative behaviors that he sees in his environment.

Building Block #5: Creation of the Perception and Understanding of Body Schema and the "Part-Whole" Relationship

"Body schema" is a kind of mental map of the body, that is, of the relationship between the various body organs and their locations. In normative development, a baby will learn about his body through recurrent experiences involving sensation and movement (crawling, climbing, pushing and pulling, touching materials and toys, etc.), thus developing knowledge about his body size and shape, body limits, and the use of each body part. Sensory-motor experiences provide the child with sensory information that is important for the development of body schema. Clear and precise senses, control of motor skills, and the ability to manipulate the environment are critical for the development of a healthy body schema. A normal body schema allows the child to understand the location of his body parts in relation to the environment, how he can use his body for a variety of activities in the space around him, and how he can move around to explore the environment efficiently and maintain personal space.

Many ASD children are affected by a sensory processing disorder. Thus, many experience significant difficulty in perceiving their body schema. The difficulty stems from deficient cognitive functions or operations that have not yet developed a strong internal representation of body schema in the brain. These deficient functions may include episodic grasp of reality, difficulties in internalization and internal representation, in distinguishing between relevant and irrelevant data, in acknowledging others, egocentricity, and more. These deficient cognitive functions make it difficult for the child to form a body schema from motor-sensory experiences, as occurs in normal development. Difficulty in perceiving body schema is expressed among ASD children in different ways. One child might try to enter through a too-narrow opening, another might try to reach an object placed too high up, and another might bump into objects or avoid physical activities.

Therapy, including sensory work, active movement and the development of body coordination, with mediation for the perception of the "part-whole," helps to develop the perception and internalization of the body schema that was not created through direct learning.

For ASD children, developing a body schema is essential for improving their impaired communication skills. Only when a person feels the limits of his body, his being, can he experience the being of others, and the sense of being separate from others (what Feuerstein called *Mediation for Individuation and Psychological Differentiation*). The distance resulting from separation is the space in which communication takes place between one person and another. Accordingly, this experience is essential for developing communication in children with ASD.

With the construction of a body schema, *separation-individuation* mediation can be provided—a process of development required for communication. *Mediation for Separation-Individuation* can be provided while carrying out movement imitation with explanations ("I do as you do, now you do as I do"), turn-taking games, or by creating personal space (e.g., each has his own mattress, and we do not touch each other during the exercises). In addition, *Mediation for Separation-Individuation* is provided by the importance that the mediator attaches to the child's curiosity, his interests, wishes and needs, thereby conveying to him a message that he is an independent person (individual). This mediation contributes to the consolidation of the self. Understanding of the part-whole is also mediated to the child in other areas (e.g., a roof, tiles, door, window, and walls together create the whole house).

The development of body schema help ASD children to have the focus and concentration necessary for learning.

Case Study: Hannah

> *Three-year-old Hannah was diagnosed with low-functioning ASD. Hannah's perception of her body's schema was not sufficiently developed. This was manifested in the fact that she tried to crawl into any small or large closet, shelf, or object that she passed. She was constantly moving; she*

would run down the corridors fast and disappear in a fraction of a second. Her mother learned to follow her all the time and lock the doors of rooms and closets where she should not go. During treatment, Hannah seemed to jump from place to place and from stimuli to stimuli. The way she studied the stimuli was very superficial. She tried several times to open the door of the room and exit. The stimuli that caught her attention and in which she showed interest was opening and closing boxes, but after a few seconds she did not want to play with them again. It was clear that in order for Hannah to benefit from the treatment, it was necessary to first work on extending her attention span so that she would begin to process the stimuli around her and be open and attentive to the mediation she was given instead of switching from stimuli to stimuli all the time. The work on extending Hannah's attention span was challenging and required great creativity and flexibility on the part of the therapist. In one session, I brought Hannah a basket containing bean bags for her to sort according to their color, and to my surprise Hannah emptied the basket quickly and immediately entered and sat down inside it. Sitting inside the basket which encircled her body seemed to provide her with sensory feedback on the limits of her body, and she seemed to be quieter and more open to learning. As soon as her body schema was clearer to her, she was able to investigate, focus on and show interest in the stimuli presented to her for longer periods of time. From that moment on, I provided Hannah with the need to feel the limits of her body in a barrel, box, or tunnel, which helped her to develop the perception of her body schema, and a meaningful learning and mediation process could take place. After about a month of treatment working on the development of the body schema with cognitive mediation in sessions at home, there was a noticeable change in Hannah's general functioning. She became much more open to mediation and made significant progress.

When a child is asked to draw himself (according to his age and ability), the drawing can give an indication of how the child perceives his body schema, and the mediator will know how best to provide cognitive mediation. Alternatively (for the child who has difficulty drawing), it is possible to use a puzzle of a child figure and see where he places each part of the puzzle. In this way, the child can be taught about the body parts and how they make up the whole body.

Mediation that helps to develop the perception of body schema in ASD children begins with work on the child's body; later, this knowledge can be transferred to the body of a child in a picture, or a doll. Mediation can be done alongside deep or shallow touch on the child's body while naming the different parts. Many children with ASD tend to focus on the details or parts, and find it hard to grasp the complete picture. In body perception, emphasis is placed on mediating synthesis—the parts make up the whole body.

Case Study: Joshua

> *Eleven-year-old Joshua is diagnosed with ASD and has been receiving treatment at the Feuerstein Institute since age six. He has learned to practice the "body awareness"' exercise, an exercise which tries to consciously develop the child's body schema and perception of the part-whole. This exercise brings the child's awareness to the parts that make up the whole body, combining touch and naming the parts. It starts with the legs: he touches the legs while saying "these are my legs," and he moves through the body from the bottom up, ending with his hands on his heart, saying "this is my heart, this is my body, this is me."*

Many ASD children prefer concrete visual information and internalize it more effectively than less concrete information. Using a mirror in which the child looks at his body and receives mediation to move, name, or point to his body parts, can strengthen his understanding of body schema. Such schema can also be internalized through kinesthetic work, in which the child experiences movement while closing his eyes. The development of a body schema is essential for a child with ASD and reinforces his ability to imitate movement, spatial perception and develops the ability to plan his movements.

Building Block #6: Developing Spatial Awareness and Acquiring Spatial Concepts

Most children with ASD experience difficulty with spatial perception and orientation, owing to a deficient cognitive function in the input phase: *lack of spatial orientation and temporal orientation.* This difficulty stems from and is affected by problems in integrating sensory-motor information and an impaired body schema, as described in the previous building blocks. A child with ASD will find it hard to consciously internalize the idea of space and to spontaneously use spatial concepts. He will have trouble moving around efficiently and independently in his surroundings and using spatial characteristics in an illustrative way (e.g., like a map), without sensory support.

In normative development, spatial perception is created and develops when an infant explores his environment. The baby is motivated by stimuli in his environment to reach out to them and to crawl towards them. Children with ASD may not feel the need for this or have the motivation or drive to reach out to a stimulus, so their spatial experience is underdeveloped. Feuerstein attributes this to lack of penetration of mediation in the child. Thus, his parents will call him, saying, "come here," and they will reach for him, but none of this penetrates him because of the difficulties of communicating with him.

We develop spatial perception in ASD children by mediating directed movement in space. In this way, the child constructs spatial perception and develops the concepts of space and the relationships between them, such as standing at different viewpoints with respect to an object and using the terms "on top," "underneath," "inside," "outside," "behind," "to the right of," and so on. With practice and the repetition of spatial concepts, the child learns to establish a relationship between himself and his environment, and then learns to move around and navigate efficiently in his surroundings.

Spatial concepts are mediated while the child moves around, so that brain connections are created between muscle memory and the cognitive concept. For example: when asking a child to raise his hands up in the air, the concept "up" is mediated and the body part that is in motion is verbalized, which internalizes the direction in muscle memory. Such tasks increase learning ability and develop the child's sensory integration.

Spatial perception begins with the body's personal space, and expands to the spatial perception of the relationship between a person, his immediate environment, and the world at large. Spatial orientation concerns the awareness of one's position as a basis for building the ability to create internal representations (the ability to conjure up spatial relationships in our minds and to assign them to a given environment that is not before us). Feuerstein calls this a "spatial frame of reference." Developing the ability to conjure up an image in thought without needing repeated sensory support is a significant stage. In this stage, the child learns to detach from sensory activity, thus reaching a higher and more abstract level of thinking in his learning process. Here the mediation is manifested in *transcendence*, through which the mediator moves away from the concrete subject at hand and extends its influence to other areas. For example, the idea of spatial concepts is transferred to create an internal spatial reference system, and to abstract thinking in general (Feuerstein & Hoffman, 2014).

Case Study: Ben

> *Ten-year-old Ben, diagnosed with ASD, has learned basic spatial concepts and uses them when needed. In a task where he had to follow a route using arrows pointing in different directions (while verbalizing the directions in which he turned), he was able to find the route's starting point and the target points to reach and to name the appropriate directions. When the task changed and he had to instruct the mediator how to follow the route and instruct her which side to turn to without sensory support, he found it very difficult to perform the task.*

Schemas, charts and maps are effective aids for the assimilation of spatial concepts and the development of internal representation. The development of spatial orientation through visual channels helps many children diagnosed with ASD overcome their *episodic grasp of reality* so that they can search for connections in their different experiences. An example of such mediation is preparing a diagram of an obstacle course on a page, and then constructing and implementing the route according to the diagram.

Spatial orientation is developed using the movement modality and the three Spatial Orientation Feuerstein Instrumental Enrichment instruments: "The Orientation in Space Basic" instrument introduces the concept of space for children in early childhood, "Orientation in Space-1" in the standard toolset teaches the school-age child the four main directions (left, right, front, back,), and "Orientation in Space-2" teaches older children about North-South-East-West. These instruments are very effective in producing a spatial reference system and for developing the child's internal representation and spatial orientation.

Alongside developing their spatial perception, the spatial orientation instruments also helps children with ASD to develop thinking skills that challenge them, such *as hypothetical thinking* (e.g., if the woman in the picture is to face the tree, to which direction she should turn?) and thought flexibility when moving between different perspectives quickly.

In our work, we have encountered children with a diagnosis of high-functioning ASD whose spatial perception was very good—even higher than average for children of their age. They remembered the names of streets and alleys in their town and could draw precise maps of bus routes and walking distances. Working on the spatial orientation instruments with these children serves as a means to achieve the relevant social and communication goals: understanding another's perspective or point of view, putting themselves in someone else's place (in the physical sense), providing principles for implementation in the social communication sphere, and especially transcendence of this principle to a more conceptual level, with examples from the child's daily life and social situations in which this principle can be applied (e.g., if I were in the role of a father, how would I react to a violent act of my son?).

Building Block #7: Constructing a Sequence/Flow of Motion

Sequence is part of the *temporal perception* process in the input phase. Most ASD children have difficulty in orientation in time, which is caused by an *episodic grasp of reality* and the lack of searching for connections. ASD children have difficulty understanding and maintaining sequences. They may find it difficult to perform an action built of several stages in a logical sequence, such as arranging blocks from largest to smallest, dressing and undressing, preparing a sandwich, brushing teeth, or following up on the order of actions required for getting ready for bed. Many parents of ASD children report that they feel that maintaining sequences is the most challenging task for their child to perform. Planning, maintaining and checking up on a sequence of activities in therapy strengthens the children's ability to build sequences.

The father of Cora, a thirteen-year-old girl diagnosed with ASD, reports:

When Cora organizes herself in the morning, it is no surprise to see her with her shirt over her sweater or walking around with a knife full of jam and looking for the slice of bread to spread it on. The whole sequence of actions that she performs is unorganized, unplanned, and fails to follow a logical sequence, which often leads her to frustration and disappointment. However, during therapy we saw Cora was able to maintain the sequence of the movement exercises in her regular personal training program. She followed a list accompanied by pictures that was prepared for her in advance and ticked off each exercise after she performed it. We therefore decided to adopt the idea of lists at home as well. We prepared a list that was hung on the refrigerator that described the order of her morning activities, the order of the activities to be performed before going to sleep, recipes broken down into simple stages and any other sequence that Cora found difficult. Initially, Cora needed intensive mediation to focus and maintain the sequence, but gradually the mediation decreased, and she became more independent in her functioning, and even remembered a sequence of activities without looking at the list.

Mediation for teaching ASD children the ability to maintain sequences begins with practicing movement sequences in the different directions and planes (e.g., raise hands up, down, backward and forward). Various motion sequences are taught that the child later reconstructs from memory. The internalization and processing of sequences will improve as the input phase becomes more active: a clear understanding of the information in all its details, systematic, accurate and planned data collection, and consideration of all sources of information.

Movement imitation exercises are performed while emphasizing the sequence of the motions, and the mediator provides verbal mediation and a breakdown of each stage. For example, regarding a sitting position where the feet face each other, the knees are bent and the legs form a kind of diamond shape, the mediator will settle in the position while emphasizing the steps as she performs the sequence of movements and simultaneously provide cognitive mediation—clear instructions for implementation emphasizing the sequence of movement in stages: 1) Sit down; 2) Bring the feet forward and together; 3) Hold your feet with your hands; and 4) Move your legs—raise your legs up and then lower them.

The execution of a sequence of motions made up of spatial and temporal elements and strength is called a flow of motion. The flow of motion reflects the quality of movement and the transition from one movement to the next. This flow develops through repetition, practice, and the internalization of movement sequences. This process can be compared to reading fluency. The reader must read the text accurately, quickly, and with appropriate intonation, while simultaneously directing resources to reading comprehension. A skilled reader can decode the text with little effort, allowing him to invest effort in the main purpose—comprehension.

The new reader, by contrast, focuses on the process of decoding words (conversion of letters to sounds). After he has acquired the groundwork for reading, he practices reading until he able to succeed in identifying the words automatically. The process of acquiring flow of motion is similar. Thus, the child performing the movement initially focuses on the planning of each stage. After internalization and practice, the adopted movement becomes an automatic and graceful movement that does not require much effort from the child, allowing him to do another action at the same time. We might think of a toddler who, while learning to walk, concentrates only on his body movements; gradually, he is able to walk while holding an object in his hand and speaking.

In order to develop the flow of motion in ASD children, work is required on the cognitive function of *use of time concepts*. Movement games incorporating timing, such as jumping until the pre-set timer rings or picking up as many rings as possible while a hoop rotates and stopping when it falls, develop the child's sense of time, *temporal orientation, regulation of behavior*, and the ability to *simultaneously consider two sources of information*.

Case Study: Jonathan

> *I worked with nine-year-old Jonathan, who is diagnosed with ASD, on the ability to maintain sequence and flow of motion. Any task that required multi-system coordination and complex movements would challenge him and we would have to break the task down into smaller components. For example, in a jumping exercise, Jonathan was initially asked to perform only the foot movements of the exercise, and then he performed only the hand movements. Next, Jonathan moved a parallel arm and leg at the same time, and only then he managed the more complex movement of moving opposite hands and legs, using a visual hint of sticking the same-colored stickers on a hand and a counter leg. After much practice, Jonathan could perform the exercise and keep to the rhythm on his own without any additional clues and help.*

The work that was done with Jonathan on motion and movement sequences became evident in his swimming. Jonathan's mother says:

> *Jonathan began to learn to swim at the age of nine. Every week I took Jonathan to a private swimming lesson with a patient instructor who was very motivated to work with children with ASD. The process of learning to swim was very slow and gradual and occasionally frustrating and exhausting. The instructor began with simple tasks like blowing bubbles underwater. We soon realized that he had to break down each task into much smaller stages and steps. At the initial breathing stage, Jonathan swallowed a lot of water and had trouble understanding when to take in air*

and when to blow out. Learning the movements in order and at the right pace was challenging for him. The verbal instructions given by the instructor were not clear to him, and he often misunderstood the instruction or found it difficult to demonstrate flexibility in implementing an instruction that was different from the one he was used to. The instructor was required to be precise and demonstrate the tasks in order for Jonathan to understand them. Four years have passed, and Jonathan has advanced at his own pace and has learned to swim front crawl and breast-stroke. He goes to swimming lessons happily and feels pleased, especially since he now swims better than his older brother…

Some children diagnosed with ASD understand sequence order well, but they find it difficult to be flexible and adapt to the order of actions or schedule according to the situation required at the time. Mediation with children of this type will emphasize the gradual introduction of variable components during treatment, while slowly "softening'" their rigidity of thought using *Mediation for Meaning* and *Mediation for Transference.* For example, a familiar personal training program for a child is performed, but with changes in the order of the exercises or in the number of repetitions that each exercise should be performed, with the addition of new exercises to the training program from time to time. When *Mediating for Meaning,* we will explain that even when there is a schedule and a prearranged timetable of activities, such as a school schedule or an agenda, there may be changes as a result of circumstances—and that is fine.

Building Block #8: Developing the Ability to Plan Movements (Praxis)

Children with ASD may have difficulty with internal representation, motor coordination, and with learning and performing complex movements that require planning. If they are significantly affected in this way, they may also be given a formal diagnosis of dyspraxia (difficulty in planning movements); the two diagnoses often appear together.

Planning movements is based on some of the previously mentioned building blocks: body schema development, spatial perception development and sequence building. Planning movements involves planning and organizing the sequence of activities required to perform the given movement, which is based on brain activity. At the execution stage, a motor command is sent to the muscles to activate them. Practice makes it possible to perform the task automatically, just like cycling allows the rider to cycle automatically without the need for as much thought and concentration as was necessary initially.

In therapy with ASD children, we mediate the ability to develop planning behaviors, which is one of the most important functions in the elaboration phase where the child learns to plan steps to solve a problem. Working on planning movements reinforces this thinking function, and it is done by maintaining a sequence of movements. To this end, we develop the ability to analyze and synthesize, and search for connections between units of information. These types of mediation are provided throughout the treatment, both in the monologue that accompanies the mediator's performance as a model and in the questions that guide the child to analyze the position of the various body parts when he is required to perform a pose. The child is asked questions that guide analysis and synthesis and seek connections between units of information: "To perform this position, do you need to stand or sit? Do your hands need to be placed in front of you or behind you?"

Clear instructions are given on how to create a particular pose through a sequence of movements which are ultimately stages of performing the pose. Spatial concepts are reiterated, as are the names of the body parts. Take, for example, instructions for the bridge position, where you lie on your back with knees bent and your feet are placed on the floor and lift up your pelvis so that your back from the height of shoulder blades, pelvis and legs are in the air. The mediator who serves as a role model will execute the position while emphasizing the stages of execution and provide cognitive mediation for movement planning and clear instructions for execution according to stages: 1) Lie down on your back; 2) Bend your knees; 3) Keep your feet down on the floor; 4) Lift your pelvis and half your back up; and so forth. Once the position has been studied and repeated, questions are asked as mediation for movement planning: "How do you perform the pose?" 'What is the first movement?' 'What do you do next?"

Case Study: Mark

> *Eight-year-old Mark, diagnosed with ASD, first raised his legs instead of his pelvis when he tried to imitate the bridge position. He was frustrated that he could not create the bridge like the mediator. He looked at the mediator demonstrating the pose but did not know how to create the position. Mark was given verbal mediation to plan movements while performing the pose in stages. Providing the sequence of movements that are the stages necessary for creating the position helped him to organize his movements and body, move the required body parts and achieve the position and a proper imitation of the model.*

Mediation is provided for the analysis and synthesis of the pose. Questions are asked to help the child analyze and synthesize the pose in order to imitate the movement—for example: "To be like the child in the picture, do you have to stand or sit? How do you place your feet and hands? Are your hands placed in front or behind?"

For exercises that require movement planning, it is important to break down the movement into stages and to verbalize the thought process that is done while moving.

Case Study: Drew

> *Four-year-old Drew, diagnosed with ASD, stood in front of the vertical barrel knowing he had to enter it, but he did not know how to proceed. With a swift movement, he jumped inside head-first with his legs dangling outside. Drew felt 'stuck' in the position and called for help. During treatment, Drew gradually learned to restrain his impulsivity, to stop and plan the moves necessary in order to enter the barrel. At first, the mediation was accompanied by verbal and motor support at each stage of the task. With repeated attempts to enter the barrel, he started to understand how to climb into it efficiently, but still needed reminders and verbal instructions from the mediator. At a later stage, Drew managed to enter the barrel by himself, while he named the active parts of his body and verbalized the stages of planned movement to himself: 'Hands, one knee, a second knee, a leg, a leg and a jump."*

Activities that require intense concentration and movement planning, like dancing which requires learning new steps, involve both physical and mental effort. Many studies confirm the effect of this type of exercise on improved brain functioning (Doidge, 2007). Movement planning becomes more complex when the child is required to relate to several sources of information simultaneously and must consider other variables (e.g., a group game that requires the child to plan and execute movements, adapt to the group, and be understood by others).

Case Study: Danny

> *Ten-year-old Danny was diagnosed with ASD and enjoys playing basketball. He began learning the rules of the game at a very young age from his father. Danny manages to play and stick to the rules of the game with another participant or two, but when more friends want to join the game it becomes too complex a game for him and he is unable to plan his moves and address many sources of information at the same time, and so he immediately gives up in such a situation.*

This ability to plan movements while exercising flexibility of thinking in a group game can improve in ASD children, thus helping them develop social communication skills. This is done through gradual practice accompanied by mediation, in which the child learns the rules and meaning of the game, and by starting to apply this in a small group that gradually expands according to the child's ability. The social situations that occur in the game have to be mediated to the child; the mediator must talk through each situation with the child and provide him with strategies to deal with the situations encountered during the game, such as victory, loss, violation of the rules, and possibly hurting a friend.

We have seen many children with dyspraxia who have been diagnosed with ASD, owing to symptoms associated with autism. However, after cognitive sensory-motor therapy with an emphasis on developing body schema and movement planning, these children have significantly improved their communication ability and adaptation to the environment. Some were even able to formally remove their autism diagnosis in their official documents and re-evaluate their source of disability.

Building Block #9: Developing the Ability to Regulate Behavior

Behavior regulation is the child's ability to maintain self-control. Mediation teaches the child how to *monitor and regulate his behavior* and acquire internal discipline. The child must learn to organize his or her behavior so that there is an effective match between stimuli (that vary according to the task requirements) and his actions.

Behavior regulation is initially built up by parents regulating their baby's behavior. With the baby's development, regulation ability gradually passes to the child. In normative development the child is open to mediation and learns to regulate his behavior. However, the child with ASD is often blocked from direct mediation from the environment and therefore requires further mediation. When parents continue to do things for the child that he has difficulty doing—such as accompanying the child in public places all the time while telling him what he is allowed to touch and what not to touch—the ability to regulate behavior is likely to remain underdeveloped. In contrast, the mediator will ask the child, for example: "Is this object yours?" "Are you allowed to touch something that is not yours?" or she will give the child the responsibility to lead.

We often see passive behavior (cognitive and behavioral) in children with ASD which is expressed as lack of initiative and difficulty initiating an action. Mediation will initially work on these areas; sometimes it is necessary to do the action with the child, by placing the therapist's hand on the client's hand, and then the mediation is slowly reduced until the child can initiate by themselves. The therapist will encourage the child's initialization by *Mediation for a Feeling of Competence* and *Mediation for Meaning*. They will develop the child's ability to start and stop behavior and activity according to his will and on demand, to control his behavior and not to be controlled by the stimuli surrounding him.

Movement exercises that require regulation of behavior develop this ability. Initially the mediator helps the child to regulate himself through mediation and exercises. It is possible to practice regulation of behavior through repetition and variation that require the child to start and stop movements according to the mediator's instructions or the initial instruction given. The mediator will provide mediation *to restrain impulsivity*, for example by slowing down the action and preventing it before pre-planning—"stop and think." When mediation is removed, the child gradually learns to regulate himself and his behavior.

The child learns from sensory-motor training with cognitive mediation that he can choose how to act in his life. He realizes that he is not activated by reality, but rather chooses how to act in it; he learns that he chooses the appropriate stimuli and not the other way around. Behavior regulation appears throughout the building blocks and is an important component of mediating learning. In the beginning we provide more mediation, and at a later stage we will bring the child to a stage of awareness of his actions. The child will realize that, in regulation of behavior, self-control is in his hands. In regulating behavior, there is a need to create a time lag between the stimulus (in the input phase) and the reaction (the output phase) for the purpose of carrying out a thought process—Mediation to Restrain Impulsiveness.

Movement activities for practicing regulation of behavior can include games involving instructions such as "jump until instructed to stop", the "musical statues," where the child moves to the rhythm of the music and freezes in position when the music stops, relay races, and so on. Tone of voice can also be used as a mediating agent for behavior regulation; according to tone of voice, the child can be calmed or activated, and his pace of action can be accelerated as needed. Treatment involves practicing the acceleration of movement and slowing and restraint of movement, freezing and resting.

Case Study: Ralf

> *At first, I gave nine-year-old Ralf, who is diagnosed with ASD, more intense mediation. With my hand on his, we initiated movements together, and learned the movements required to produce a sound from the Tibetan bowl. Raphael then tapped the bowl back and forth. He found it difficult to restrain his behavior and to pass the bowl to the mediator. Slowly and gradually, as he was practicing, Ralf learned to regulate his behavior, to tap once in turn, listen to the long sound and pass the bowl and the stick to the mediator, in order to listen to the sound and wait for his turn. He enjoyed this activity for a few minutes!*

Building Block #10: Implementation and Transfer of Treatment Content to other Areas

An important component expressed throughout the therapy process is Transcendence—the ability to transfer, connect, and associate what was mediated in the treatment framework to situations that the child encounters in daily life. Children with ASD may find it difficult to seek connections between new experiences and existing ones, and they may not make the transfer from one field of knowledge to another independently. They often need mediation to find a point of comparison between events and do not know how to transfer what they have learned in other similar tasks that are not directly in their field of vision. The mediator has the responsibility to create these "bridges" for the child for purposes that are relevant to the child and which can serve him in his future functioning. For example, in cognitive therapy using the motor modality, where the goal is to develop the child's strength regulation while in motion, it is difficult for the child to know how powerful each action should be. Implementation will be linked to situations the child will meet in reality, such as "you can press the ball hard if you like it, but you should squeeze your mother's hands gently without too much strength, so your touch will be pleasant for her." For a child who has difficulty internalizing and applying rules, and keeping to the limits that are set for him, we will teach him movement games with clear rules, explain his successes and connect this ability to everyday life; in daily life and at home, there are rules that we must abide by, such as stopping at a red light or going to sleep on time. In this way, we encourage the child to try to apply the learned principle outside of the treatment framework.

Treatment is usually provided in the presence of a parent (especially for preschoolers), since collaboration with the parents is vital. Parents have specific goals in mind for their child that they see as most important, and parents who watch the therapist's mediation model see for themselves what mediation is given to the child and how their child reacts to it. During the course of the treatment, parents will be instructed in how to transfer the learning that has been found to be effective for the child to his daily life. The parents will be guided as to which types of mediation to use, how to persuade the child to carry out complex new tasks, how to proceed with the child's current learning process, and why this is important. The transfer and implementation of learned skills and continuing work on them within the child's school framework and home, are a necessary condition for achieving the set treatment goals and improving the overall functioning of the child.

Case Study: Henry

> *Henry, eleven years old, was diagnosed with Down Syndrome and ASD. He also has significant sensory processing difficulties. Henry's*

mother, a teacher and a cognitive therapist, was very receptive during therapy to learn and apply the treatment methods and objectives at home. When she observed Henry's cognitive therapy through the motor modality, she saw how he enthusiastically carried out the body-awareness exercise which aims to develop sensory-motor integration and teach him about body limits. In the mediating exercise, Henry rolled a small soft ball over his limbs and named the body parts while listening to a song about body awareness. That evening when Henry objected to putting soap on his body during his shower, which often happened because of his sensory difficulties, his mother began singing the body awareness song from his treatment session that day. Henry remembered the melody well and to the beat of the song he started to put soap on his body with his sponge and name the limbs, just like in the treatment exercise. At the end of the song he had a big smile and wanted to do it all over again...

When dynamic cognitive therapy through the motor modality is completed, recommendations for applications outside the treatment framework are adapted and varied according to the needs of each child. However, there are general recommendations that can be repeated in the ASD population. These include:

- Encouraging and maintaining the child's active life. Outdoor leisure activities are preferred as an extension of the communication and initiating skills taught to them in the course of the treatment: in the playground, garden, etcetera, for prolonged time frames. Active breaks during the day, especially in their educational setting, will help their concentration and learning.
- Participation in an after-school activity or class based on movement that is suitable to the child for social integration and communication development. In some cultures, participation in a sports group is very common and prevents social isolation.

Case Study: Isabella

Isabella is a sixteen-year-old girl diagnosed with ASD. She studies at a special education school. The school day is long, and when she comes home, she receives one-on-one paramedical treatments. Therefore, Isabella is very busy during the week, which her parents say gives her stability and a sense of security. On weekends, however, Isabella has a lot of free time, most of which she spends with her parents. Isabella's parents try to offer her different activities and encourage her to develop a variety of interests, but she abandons all activities after a short period of time. Her lack of framework makes her wander around in circles aimlessly. Most of the boys and girls of Isabella's age who live in their city spend weekends participating in various sports and leisure activities such as volleyball, tennis, golf, and more. Isabella's parents dream and hope that someday her social isolation on weekends will stop, and she too will be able to take part in sports activities she likes and participate in a sports club just like others in their culture. We recommended that Isabella join a small sports group, which would contribute to her social integration, while emphasizing the adaptations, mediation methods and emphases that must be taken into consideration when composing the optimal group for Isabella. This recommendation is intended to transfer the change created in Isabella throughout the treatment to her daily life.

The element of transcendence is also expressed in the context of multi-disciplinary work. As a multidisciplinary team treating the child, it is important to provide progress reports to all the professional staff using FM language in order to see the work with the child in a broader perspective and to work collaboratively toward common goals. For example, if in dynamic cognitive therapy through the motor modality we notice that a particular child benefits from deep pressure that helps him concentrate and be more focused for learning and receiving mediation, we pass on this information and demonstrate how to do this to the therapists in other areas so that they can also use this stimulation in their sessions. When a speech therapist reports that her current goal with a child with ASD is to teach him to point accurately to his choice between two objects and explain how to do this, the other therapists treating this child will try to encourage and reinforce this goal and continue this communication process in collaboration.

Conclusion

This chapter discussed the main goals and components of dynamic cognitive therapy through the motor modality. Its purpose was to present a unique field of treatment for ASD children as part of a multi-disciplinary team using the FM.

Dynamic cognitive therapy through the motor modality is based on the SCM theory. In this theory, we view the child with ASD in the present as well as the future and believe in his ability to make a structural change that will affect his functioning in all areas. The pace and quality of the ASD child's changes vary from child to child. Those in his immediate environment need to make themselves aware of every small change that he demonstrates.

Treatment is carried out with a dynamic approach, which seeks to identify the child's abilities. The therapist sets herself the goal of expanding these abilities and bringing them to expression outside of the therapeutic framework. In the treatment of ASD children, the source of the child's difficulty—the cognitive functions and operations that are the source of learning and thinking is identified. Through mediated learning, we develop the child's deficient functions and provide him with the mediation that is uniquely effective for him.

Dynamic cognitive therapy through the motor modality is designed to enable ASD children to explore, discover and experience the world as a safe place full of meaningful experiences. This is done by mediating a variety of tasks and cognitive, motor, sensory and emotional stimuli during therapy.

The main advantages of this type of therapy are that the motor and sensory modalities are natural and enjoyable for children with ASD, and they help the brain regulate sensory information that affects its functioning. This type of therapy enables children who have difficulty learning directly from stimuli to learn and internalize skills with the help of mediation and a motor-sensory experience. Furthermore, the motor modality is suitable for children with ASD because therapy does not necessarily require language. It therefore allows this population to take an active part in the treatment, and the therapy promotes verbal and nonverbal communication skills. Only in this modality do ASD children experience content that requires thinking and developing cognitive skills in motion, which leads them to internalize and store complex and abstract ideas physically and mentally.

We have seen in this chapter the ten building blocks that comprise the goals of intervention in dynamic cognitive therapy through the motor modality: 1) Building communication ability; 2) Building an understanding of the therapeutic framework; 3) Developing sensory movement; 4) Developing the ability to imitate; 5) Creating the perception and understanding of body schema and the "part-whole" relationship; 6) Developing spatial awareness and acquiring spatial concepts; 7) Constructing a sequence and flow of motion; 8) Developing the ability to plan movements; 9) Developing ability to regulate behaviour; and 10) Implementation and transfer of treatment content to other areas. Work on these building blocks is carried out in an integrated and parallel manner—all the blocks are related. The interaction and development of the building blocks are not random but are a direct result of the mediation process.

In our clinical work over the years, we have treated many children and adolescents diagnosed with ASD at various levels of functioning. Children who participated in the FM multi- disciplinary program and received systematic and intensive treatment that reached beyond the therapeutic framework to their immediate surroundings achieved far-reaching results, became more involved in their surroundings, and experienced a change in their perception of the world. We can clearly point to significant changes in the cognitive, communicative, emotional, and motor functioning of children that occurred following dynamic cognitive therapy through the motor modality.

Note

1 Rabbi Nachman of Breslau (1772–1810) was a spiritual teacher in Ukraine.

References

Doidge, N. *The Brain that Changes Itself: Stories of Personal Triumph from the Frontiers of Brain Science.* New York: Penguin Books, 2007.
Feuerstein, R. & M. Hoffman. *Orientation in space: Teacher's guide.* Jerusalem: ICELP, 2014.
Feuerstein, R, Y. Mintzker, R. S. Feuerstein, et al. *Mediated Learning Experience: Guidelines for Parents.* Jerusalem: ICELP, 2006.
Hazan, A. *Kochavai Or.* Machon Bashan, 1896. (Hebrew).
Kranowitz, C. S. *The out-of-sync child: Recognizing and coping with sensory processing disorder.* New York: Penguin Group, 2005.
Prostig, M. *Noa Grew Up and Learnt.* Tel Aviv: National Center for Special Education and Rehabilitation, 1994.

Chapter 10

Mediated Learning Experience as a Treatment Modality with Families of ASD Children

Betty Brodsky Cohen[1]

Mediated Learning Experience (MLE) is based on the premise that all children learn from direct exposure to stimuli in their environment as well as from mediated learning in which the mediator (e.g., parent, teacher, or other caretaker) places himself between the child and the stimuli in order to make the world more understandable. Children whose cognitive abilities are limited are in greater need of such mediation. The hope is that the child will eventually develop the capacity to engage in more independent and direct learning. In my many years of work with parents of special children, I have often presented MLE (see Introduction to the Theory) as a powerful method to break down the walls and barriers around the child, with the mediators using themselves as the hammers to do so. With its emphasis on activity and engagement by a therapist who does not reject educative tasks as part of his work, the opportunities for competence-enhancement of parents that can be provided by a model of practice based on MLE are both numerous and powerful.

In my use of MLE instruction when working with families of autistic children, modeling, and the abundant provision of examples for each criterion were an inherent part of my work. For example, my own voice (with it's varied intonation and volume) was often used to demonstrate *Mediation for Meaning,* the attribution of feelings, beliefs, and values to the mediated content.

Mediation for Intentionality relates to the mediator's commitment to help the child understand the message being communicated. When working with a parent who has difficulty in this area, non- verbal modeling can be used to bring about improved focusing behavior critical for mediation of this criterion.

Let us turn to the criterion of *Mediation for Reciprocity*, where the parent acts and the child responds, signaling that he truly relates to his parents' actions. A brief example illustrates this criterion. A child began to attend a regular educational setting after years in a special school. After working intensively on focusing behavior, the parents expressed

DOI: 10.4324/9781003451136-11

astonishment that their son would approach them and say: "Mommy/ Daddy, I'm looking at you. Look at me. I want..."

In order to engage in *Mediation for a Feeling of Competence,* which deals with the child's self-image, the mediator sets up the conditions for the child to experience success, as well as to interpret his success or failure in a constructive way. In keeping with the active, participatory approach suggested by a practice model based on Mediated Learning, a parent can be engaged in role-playing behavior as to how a child's drawing may be commented on in a way that builds self-esteem.

In *Mediation for Transcendence,* the mediator goes beyond the immediate goal by explaining, expanding on, and connecting activities, objects and events to larger systems in the child's environment. One of my favorite examples of this criterion emerged from my work with parents who lived in fear for their ten-year-old autistic daughter's safety due to her long-standing habit of darting into the street. After years of intervening with a flat "NO!" at the time of each incident, the parents were helped to grasp the importance of explaining to their child, in language she would understand, the likely consequences of her actions. Only then were they able to help her stop engaging in this dangerous behavior.

One of the social worker's tasks is to assist families with prioritizing problems in order to bring organization to their lives. During this prioritization process, the client is helped to identify and categorize. A practice model based on MLE tends to have a calming, organizing effect on overwhelmed parents. Asking them to purchase a notebook (or to open a digital file), in which their own mediation efforts are jotted down and categorized for the purpose of later review and discussion may reduce feelings of powerlessness and of being overwhelmed. Parents themselves often reported experiencing new-found feelings of competence as their own successes in mediating to their children were charted in a concrete yet reflective manner. A side effect of keeping such a journal is that it propels parents to seek out and actively create situations in which mediation can take place. For example, reflecting on their documented efforts toward *Mediation for a Feeling of Competence* to their eleven-year-old autistic son, one set of parents reported that the review of their own success with this particular criterion prompted them to think of further ways to create viable competence and self-image enhancing opportunities for success. Some of these opportunities included the assigning of household chores, sending the child on his own to the supermarket, and requesting that he read to his younger brother.

In order to illustrate the opportunities for successful therapeutic work with families of children exhibiting autism or autistic states, two case studies are presented below. They describe work with two sets of parents of five-year-old children, each from a vastly different part of the world.

Case Studies

Case Study: Alan

> *The following case study illustrates what is possible to achieve within an extremely limited timeframe when MLE is used as a treatment modality. The parents of Alan, a five-year-old boy from Italy, were seen at the Feuerstein Institute over a period of three weeks. Although the child was diagnosed as autistic, Alan's early developmental tasks in all areas were reported to have occurred at age-appropriate times. Interviewing the parents, I learned that at the age of two and a half, a severe regression occurred in the area of verbal communication. An almost complete discontinuation of speech was reported to have taken place four months after a sibling's birth. Learning more about the events surrounding the sister's arrival, I became convinced of at least some correlation between this child's expressive language output and the amount and quality of parental mediation.*

With Alan's use of speech coming almost completely to a halt shortly after his sibling's arrival, the mother was aware of having decreased her availability to her son at the time. In addition, while she had previously been the primary caretaker for Alan with minimal help in the mornings from a young girl, two months prior to her daughter's birth the assistant of several years was replaced by a full-time, live-in nanny-housekeeper who had arrived from Africa who did not speak Italian. With the mother now preoccupied with the care of his sister (who remained in the parents' bedroom until the age of one-and-a-half), and abruptly separated from his former babysitter with whom he had developed a close and warm relationship, Alan was now entrusted to a total stranger with whom he had no common language. Busy with his business and working long hours, Alan's father is also reported to have spent little time with him during his early years, usually arriving home after his son's bedtime.

Deciding to use MLE as a tool to repair what I viewed as a sudden break in whatever emotional bonding had taken place prior to the sister's birth, I found it extremely easy to engage the parents in our cognitively based work together. Had I chosen a more traditional introspective treatment approach in which the parents would have been assigned the role of clients, self-blame and use of defense mechanisms might well have arisen around any part they may have played in contributing to Alan's difficulties. In an atmosphere characterized by the optimism, activity, and learning dictated by MLE, a therapist's efforts are much less likely to be met with resistance.

In my work with his parents, Alan was observed to be more likely to listen to his father—who used his voice and facial expression to mediate both *Intentionality* and *Meaning*—than his mother. Although eye contact was fleeting at best in the interactions of both parents with Alan, the father was more likely to engage his son's attention through the use of his voice.

With the *Mediation for Intentionality* discussed as a crucial component for Alan's development, suggestions were made as to how to achieve mediation in this area through use of themselves as objects of focus. With the parents noting that the youngster enjoyed watching his father make faces, recommendations were made as to how to incorporate such play while mediating to Alan. The use of proximity, physical contact, as well as face-to-face sitting positions were also discussed for mediation of this criterion, with its emphasis on focusing behavior.

Relating their son's long-standing fears of attempting new tasks, when this area was explored it became apparent that there had been little, if any, *Mediation for a Feeling of Competence*. On the contrary, prior to their consultation at the Feuerstein Institute, the parents tended to communicate Alan's deficiencies to him as well as to his two-and-a-half-year-old sister by allowing the latter to watch over him, and by generally conveying the message that "something's wrong" with her brother. In addition to discussing the general importance of this criterion, specific suggestions were made; for example, to refer to Alan as the "big brother" who deserves special privileges (e.g., a later bedtime) by virtue of his position in the family.

Relating their son's long-standing fears of attempting new tasks, when this area was explored with the parents it became apparent that there had been little, if any, *Mediation for Individuation and Psychological Differentiation*. With Alan and his sister having shared the same toys, neither appeared to have developed a sense of possession. It was decided that upon the family's return to Italy, both children would be given separate boxes and shelves labeled with pictures of themselves as a means of identification of ownership. Boxes and shelves for items to be shared were also marked.

Extremely eager to put into practice all the recommendations made, the parents were already able to note several meaningful changes in their interactions with Alan after only a few sessions. Having learned to encourage on eye contact in all their communications with him, no longer did they take for granted his understanding of instructions until such contact was established and Alan's eyes searched to confirm comprehension. Parental instructions were reportedly more likely to be fulfilled (e.g., to pass items between family members, to throw garbage in the trash, to remove chewing- gum wrappers independently).

It is through the *Mediation for Goal Seeking, Goal Planning* and *Goal Achieving Behavior* that the child learns to delay immediate gratification, to choose goals, and to plan how they may be achieved. After working with his parents in this area, Alan began to plan independently and carry out several operations involved in completing a task. In his work with the Institute's movement therapist, Alan no longer panicked when requested to engage in new exercises, followed instructions with newly acquired ease, and even participated in a group. Perhaps most meaningfully, Alan began to spontaneously allow his parents to hug him! |In addition, how much more rewarding it must have been for them to receive such a reward than to spend time discussing how painful it was that such affection was lacking.

Case Study: Paul

> *Paul, a five-year-old boy from a prosperous family, was seen at the Feuerstein Institute for the purpose of evaluation and treatment. He was accompanied by his parents and seven-year-old brother. According to the parents, his wide-ranging developmental delays had reportedly been attributed to autism by a visiting psychiatrist. The family history revealed an early symbiotic-like bond between mother and son as well as over- indulgence on the part of the father. Paul had his own carer responsible for his wellbeing in the absence of the parents. While the latter communicated in English with Paul and his brother, his carer had a poor command of English and little ability to stimulate Paul, and he was fearful of making demands on Paul. At the age of five, Paul had not yet attended kindergarten and spent his days wandering aimlessly, with no one expecting him to follow instructions. In spite of Paul's severe delays of language skills, there was no need for him to use language. The mother reported that she "could understand what no one else [could]" from her son's facial expressions and gestures. Although Paul had begun to walk between 12 and 18 months, he was unaccustomed to walking any distances and was consistently carried by his parents and caregivers.*
>
> *Instruction in MLE began shortly after Paul's arrival at the Feuerstein Institute, and both parents participated actively in the process, bringing daily examples of the criteria covered as well as questions and concerns. Intentionality was an extremely important category for these parents, who had never before made the effort to have their intentions known to a son previously thought of as incapable of understanding. Learning to follow through with any request made of Paul, the parents rapidly noted an improvement in his ability to engage in eye contact as they learned to turn his face while saying "Look at me." Although accustomed to being called twice, Paul soon started to respond after hearing his name called only once. Noting that he had begun to seek mediation from his brother, the parents were encouraged to incorporate their son's desire for physical contact in all their communications with him. While he initially expressed concern that warm, physical contact would contradict the new emphasis on independence, the father was helped to balance a less indulgent, more demanding demeanor with Paul's continuing needs for age- appropriate displays of affection.*

Paul had never played with many of toys that had been bought for him, and his parents had been unaware of the importance of play. Their newly acquired appreciation of focused play as a precursor for learning seemed to be reflected in Paul's obvious joy while beginning to engage in symbolic play.

Mediation for the Search of an Optimistic Alternative relates to the belief that circumstances can be improved, problems can be solved, and hurdles can be overcome. Such a hopeful attitude leads to greater possibilities of behavioral and cognitive change than belief systems in which passivity and acceptance are the norm. Learning to adapt his speech and rhythm to sit down and begin to engage Paul in *reciprocal* communication, the father noted a turning point in his own ability to believe in and mediate for an *optimistic alternative* for his son's future. Following the family's return from a vacation, he emotionally expressed a new feeling of certainty that he will, after all, "have two sons to share his family time with." It was with great pride that he related that Paul was able to respond to the question "What did you do yesterday?" by answering "Paul went to the zoo yesterday."

The *Mediation for Sharing Behavior* relates to the individual's participation with others. It encourages sensitivity, helps the child be less self-centered and more aware of other people's feelings and desires. With Paul's growing ability to engage in eye contact matched by his increasing responsiveness to mediation in the area of sharing, the parents noted their son's apparent development of such empathy and that he had begun to react to the cries of his brother by crying himself. Both mother and father appeared to make a real effort in mediating sharing by encouraging Paul's participation in family conversations as well as in play situations with his brother. Acknowledging the importance of such behavior, the parents began to make a "game" out of sharing whenever possible. For example, the children began to take turns pressing buttons in elevators and turning pages while being read to, which also led to improved **behavior regulation.** The objective of *Mediation of Regulation and Control of Behavior* is for the child to take control of his own actions rather than having his behavior managed and directed by others. An indication of the improved parental mediation in this area was the suggestion of Paul's parents that their son take on the responsibility for feeding the family pet upon their return home. This task would incorporate both Paul's great pleasure in playing with animals as well as their new-found optimism that their son was now capable of taking on such a chore with its requisite planning and organization.

It is through the *Mediation for Individuation and Psychological Differentiation* that the child learns that he is unique, unlike anyone else, and equipped with boundaries, both external and internal, which separate him from others. After receiving mediation in this area, the parents reported their son's new sense of embarrassment while undressing in front of strangers on the beach as well as his proud proclamations upon greeting others: "Hi, I'm Paul."

With both parents exhilarated by their son's newly apparent ability to understand abstract concepts such as temporal relations and gradation (he had begun to use the word "almost"), they began to quite naturally incorporate communications involving *transcendence* in their interactions with him. Realizing that he was capable of understanding "why" and of connecting isolated activities to the larger environment, they were encouraged to find a kindergarten placement which would mesh his newly discovered cognitive needs with play activities. The need for a more appropriate caretaker was also discussed with the parents, who accepted the recommendation to hire a personal care giver with an educational background who would not be fearful of making demands of Paul.

Having learned how to engage in *Mediation for a Feeling of Competence* with Paul by both interpreting success and conscientiously creating conditions for accomplishment, the parents were asked to make a list of their son's successes, both for their own development of feelings of competence as mediators and for their *mediation to Paul of himself as a changing entity. The Human Being as a Changing Entity* is critical if the child is to believe that he is capable of positive change, that he can be modified in meaningful ways, and that he is not destined to remain as he is at any given moment. In the case of Paul, the parents were urged to continue keeping a daily diary of all mediational criteria used, as well as of all related responses. They departed the Feuerstein Institute with the sense that they had changed as much as their son had. Initially ambivalent about their son's development, they were helped to mourn the loss of "Baby Paul" and left the Feuerstein Institute looking forward to his continued growth in all areas.

Conclusion

The above two case studies reveal MLE as an extraordinarily effective tool by which a wide range of competencies can be brought out in youngsters considered to be autistic or having autistic tendencies. Daily life for children with such diagnoses can be vastly improved if social workers and other therapists are willing to integrate an educational role based on MLE into their practice. This role should not be considered incongruous for the therapist who has been taught that his or her primary task is to help clients gain insight into their feelings and behaviors. When working with families of autistic children, such reflection alone is not enough; it must be accompanied by the activity and optimism that is brought to the fore by an approach integrating Mediated Learning into the clinical setting.

Note

1 In my nearly thirty years as Senior Social Worker at the Feuerstein Institute, I had the honor of working extremely closely with Professor Feuerstein while being the primary therapist for the families of the many children diagnosed as autistic, who came for help from all over the world. Working with the parents of these children, I have found MLE to be highly effective as a treatment modality. With its emphasis on treatment and engagement with a therapist who welcomes educative tasks as part of her work.

Chapter 11

Brief Case Studies

Reuven Feuerstein, Louis H. Falik and Refael S. Feuerstein

The following brief case studies illustrate the Feuerstein Method applied to a variety of children presenting with behavior identified as ASD. Notably, these studies were carried out directly by Prof. Reuven Feuerstein (the founder of the system named after him) and his team.

Danny: The Long, Slow, Upward Journey

Our first vignette gives us a snapshot of the process of progress. Hannah Brown here writes of her son, who began to work with the late Reuven Feuerstein and the treatment team when he was quite young.

At age seven, my son could not even play with a single toy for more than 10 seconds, let alone do complex exercises involving organizing and finding shapes in groups of dots, typically the first workbook therapists use (from the Feuerstein Instrumental Enrichment Program; Feuerstein, Feuerstein, Falik & Rand, 2006). Until a few years ago when his health began to fade, the Professor was closely involved in every student's treatment and he was always interested in my son... Under Feuerstein's guidance, the staff (of the Feuerstein Institute) spent the better part of a decade investing a great deal of time, energy and skill teaching my son first to play with each toy for a few minutes at a time, then to spend entire sessions playing with one or two toys. Gradually, Danny developed what is called "functional play": instead of simply rolling a car back and forth, he would put a car into a garage, take it to a toy car wash, and build bridges and tunnels out of books. He became interested in books and began to study children's encyclopedias at a table [while]guided by a therapist. He internalized the therapists' mediation and his motivation changed. He actually wanted to play in a more focused, varied way. Only after years was he able to sit still and work the Instrumental Enrichment tools, but when he was ready, he was eager to learn. He still is. (The Jerusalem Post, 5/1/2014.)

DOI: 10.4324/9781003451136-12

The contribution of the cognitive elements and how they are related to emotional/social variables are clearly evident in Hannah's description of the process of his development.

Ben: Effects on Parent Expectations and Interaction

Ben had received an early diagnostic evaluation that indicated that he was within the autistic spectrum. By the age of 7, he was echolalic, referred to himself in the third person, and had some other mild stereotyped behaviors. They were easily controlled and modified by minimal intervention, either by the parents or when he was given something to do which was interesting. In an early observational assessment, within a brief interaction, it was *clear* that these so-called "autistic" behaviors could be modified by engaging him and focusing his behavior. When it was demonstrated to the parents how easy it was to change Ben's responses, and how happy he was to give up his previously dysfunctional communication, he ran to his mother and began to enthusiastically kiss her and express intense joy in his sharing with her his pleasure and accomplishments. Interestingly, the mother did not turn her face to the child and showed great difficulties in accepting his expression of affection. It soon became clear, however, that his mother's reaction was not her natural tendency.

After Ben left the room his mother broke down in tears, saying: "this child is closest to my heart, but I've been told that this is his condition. I felt so much distance from him, and this made me hold back from the way I want to be. I could not be comfortable with him. I felt that I had to put distance between him and me in order not to cause him to feel the suffering that his distance inflicted on me. I needed to protect *myself* from the pain that this distance caused!"

Here, the child's behavioral reactions had caused responses in the parent that both confirmed the child's behavior and prevented the natural mediation that occurs between parent and child. It is as if one says to oneself, my child cannot or does not respond, so I will retreat from interactions — at first with disappointment and pain, and eventually with sad acceptance.

Sally: Reducing Social Distance and Creating Human Interaction

Four-year-old Sally came to us with the usual autistic features of detachment from the social interaction taking place around her. She seemed unaware of the objects and events that she was experiencing. As her mother and grandmother watched during one assessment session, she resisted sitting at the table with the assessor and instead walked about the room, paying fleeting attention to various objects. At one point in her wandering, she brushed against the assessor's shoulder. He took this opportunity to feign surprise and fear. This was done in an exaggerated manner, loudly and with much verbal accompaniment ("oh, you frightened me! I hope you won't do it again, etc."), conveyed in a pleasant and playful way, with a smiling face. He repeated this reaction several times, which Sally noticed, and, returning from a far corner of the room, repeated the arm movement that had elicited the first reaction. This was mediated, even elaborated— vocal elements were added, in an equally embellished way, as the assessor "screamed" and "cried"—such that Sally first noticed, then became curious but not frightened, and her detachment subsided and was replaced by interest and focus. Her random movement in the room was substantially reduced as she became profoundly involved in producing the simulated "panic" in the adult. It had become clear to Sally that she and the observer were "playing a game." They certainly were interacting!

A lively game ensued: the adult would "hide" under the table when Sally came closer, feigning the fear reaction but with a smile on his face, verbalizing how "frightened" he was. After several repetitions that Sally initiated and clearly enjoyed, the adult stopped, saying, "I want a kiss from you, if you want me to continue." She came over, gave him a kiss on his cheek, and the play continued. Following this, each time that the assessor quieted down and discontinued the play, the child returned and was ready to resume the interaction. Observing everything, mother and grandmother were visibly touched. They had never gotten such a kiss from the child, and they may have thought that they never would. After further repetitions of the "game," Sally was asked to kiss her mother if she wanted the game to continue. She went over to her mother, climbed into her lap, and kissed her. The mother began crying.in her daughter's four years of life, she had never kissed her mother!

The goal of this interaction was to demonstrate that Sally was open to affective responding (the kissing behavior), and its underlying interactive meaning, extended into a larger and more ultimately meaningful interaction. Her mother observed what was possible, and how it was produced, and ultimately was encouraged and instructed how to produce similar interactions. In this situation with Sally, a behavior was *detected,* it was *reinforced* through the mediation of repeated behavioral interactions, and it was *generalized* to include a variety of other elements that are considered important. Thus, in this instance, Sally was able to acquire and then generalize a behavior that was previously totally absent from her repertoire. The joy experienced by the child (despite her clear autistic features) became a way to penetrate the barrier creating the distance in her responding repertoire, and to make her amenable to the mediated learning experience (MLE). The MLE was focused on producing a reaction to an observed subjective condition in the other (the assessor/mediator), eliciting in another human being a condition that gave the child a positive feeling that she wanted to continue, and even make stronger. The kiss became, a kind of reward, creating a reciprocity which brings the child into contact with the world of interaction outside of herself, and makes her ready to "pay the price" of further contacts which continue into new—but increasingly satisfying—interactions. In a sense, the kiss—a carefully selected behavior, bringing her into a socially relevant and presumably satisfying interaction—was a first engagement with the "other" and generated *mutual* satisfaction once experienced (certainly with her mother).

Max: Autism in the Context of Profound Sensory Deprivation

Max was seventeen years old when he was referred for dynamic assessment, using the *Learning Propensity Assessment Device (LPAD)*. This procedure is based on the application of mediated learning experience to assess cognitive functions and learning/adaptation potential. Max's mother had contracted rubella during the first trimester of her pregnancy with him, and he was born deaf. At the age of two, he was diagnosed as "autistic." Max had lived for many years in group residential settings, first at a school for the deaf and then, because of his behavior problems, in a school for the mentally retarded. His group home director made the referral to us because of her feeling that he had untapped potential beneath his complex presenting behavior. The director's hope was that the dynamic assessment might assist in the process of removing him from the school for the retarded and placing him in a higher functioning setting. (She had detected, as the Feuerstein Method terms it, "islets of normalcy"; see Chapter 4.)

Upon first observation, Max appeared to fit the classic autistic profile. He lacked expressive language, showed intermittent eye contact, made minimal vocalizations, engaged in intense upper body rocking, and had a large welt on his forehead from frequent and severe head banging. In his educational setting, he, was considered "a hopeless case." Max had some basic reading and writing skills, including recognizing his name and some simple words, and could do some number series. His "hobby" was to take apart the plumbing connections in the school lavatories—which he could correctly put back together when persuaded to do so by the staff.

The dynamic assessment searched for Max's "islets of normalcy." The examiner noted intermittent eye contact, indicating some small sense of human contact and recognition. Nonetheless, he appeared to be very difficult to assess on the LPAD. How could we assess a young man with profound deafness, no systematic sign language, and barely any contact skills? With the house manager present in the assessment, using minimal manual signs and contact modalities, tasks from the LPAD battery were selected that could be administered non-verbally. It was necessary to creatively adapt the initial presentation of tasks so that Max would understand what was required and acquire the appropriate response set. For example, on the *Mazes* test, pictures of a mouse and cheese were placed at the starting and stopping points to convey the idea of moving through the pathways in a purposeful manner.

On a *Mazes* task, Max quickly understood what he was expected to do, and moved through simple mazes, and within minutes had accurately traced the routes of the most complex tasks. On the difficult problems, he was observed to pause before drawing the line, appearing to plan visually before acting motorically. When the *Organization of Dots* task was demonstrated, Max watched intently (rocking his body back and forth). When the training page was placed in front of him, he clearly understood the task, and completed the frames rapidly and correctly. He varied his pace— doing the simpler (for him) frames rapidly and slowing down to visually check and plan before drawing lines on the complex problems. His facility with the training page was so impressive that he was given several of the advanced pages of the Instrumental Enrichment "Organization of Dots" instrument, which he completed with speed, accuracy, and an apparent sense of ease. On the *Raven's Matrices,* Max understood the tasks immediately, was absorbed in them, and accurately solved a majority of the problems through three levels of increasing difficulty. His performance was mediated by pointing, focusing, and much acknowledgment of his successes- -stroking his hand, applauding (and making sure he observed it). He appeared to be learning so much from the process that the tasks were repeated, with improvement on problems that had previously been difficult for him. On several other very complex LPAD instruments Max showed similar propensities to focus, learn the nature of the task, and respond to mediation which showed capacities for cognitive functioning to a much higher degree than his manifest (unmediated) behavior suggested, both in the assessment sessions, but more importantly in the larger issues of his functioning in his environment.

Beyond our expectations, this profoundly deaf young man who was considered retarded performed brilliantly, in spite of the limitations of communication, and with relatively "light" mediation overcame his "autistic" behavioral symptoms. Max enjoyed the situation, the interpersonal contact, responded to the praise given to him (e.g., writing "well done," stroking his arm), and even the mental challenge of the complex tasks presented to him.

We include this case here to illustrate a metaphor that was offered by Piaget and adapted by Feuerstein, that of the *two-sided coin,* the relationship between cognition and affect. Max shows well how working with his cognitive functions unlocks and modifies aspects of long held and seemingly persistent social and emotional dysfunction. The dynamic assessment process indicated that Max had a great deal of latent intelligence that could be tapped. We observed his responses to complex and abstract tasks. His demeanor and eye contact changed as nonverbal mediation was offered to support and extend his responses. We concluded that Max's symptoms were "autistiform" rather than classically autistic.

Max was referred to a computer training program, where his teacher marveled at the complexity of the tasks he could undertake and understand. One day, working in the instructor's apartment, the sound of an ice cream truck became audible, and Max stopped working and smiled. Was he truly deaf? Perhaps he was neither deaf nor autistic. It is entirely possible that his autistiform behavior was a secondary effect of an under-mediated and under-stimulated condition, hypothetically having a hearing loss, who never learned to use what residual hearing might have been available. Whatever the case, in Max the islets of normalcy were clearly present, and we harnessed them to identify and develop his perceptual, intellectual, and cognitive propensities.

Sam: Overcoming Early ASD Behavior

We began to work with Sam at age three and a half.[1] He had been assessed previously by many specialists, each of whom had diagnosed him as on the autistic spectrum. His mother, however, was determined that her son would not remain autistic.

At the age of two, Sam had been diagnosed as "possessing the criteria of autism" as manifested by observations of "impaired interpersonal contact, lack of development of language and communication, lack of imitative behavior, and lack of interest in peers." He was deemed needing an "intensive therapeutic (educational) intervention to meet his needs." His mother steadfastly refused to place him in such a setting, believing that he would gain more from integration among typical children, with the assistance of an integration aide that the parents provided. The mother supplemented this with a program of private intensive therapy for several hours each day, involving speech, occupational therapy, music and movement.

When the mother arrived with Sam at the center, she brought the integration aide a thick notebook detailing his "afternoon program," and a comprehensive articulation of goals to be completed. It is our belief, however, that when assessing children with severe and complex language and developmental impairments, we need to temporarily put aside the prior "data" even though we know it contains important information, and engage in a dynamic interaction—framed from the perspective of "how can we help this child improve" without any preconceived notions that might block our vision and search. Rather than a focus on "what do we call this (based on observable symptoms)," we want to be open to observing and experiencing directly the strengths and gifts of the child. We want to be alert to the *islets of normalcy*, however subtle they may be.

Assessment with severely communication-impaired children consists of two phases: observation and interaction. When the child's skill levels and abilities to cooperate on structured tasks are routinely low, it is observation of the child in a free-play setting and relaxed atmosphere that provides the key qualitative information we are seeking.

When Sam entered the room, it was observed that his eye contact was highly avoidant. He appeared to avoid the assessor, preferring to examine a basket of miniature animals and a small doll house placed for him on the carpet. He uttered a word here and there, such as the name of an animal, but his speech was garbled and difficult to understand. Sam handled the animals, pushing the smallest of them into hole in the cupboard, making them disappear. His spontaneous play appeared to be two dimensional and fairly mechanical. However, as he looked at the play objects, his body language communicated a sense of comprehension. For example, he responded to the doll house by appropriately placing objects in it and exploring the windows and other details.

As the assessor watched, Sam looked with interest and intent at the play materials. We noted that despite his very limited language and eye contact, his play indicated that he was alert, exploratory, aware of details, and capable of purposeful rather than simply rote, random, and repetitive behavior. There were no stereotypical behaviors of spinning, hand flapping, or other self-stimulatory responses, and only the mild instance of stuffing the little animals into the hole. It was clear that Sam's behavior did not conform to the traditional diagnostic indicators of autism—extreme emotional cutting off from the environment, obsessive insistence on sameness.

As the session progressed, Sam's gaze toward the familiar figures of mother and aide softened and warmed, while he continued to avoid the gaze of the assessor. This indicated (1) an accommodation to the strange situation, as Sam was recovering some basic eye contact with those familiar to him, and (2) distinguishing between familiar people and strangers. As the observation period continued, Sam began to show some differentiated emotions, moving closer to the aide, brushing against her in an almost affectionate way, and whining in frustration when he went to the locked office door and it wouldn't open. *Emotional differentiation is an islet of normalcy.*

At the level of interaction, the FM assessor used the modality of play. Within the context of dynamic assessment, play provides the opportunities to examine both cognitive tools (such as cause, and effect, symbolic fluency, latent imagination, labeling behavior), and social dimensions (eye contact, emotional responsiveness). The assessor, in this context, was curious to observe the effect of introducing an imaginative theme. Several human figures were arranged around a tiny table with chairs. With clay a birthday cake was fashioned, and the "happy birthday" song was quietly sung. Sam began to mumble and repeat "happy birthday." Another islet manifested and detected: Sam was comprehending the symbolic expression and responding to it. For 20 minutes during that session Sam watched, sometimes repeating the words of the birthday scenario, and then he began to place other objects in the scene. When Sam finally tired of this activity, he returned to stuffing animals through the hole in the cupboard door. The intervention was elaborated, consistent with Feuerstein's concept of *Mediation for Meaning*, and Greenspan and Weider's principle of "floor time." The assessor took turns pushing the animals into the hole, and added verbal and imaginative meaning to the activity, saying "Goodbye animals. Where are you going? You're disappearing." Sam did not repeat the words, but his eye contact and focusing noticeably increased as he clearly listened to this interaction. Yet another *islet:* Sam could be pulled into further contact if his play was joined, and verbal meaning was added.

At the end of a nearly two-hour session, numerous islets of normalcy had been observed, and clear evidence of modifiability had been noted. On the indices of eye contact, accommodation to a strange situation, differentiated emotions, and openness to symbolic ideation and play, Sam was not cut off from contact, and did not meet the classical criteria for autism. He was quiet, subdued, under-confident, sometimes avoidant—but not autistic. It might be mentioned that although Sam may not fit the autistic diagnosis, he might still greatly benefit from treatment, expanding and consolidating newly acquired behaviors.

The dynamic assessment perspective indicated that Sam's development was imbalanced. His program had completely stressed skill acquisition. With the addition of opportunities for symbolic play, integrated with verbal and behavioral skills, his imbalances could be corrected. His mother and the aide were open to this recommendation and received further instruction regarding its implementation.

For three years, follow-up contact was maintained through periodic return visits (every' 4 to 8 weeks at the outset, less frequently later). Recommendations were: (1) reduce the amount of time on skill-based therapies, (2) maintain Sam in regular educational settings, (3) and initiate a regular expressive play therapy interaction. Process consultation was reflected in such suggestions as inviting peers home for play experiences that modeled safe and familiar acquisition of social skills.

As an almost seven-year-old boy, Sam was virtually unrecognizable from the subdued and avoidant little boy who first arrived at the Feuerstein Institute. He spoke in full sentences, with excellent grammar and syntax. He had a sense of humor, and he spoke happily about his kindergarten. At this point, Sam enjoyed making up simple stories and illustrating them with line drawings. He was on the verge of learning to read—he knew the alphabet and could write many words. Sam further enjoyed entertaining his parents with his acquired vocabulary of new words. He took judo lessons at the local community center. His parents opted to have him repeat kindergarten, without his integration aide, to strengthen his skills. He was thriving under his "own steam." On his most recent visit to the center, Sam found a pair of roller skates under the cupboard, asked his father to put them on him, and went for a spin around the waiting room area.

Conclusion

The brief case descriptions offered in this chapter disclose a simple truth: conventional methods of assessing children with autism and autistic spectrum disorders that are based primarily on symptomology simply serve to label individuals. They fail to capitalize on the child's potential for modifiability which may invalidate the diagnosis, or at best, open up options for meaningful treatment that will make a difference. Even in situations where well-established autistic behavior is present, mediated learning experience interventions have the power to reduce symptoms, improve quality of life, and change underlying cognitive and behavioral structures. Dynamic assessment represents a qualitative and interactive search for the individual's islets of normalcy, searches for samples of modifiability, and then elaborates and generalizes them, leading to implementable recommendations and interventions. As an initial experience of mediation, prior to the initiation of a treatment plan, they provide a first window on the child's availability for mediation. In this chapter, we saw how children like Sam and Sally, and Max and Ben were helped to leave the realm of pathology and begin to realize their underlying potential beneath their exceedingly debilitating symptoms and histories of responding. As an aside, one might note that when parents, teachers, and peers observe the changes in the child, a positive self-fulfilling prophesy is generated, based on revised expectations. In this vein, we might say: *You act normally, I treat you normally, and you are normal.*

Note

1 This case study owes its attribution to Shoshana Levin Fox.

Index

For Product Safety Concerns and Information please contact our EU
representative GPSR@taylorandfrancis.com
Taylor & Francis Verlag GmbH, Kaufingerstraße 24, 80331 München, Germany

9 781032 587042